Urban Bikeway Design Guide

About Island Press

Since 1984, the nonprofit Island Press has been stimulating, shaping, and communicating the ideas that are essential for solving environmental problems worldwide. With more than 800 titles in print and some 40 new releases each year, we are the nation's leading publisher on environmental issues. We identify innovative thinkers and emerging trends in the environmental field. We work with world-renowned experts and authors to develop cross-disciplinary solutions to environmental challenges.

Island Press designs and executes educational campaigns in conjunction with our authors to communicate their critical messages in print, in person, and online using the latest technologies, innovative programs, and the media. Our goal is to reach targeted audiences—scientists, policymakers, environmental advocates, urban planners, the media, and concerned citizens—with information that can be used to create the framework for long-term ecological health and human well-being.

Island Press gratefully acknowledges major support of our work by The Agua Fund, Inc., The Andrew W. Mellon Foundation, Betsy and Jesse Fink Foundation, The Bobolink Foundation, The Curtis and Edith Munson Foundation, Forrest C. and Frances H. Lattner Foundation, G.O. Forward Fund of the Saint Paul Foundation, Gordon and Betty Moore Foundation, The Kresge Foundation, The Margaret A. Cargill Foundation, New Mexico Water Initiative, a project of Hanuman Foundation, The Overbrook Foundation, The S.D. Bechtel, Jr. Foundation, The Summit Charitable Foundation, Inc., V. Kann Rasmussen Foundation, The Wallace Alexander Gerbode Foundation, and other generous supporters.

The Opinions expressed in this book are those of the author(s) and do not necessarily reflect the views of our supporters.

Urban Bikeway Design Guide

 National Association of
City Transportation Officials

 Washington | Covelo | London

National Association of
City Transportation Officials

 Bikes Belong COALITION   SRAM CYCLING FUND   THE SUMMIT FOUNDATION

Edward Reiskin, President,
NACTO, Director, San Francisco Municipal
Transportation Agency

Janette Sadik-Khan,
Chair, Strategic Advisory Board

Linda Bailey,
Acting Executive Director

David Vega-Barachowitz,
Director, Designing Cities initiative

NACTO encourages the exchange of
transportation ideas, insights and practices
among large cities while advocating for a
federal transportation policy that prioritizes
investment in infrastructure in the nation's
cities and their metropolitan areas—home
to a majority of Americans and hubs of
economic activity. Large city transportation
officials are investing in innovative public
transportation, bike, pedestrian and public
space projects to create more sustainable,
livable, healthy, and economically
competitive cities.

**National Association of City
Transportation Officials**
55 Water Street, 9th Floor
New York, NY 10041
www.nacto.org

Cataloging-in-Publication Data has been
applied for and may be obtained from the
Library of Congress.
ISBN: 978–1–61091–436–9

© Copyright 2014 National Association of City
Transportation Officials

Second Edition
The most current version of the Guide is
available at c4cguide.org. Copies may be
purchased through the National Association
of City Transportation Officials (www.nacto.
org/print-guide/). Updates and addenda
to the Urban Bikeway Design Guide will be
posted on the NACTO website.

Design: Pure+Applied (pureandapplied.com)

 **ISLAND**PRESS

Washington | Covelo | London
www.islandpress.org
All Island Press books are printed on
recycled, acid-free paper.

Contents

Foreword   vii
Introduction   ix

Bike Lanes   1
Conventional Bike Lanes   3
Buffered Bike Lanes   9
Contra-Flow Bike Lanes   15
Left-Side Bike Lanes   21

Cycle Tracks   27
One-Way Protected Cycle Tracks   29
Raised Cycle Tracks   35
Two-Way Cycle Tracks   41

Intersections   47
Bike Boxes   49
Intersection Crossing Markings   55
Two-Stage Turn Queue Boxes   61
Median Refuge Island   67
Through Bike Lanes   73
Combined Bike Lane/Turn Lane   79
Cycle Track Intersection Approach   85

Signals   91
Bicycle Signal Heads   93
Signal Detection and Actuation   99
Active Warning Beacon for Bike Route at
Unsignalized Intersection   105
Hybrid Beacon for Bike Route Crossing of Major Street   111

Signing and Marking 117

Colored Bike Facilities 119

Colored Pavement Material Guidance 125

Shared Lane Markings 133

Bike Route Wayfinding 139

Bicycle Boulevards 145

Route Planning 149

Signs and Pavement Markings 161

Speed Management 167

Volume Management 177

Minor Street Crossings 185

Major Street Crossings 191

Offset Intersections 201

Green Infrastructure 209

Resources 215

Notes 217

Design Guide Project Teams 236

References 237

Foreword

Since the publication of the first edition of the NACTO *Urban Bikeway Design Guide* in 2011, the progress made for bicycle safety in US cities had been nothing short of astonishing. The number of miles of protected bike lanes across the country has grown exponentially. Cities from Houston to Lincoln, Nebraska to San Diego are now proactively redesigning their streets for bicyclists, using the NACTO Guide as their go-to source for world-class design. At the same time, support has steadily grown among some of NACTO's key partners, culminating in an August 2013 FHWA Memorandum that expresses full support and endorsement for the Bike Guide itself. Two states, Massachusetts DOT and Georgia DOT, officially adopted the Bike Guide in 2013.

As the landscape changes for bicycling on US streets, so too has NACTO witnessed a year of transitions. Longtime NACTO President and former NYC DOT Commissioner Janette Sadik-Khan has passed the baton to me, as she moves into a new position with NACTO as the chair of the organization's new strategic advisory board. Under her leadership, NACTO has grown from a shoestring operation into a leader in transportation policymaking and a barometer for innovation at the local level. In fall 2013, under NACTO's Designing Cities initiative, NACTO released its first companion volume to the Bike Guide, the *Urban Street Design Guide.* That document is the first of its kind to comprehensively integrate the most up-to-date bicycling infrastructure guidance into a document that addresses pedestrian, bicycle, transit, and motorist design issues.

The product of an unprecedented coalition of local actors and designers, the NACTO *Urban Bikeway Design Guide* is actively transforming how our cities think about streets—whom they are for, and how they might be best used. In our member cities, this design guidance is being translated into a series of game-changing street projects—bikeways that funnel people through the heart of the city into our cherished neighborhoods, from greenways to waterfronts, and from homes to businesses. While our efforts in this arena are just getting started, NACTO is fully committed to accelerating innovation and world-class design in this exciting field.

In 2014, NACTO will focus on encouraging federal, state, and local adoption of this Guide, as well as the *Urban Street Design Guide.* We will also continue our work to support cities in their implementation of projects, providing tools and sharing best practices to get these projects built. We welcome your participation in helping us to make the public realms of our cities safer and more enjoyable.

Edward Reiskin

NACTO President

Director, SFMTA

Introduction

The purpose of the *NACTO Urban Bikeway Design Guide* (part of the Cities for Cycling initiative) is to provide cities with state-of-the-practice solutions that can help create complete streets that are safe and enjoyable for bicyclists.

The *NACTO Urban Bikeway Design Guide* is based on the experience of the best cycling cities in the world. The designs in this document were developed by cities for cities, since unique urban streets require innovative solutions. Most of these treatments are not directly referenced in the current version of the AASHTO Guide to Bikeway Facilities, although they are virtually all (with two exceptions) permitted under the Manual on Uniform Traffic Control Devices (MUTCD). The Federal Highway Administration has posted information regarding MUTCD approval status of all of the bicycle related treatments in this guide. All of the NACTO Urban Bikeway Design Guide treatments are in use internationally and in many cities around the US.[1]

To create the Guide, the authors have conducted an extensive worldwide literature search from design guidelines and real-life experience. They have worked closely with a panel of urban bikeway planning professionals from NACTO member cities, as well as traffic engineers, planners, and academics with deep experience in urban bikeway applications.

NEW YORK, NY

For each treatment in the Guide, the reader will find three levels of guidance:

Required Features

Elements for which there is a strong consensus that the treatment cannot be implemented without

Recommended Features

Elements for which there is a strong consensus of added value.

Optional Features

Elements that vary across cities and may add value depending on the situation.

In all cases, we encourage engineering judgment to ensure that the application makes sense for the context of each treatment, given the many complexities of urban streets.

It is important to note that many urban situations are complex; treatments must be tailored to the individual situation. Good engineering judgment based on deep knowledge of bicycle transportation should be a part of bikeway design. Decisions should be thoroughly documented. To assist with this, the NACTO Urban Bikeway Design Guide links to companion reference material and studies.

VANCOUVER, BC

Bike Lanes

Conventional Bike Lanes   3

Buffered Bike Lanes   9

Contra-Flow Bike Lanes   15

Left-Side Bike Lanes   21

A bike lane is defined as a portion of the roadway that has been designated by striping, signage, and pavement markings for the preferential or exclusive use of bicyclists. Bike lanes enable bicyclists to ride at their preferred speed without interference from prevailing traffic conditions and facilitate predictable behavior and movements between bicyclists and motorists. A bike lane is distinguished from a cycle track in that it has no physical barrier (bollards, medians, raised curbs, etc.) that restricts the encroachment of motorized traffic. Conventional bike lanes run curbside when no parking is present, adjacent to parked cars on the right-hand side of the street or on the left-hand side of the street in specific traffic, though they may be configured in the contra-flow direction on low-traffic corridors necessary for the connectivity of a particular bicycle route.

The configuration of a bike lane requires a thorough consideration of existing traffic levels and behaviors, adequate safety buffers to protect bicyclists from parked and moving vehicles, and enforcement to prohibit motorized vehicle encroachment and double-parking. Bike lanes may be distinguished using color, lane markings, signage, and intersection treatments.

Contra-flow bike lanes in Baltimore facilitate key connections in the city's bicycle network. Shared lane markings reinforce the two-way nature of bicycle traffic, while serving as an effective wayfinding tool for cyclists.

IMAGE: BALTIMORE, MD

Conventional Bike Lanes

OLYMPIA, WA (PHOTO: WWW.PEDBIKEIMAGES.ORG, DAN BURDEN)

Bike lanes designate an exclusive space for bicyclists through the use of pavement markings and signage. The bike lane is located adjacent to motor vehicle travel lanes and flows in the same direction as motor vehicle traffic. Bike lanes are typically on the right side of the street, between the adjacent travel lane and curb, road edge, or parking lane. This facility type may be located on the left side when installed on one-way streets, or may be buffered if space permits. See contra-flow bike lanes for a discussion of alternate direction flow.

Bike lanes enable bicyclists to ride at their preferred speed without interference from prevailing traffic conditions. Bike lanes also facilitate predictable behavior and movements between bicyclists and motorists. Bicyclists may leave the bike lane to pass other bicyclists, make left turns, avoid obstacles or debris, and avoid other conflicts with other users of the street.

PORTLAND, OR

Benefits

Increases bicyclist comfort and
confidence on busy streets.

Creates separation between bicyclists
and automobiles.

Increases predictability of bicyclist and
motorist positioning and interaction.
Increases total capacities of streets
carrying mixed bicycle and motor
vehicle traffic.

Visually reminds motorists of bicyclists'
right to the street.

Typical Applications

Bike lanes are most helpful on streets
with ≥ 3,000 motor vehicle average
daily traffic.

Bike lanes are most helpful
on streets with a posted speed
≥ 25 mph.

On streets with high transit vehicle
volume.

On streets with high traffic volume,
regular truck traffic, high parking
turnover, or speed limit > 35 mph,
consider treatments that provide
greater separation between bicycles
and motor traffic such as:

NEW YORK, NY

NEW YORK, NY

In a case study looking at the influence of pavement markings and bicyclist positioning, researchers found that, "the bicycle lane [with an edge line demarcating the parking lane] was the most effective at keeping cars parked closer to the curb and encouraging cyclists to ride in a consistent position at intersections."

Pedestrian and Bicycle Information Center. (2006). BIKESAFE: Bicycle Countermeasure Selection System. Publication No. FHWA–SA–05–006, Federal Highway Administration, Washington, DC.

SAN MARCOS, TX (PHOTO: WWW.PEDBIKEIMAGES.ORG, GREG GRIFFIN)

Design Guidance

Conventional Bike Lanes

Required Features

1 The desirable bike lane width adjacent to a curbface is 6 feet. The desirable ridable surface adjacent to a street edge or longitudinal joint is 4 feet, with a minimum width of 3 feet. In cities where illegal parking in bike lanes is an concern, 5 foot wide bike lanes may be preferred.[2]

2 When placed adjacent to a parking lane, the desirable reach from the curb face to the edge of the bike lane (including the parking lane, bike lane, and optional buffer between them) is 14.5 feet; the absolute minimum reach is 12 feet. A bike lane next to a parking lane shall be at least 5 feet wide, unless there is a marked buffer between them. Wherever possible, minimize parking lane width in favor of increased bike lane width.[3]

3 The desirable bike lane width adjacent to a guardrail or other physical barrier is 2 feet wider than otherwise in order to provide a minimum shy distance from the barrier.[4]

4 Bicycle lane word and/or symbol and arrow markings (MUTCD Figure 9C–3) shall be used to define the bike lane and designate that portion of the street for preferential use by bicyclists.[5]

5 Bike lane word, symbol, and/ or arrow markings (MUTCD Figure 9C–3) shall be placed outside of the motor vehicle tread path at intersections, driveways, and merging areas in order to minimize wear from the motor vehicle path.

6 A solid white lane line marking shall be used to separate motor vehicle travel lanes from the bike lane. Most jurisdictions use a 6 to 8 inch line.[6]

7 A through bike lane shall not be positioned to the right of a right turn only lane or to the left of a left turn only lane (MUTCD 9C.04). A bike lane may be positioned to the right of a right turn only lane if split-phase signal timing is used. For additional information, see bicycle signal heads. For additional strategies for managing bikeways and right turn lanes, see through bike lanes in this guide.

Recommended Features

8 Bike lanes should be made wider than minimum widths wherever possible to provide space for bicyclists to ride side-by-side and in comfort. If sufficient space exists to exceed desirable widths, see buffered bike lanes. Very wide bike lanes may encourage illegal parking or motor vehicle use of the bike lane.

9 When placed adjacent to parking, a solid white line marking of 4 inch width should be used between the parking lane and the bike lane to minimize encroachment of parked cars into the bike lane.[7]

10 Gutter seams, drainage inlets, and utility covers should be flush with the ground and oriented to prevent conflicts with bicycle tires.[8]

11 If sufficient space exists, separation should be provided between bike lane striping and parking boundary markings to reduce door zone conflicts. Providing a wide parking lane may offer similar benefits. Refer to buffered bike lanes for additional strategies.

12 If sufficient space exists and increased separation from motor vehicle travel is desired, a travel side buffer should be used. Refer to buffered bike lanes for additional details.

13 Lane striping should be dashed through high traffic merging areas. See through bike lanes for more information.

14 The desirable dimensions should be used unless other street elements (e.g., travel lanes, medians, median offsets) have been reduced to their minimum dimensions.

15 In cities where local vehicle codes require motor vehicles to merge into the bike lane in advance of a turn movement, lane striping should be dashed from 50 to 200 feet in advance of intersections to the intersection. Different states have varying requirements.

Optional Features

16 "Bike lane" signs (MUTCD R3–17) may be located prior to the beginning of a marked bike lane to designate that portion of the street for preferential use by bicyclists. The 2009 MUTCD lists bike lane signs as optional; however, some states still require their use.

17 On bike lanes adjacent to a curb, "No Parking" signs (MUTCD R8–3) may be used to discourage parking within the bike lane.

1 Desired width: 6 feet

2 Wherever possible, minimize parking lane width in favor of increased bike lane width.

9 4 inch solid white line

6 6- to 8-inch solid white line

11 Separation between bike lane striping and parking boundary reduces risk of door zone conflicts.

16 BIKE LANE
MUTCD R3–17

Maintenance

Lane lines and stencil markings should be maintained to clear and legible standards.

Bike lanes should be plowed clear of snow by crews.

Bike lanes should be maintained to be free of potholes, broken glass, and other debris.

Utility cuts should be back-filled to the same degree of smoothness as the original surface. Take care not to leave ridges or other surface irregularities in the area where bicyclists ride.

If chip sealing, consider providing new surfacing only to the edge of the bike lane. This results in a smoother surface for bicyclists with less debris. Sweep bike lanes clear of loose chip in the weeks following chip sealing.

If trenching is to be done in the bike lane, the entire bike lane should be trenched so that there is not an uneven surface or longitudinal joints.

Treatment Adoption and Professional Consensus

Bicycle lanes are the most common bicycle facility in use in the US, and most jurisdictions are familiar with their design and application as described in the MUTCD and AASHTO Guide for the Development of Bicycle Facilities. To offer increased levels of comfort and security to bicyclists, some cities have exceeded the minimum dimensions required in these guides.

CHAPEL HILL, NC (PHOTO: WWW.PEDBIKEIMAGES.ORG, LIBBY THOMAS)

MADISON, WI (PHOTO: WWW.PEDBIKEIMAGES.ORG, MARGARET GIBBS)

BALDWIN PARK, CA (PHOTO: WWW.PEDBIKEIMAGES.ORG, DAN BURDEN)

DEL MAR, CA

Buffered Bike Lanes

SEATTLE, WA

Buffered bike lanes are conventional bicycle lanes paired with a designated buffer space separating the bicycle lane from the adjacent motor vehicle travel lane and/or parking lane. A buffered bike lane is allowed as per MUTCD guidelines for buffered preferential lanes (section 3D–01).

NEW YORK, NY

PHILADELPHIA, PA (PHOTO: PHILADELPHIA BICYCLE COALITION)

Cyclists indicated they feel lower risk of being 'doored' in the buffered bike lanes and nearly nine in 10 cyclists preferred a buffered bike lane to a standard lane. Seven in 10 cyclists indicated they would go out of their way to ride on a buffered bike lane over a standard bike lane, ...

Portland State University, Center for Transportation Studies. (2011). Evaluation of Innovative Bicycle Facilities: SW Broadway Cycle Track & SW Stark/Oak Street Buffered Bike Lanes FINAL REPORT. Portland Bureau of Transportation, Portland, OR.

Benefits

Provides greater shy distance between motor vehicles and bicyclists.

Provides space for bicyclists to pass another bicyclist without encroaching into the adjacent motor vehicle travel lane.

Encourages bicyclists to ride outside of the door zone when buffer is between parked cars and bike lane.

Provides a greater space for bicycling without making the bike lane appear so wide that it might be mistaken for a travel lane or a parking lane.

Appeals to a wider cross-section of bicycle users.

Encourages bicycling by contributing to the perception of safety among users of the bicycle network.

Typical Applications

Anywhere a standard bike lane is being considered.

On streets with extra lanes or extra lane width.

On streets with high travel speeds, high travel volumes, and/or high amounts of truck traffic.

Special consideration should be given at transit stops to manage bicycle and pedestrian interactions.

CAPE CORAL, FL (PHOTO: WWW.PEDBIKEIMAGES.ORG, DAN MOSER)

AUSTIN, TX

BILLINGS, MT

SEATTLE, WA

Design Guidance

Buffered Bike Lanes

Required Features

① Bicycle lane word and/or symbol and arrow markings (MUTCD Figure 9C–3) shall be used to define the bike lane and designate that portion of the street for preferential use by bicyclists.[9]

② The buffer shall be marked with 2 solid white lines, with diagonal hatching if 3 feet in width or wider. White lines on both edges of the buffer space indicate lanes where crossing is discouraged, though not prohibited. For clarity, consider dashing the buffer boundary where cars are expected to cross at driveways.[10]

③ The buffer area shall have interior diagonal cross hatching or chevron markings if 3 feet in width or wider.[11]

Recommended Features

④ If used, interior diagonal cross hatching should consist of 4 inch

lines angled at 30 to 45 degrees and striped at intervals of 10 to 40 feet. Increased striping frequency may increase motorist compliance.[12]

⑤ The combined width of the buffer(s) and bike lane should be considered "bike lane width" with respect to guidance given in other documents that don't recognize the existence of buffers. Where buffers are used, bike lanes can be narrower because the shy distance function is assumed by the buffer. For example, a 3 foot buffer and 4 foot bike lane next to a curb can be considered a 7 foot bike lane. For travel side buffered lanes next to on street parking, a 5 foot minimum

② ⑦ The buffer shall be marked with 2 solid white lines. Minimum buffer width: 18 inches

⑤ The combined wi of the buffer(s) and bike lane should be considered "bike lane width" with respect to other guidance.

③ The buffer area shall have interior diagonal cross hatching or chevron markings if 3 feet in width or wider

Parking Side Buffer Configuration

width is recommended to encourage bicyclists to ride outside of the door zone.

6 Where bicyclist volumes are high, bicyclist speed differentials are significant, or where side-by-side riding is desired, the desired bicycle travel area width is 7 feet.

7 Buffers should be at least 18 inches wide because it is impractical to mark a zone narrower than that.

8 On intersection approaches with right turn only lanes, the bike lane should be transitioned to a through bike

lane to the left of the right turn only lane, or a combined bike lane/turn lane should be used if available road space does not permit a dedicated bike lane.

9 On intersection approaches with no dedicated right turn only lane the buffer markings should transition to a conventional dashed line. Consider the use of a bike box at these locations.

Optional Features

10 Like a conventional bike lane, a wide (6 to 8 inch) solid white line may be used to mark the edge adjacent to a motor vehicle travel lane. For a parking side buffer, parking T's or a solid line are acceptable to mark between a parking lane and the buffer.

11 For travel lane buffer configurations, separation may also be provided between bike lane striping and the parking boundary to reduce door zone conflicts. This creates a type of parking-side buffer.

12 On wide one-way streets with buffered bike lanes, consider adding a buffer to the opposite side parking lane if the roadway appears too wide. This will further narrow the motor vehicle lanes and encourage drivers to maintain lower speeds.

13 The interior of the buffer area may use different paving materials to separate it from the bike lane. Textured surface materials may cause difficulties for bicyclists as surfaces may be rough. Increased maintenance requirements are likely.

14 Color may be used at the beginning of each block to discourage motorists from entering the buffered lane. For other uses of color in buffered bike lanes see colored bike facilities.

5 Desired minimum next to on street parking: 5 feet

11 Separation may also be provided between bike lane striping and the parking boundary to reduce door zone conflicts.

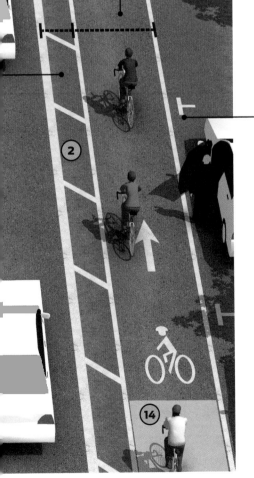

Travel Side Buffer Configuration

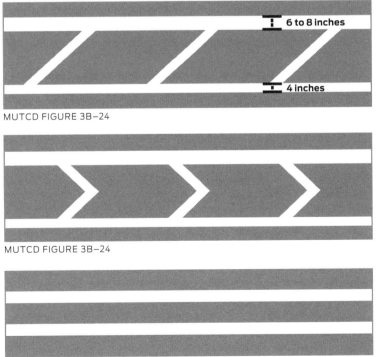

MUTCD FIGURE 3B–24

6 to 8 inches

4 inches

MUTCD FIGURE 3B–24

MUTCD FIGURE 3D–2

NEW YORK, NY

Maintenance

Buffer striping may require additional maintenance when compared to a conventional bicycle lane.

Buffered bike lanes should be maintained free of potholes, broken glass, and other debris.

If trenching is to be done in the bicycle lane, the entire bicycle lane should be trenched so that there is not an uneven surface or longitudinal joints.

See conventional bicycle lanes for additional maintenance issues that may apply.

Treatment Adoption and Professional Consensus

Buffered bike lanes are used in the following US cities and counties:

- Austin, TX
- Billings, MT
- Boston, MA
- Cape Coral, FL
- Los Angeles, CA
- Marin County, CA
- Minneapolis, MN
- New Orleans, LA
- New York, NY
- Philadelphia, PA
- Phoenix, AZ
- Portland, OR
- San Francisco, CA
- Seattle, WA
- Tucson, AZ

Contra-Flow Bike Lanes

BALTIMORE, MD

Contra-flow bicycle lanes are bicycle lanes designed to allow bicyclists to ride in the opposite direction of motor vehicle traffic. They convert a one-way traffic street into a two-way street: one direction for motor vehicles and bikes, and the other for bikes only. Contra-flow lanes are separated with yellow center lane striping. Combining both direction bicycle travel on one side of the street to accommodate contra-flow movement results in a two-way cycle track.

The contra-flow design introduces new design challenges and may introduce additional conflict points as motorists may not expect on-coming bicyclists.

CHICAGO, IL

WASHINGTON, DC

EUGENE, OR

Benefits

Provides connectivity and access to bicyclists traveling in both directions.

Reduces dangerous wrong-way riding. Decreases sidewalk riding.

Influences motorist choice of routes without limiting bicycle traffic.

Decreases trip distance, the number of intersections encountered, and travel times for bicyclists by eliminating out-of-direction travel.

Allows bicyclists to use safer, less trafficked streets.

SAN FRANCISCO, CA

BOISE, ID

CHICAGO, IL

DENVER, CO

Typical Applications

On streets where large numbers of bicyclists are already riding the wrong way.

On corridors where alternate routes require excessive out-of-direction travel.

On corridors where alternate routes include unsafe or uncomfortable streets with high traffic volumes and/or no bicycle facilities.

On corridors where the contra-flow lane provides direct access to destinations on the street under consideration.

Where two-way connections between bicycle facilities are needed along one-way streets.

Works best on low-speed, low-volume streets, unless buffer separation or physical protection is provided.

Design Guidance

Contra-Flow Bike Lanes

Required Features

(1) Bicycle lane word, symbol, and arrow markings (MUTCD Figure 9C–3) shall be used to define the bike lane direction and designate that portion of the street for preferential use by bicyclists.

(2) "One Way" sign (MTCD R6–1, R6–2) with "Except Bikes" plaque shall be posted along the facility and at intersecting streets, alleys, and driveways informing motorists to expect two-way traffic.

MUTCD R6-1, R6-2

(3) Intersection traffic controls along the street (e.g., stop signs and traffic signals) shall also be installed and oriented toward bicyclists in the contra-flow lane.

Recommended Features

(4) "Do Not Enter" sign (MUTCD R5–1) with "Except Bikes" plaque should be posted along the facility to only permit use by bicycles.

MUTCD R5-1, R6-2

(5) When configured without parking, a solid double yellow lane line marking should be used to separate opposing motor vehicle travel lanes from the contraflow bicycle lane.[13]

(6) Consider a No Turn on Red restriction by installing a "No Turn on Red" sign (MUTCD R10–11) on cross streets to minimize potential conflicts with turning vehicles. Cross street traffic may not look for or anticipate contraflow bicycle travel.

MUTCD R10-11

(7) Where there is room, bike lanes should be used on both sides. When there is no room for a with-flow lane, shared lane markings should be used to guide with-flow bicyclists to keep to the right side of the road.[14]

(8) If sufficient space exists, a buffered bike lane design should be used. The buffer should conform with Figure 3D-4 of the MUTCD. A broken buffer may be used if on-street parking is present.

(9) Contra-flow bike lane markings should be extended across the intersection, especially for contra-flow lanes against the curb, as a way of alerting cross street traffic to look for contra-flow bicyclists.

Optional Features

(10) Warning signage, such as a modified "Two Way" sign (MUTCD W6-3) may be posted along the facility to inform motorists to expect two-way traffic.

MUTCD W6-3

(5) A solid double yellow lane line marking should be used to demarcate the lane from opposing traffic.

(8) If sufficient space exists, a buffered bike lane design should be used.

(7) Where there is no room for a with-flow bike lane, shared lane markings should be used.

(11) Colored pavement may be used along the facility to draw attention to the unique function of the lane, or in areas with cross traffic, such as at driveway exits, for increased visibility of bicyclists.

(12) Small versions of "Stop" signs (18 x 18 inches) and other regulatory signage may be used along the contra-flow lane to emphasize that only bike traffic is permitted to travel in the contra-flow direction.

(13) Special consideration should be given before implementing contra-flow bike lanes adjacent to parking. Cars entering and exiting the parking lane will be maneuvering head-on with oncoming bicyclists, introducing an increased speed differential and potentially unfamiliar traffic operations. The driver of a vehicle parked adjacent to a contra-flow lane will have reduced visibility of oncoming bicyclists when compared to parking adjacent to a with-flow bike lane. Increased bike lane width paired with parking-side buffer striping may be used to increase maneuvering space and sight distance.

Most existing installations use a double yellow line to separate the contra-flow bicycle lane, however local ordinance may prohibit parking in the opposite direction of the contra-flow travel lane. A dashed yellow line, or dashed white line may also used to separate the contra-flow bicycle lane. Local urban practitioners should use best engineering judgment to determine which strategy to implement.

(14) A curb or a raised median may be used in place of double yellow striping to separate the contra-flow lane from opposing vehicle traffic. Such a facility becomes a contra-flow protected cycle track.

OLYMPIA, WA (PHOTO: WWW.PEDBIKEIMAGES.ORG, DAN BURDEN)

Maintenance

Like all bicycle lanes, contra-flow bike lanes should be maintained to be free of potholes, broken glass, and other debris.

If trenching is to be done in the bicycle lane, the entire bicycle lane should be trenched so that there is not an uneven surface or longitudinal joints.

Please see guidance for conventional bike lanes.

Treatment Adoption and Professional Consensus

Contra-flow bike lanes are used in the following US cities:

- Austin, TX
- Baltimore, MD
- Boise, ID
- Boulder, CO
- Brookline, MA
- Cambridge, MA
- Chicago, IL
- Denver, CO
- Eugene, OR
- Madison, WI
- Minneapolis, MN
- Olympia, WA
- Portland, OR
- San Francisco, CA
- Seattle, WA
- Washington, DC

Left-Side Bike Lanes

SAN FRANCISCO, CA

Left-side bike lanes are conventional bike lanes placed on the left side of one-way streets or two-way median divided streets.

Left-side bike lanes offer advantages along streets with heavy delivery or transit use, frequent parking turnover on the right side, or other potential conflicts that could be associated with right-side bicycle lanes. The reduced frequency of right-side door openings lowers dooring risk.

NEW YORK, NY

NEW YORK, NY

Benefits

Avoids potential right-side bike lane conflicts on streets.

Improves bicyclist visibility by motorists by having the bike lane on the driver's side.

Provides consistent facility configuration in locations where right-side travel lanes are subject to rush hour parking restrictions and other flexible uses.

Minimizes door zone conflicts next to parking because of fewer door openings on the passenger side of vehicles.

Fewer bus and truck conflicts as most bus stops and loading zones are on the right side of the street.

Typical Applications

On one-way streets or median divided streets with frequent bus stops or truck loading zones on the right side of the street.

On streets with high parking turnover.

On streets with rush hour parking restrictions.

On streets with high volumes of right turn movements by motor vehicles.

On streets with a significant number of left-turning bicyclists.

On streets where traffic enters into an add lane on the right-hand side, as from a freeway off-ramp.

For favorable alignment to connect to a path, two-way cycle track, or other bicycle facility.

Design Guidance

Left-Side Bike Lanes

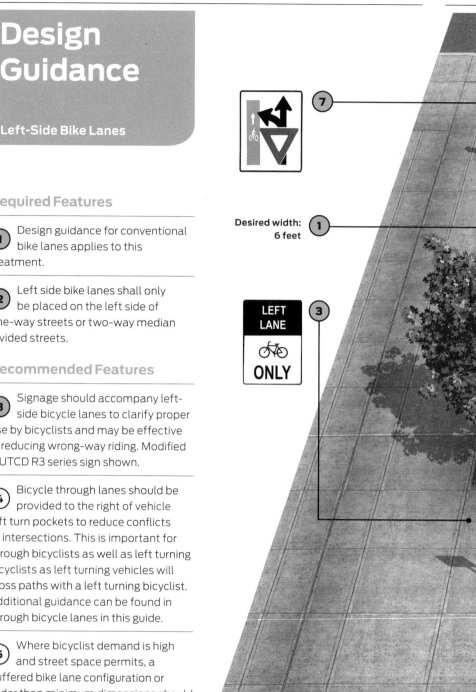

Required Features

1 Design guidance for conventional bike lanes applies to this treatment.

2 Left side bike lanes shall only be placed on the left side of one-way streets or two-way median divided streets.

Recommended Features

3 Signage should accompany left-side bicycle lanes to clarify proper use by bicyclists and may be effective in reducing wrong-way riding. Modified MUTCD R3 series sign shown.

4 Bicycle through lanes should be provided to the right of vehicle left turn pockets to reduce conflicts at intersections. This is important for through bicyclists as well as left turning bicyclists as left turning vehicles will cross paths with a left turning bicyclist. Additional guidance can be found in through bicycle lanes in this guide.

5 Where bicyclist demand is high and street space permits, a buffered bike lane configuration or wider than minimum dimensions should be used to allow bicyclists to pass one another without encroaching upon the adjacent travel lane.

6 Intersection treatments such as bike boxes and bike signals, should be considered to assist in the transition from left-side bike lanes to right-side bike lanes.

7 A "Yield to Bikes" sign should be post-mounted in advance of and in conjunction with a left turn lane to reinforce that bicyclists have the right-of-way going through the intersection.[15]

Optional Features

8 Colored pavement may be used along the facility to draw attention to the unique function of the lane, or within conflict areas for increased visibility of bicyclists.

SAN FRANCISCO, CA

BOSTON, MA

SACRAMENTO, CA

NEW YORK, NY

BOSTON, MA

NAPLES, FL (PHOTO: WWW.
PEDBIKEIMAGES.ORG, DAN BURDEN)

Maintenance

Like all bicycle lanes, left-side bike lanes should be maintained to be free of potholes, broken glass, and other debris.

If trenching is to be done in the bicycle lane, the entire lane should be trenched so that there is not an uneven surface or longitudinal joints.

Please see guidance for conventional bike lanes.

Treatment Adoption and Professional Consensus

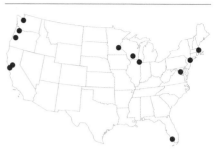

Left-side bike lanes are used in the following US cities:

- Berkeley, CA
- Boston, MA
- Chicago, IL
- Eugene, OR
- Madison, WI
- Minneapolis, MN
- Naples, FL
- New York, NY
- Portland, OR
- Sacramento, CA
- San Francisco, CA
- Seattle, WA
- Washington, DC

Cycle Tracks

One-Way Protected Cycle Tracks · · · · · · · · · · · · · · · · 29

Raised Cycle Tracks · 35

Two-Way Cycle Tracks · 41

A cycle track is an exclusive bike facility that combines the user experience of a separated path with the on-street infrastructure of a conventional bike lane. A cycle track is physically separated from motor traffic and distinct from the sidewalk. Cycle tracks have different forms but all share common elements—they provide space that is intended to be exclusively or primarily used for bicycles, and are separated from motor vehicle travel lanes, parking lanes, and sidewalks. In situations where on-street parking is allowed cycle tracks are located to the curb-side of the parking (in contrast to bike lanes).

Cycle tracks may be one-way or two-way, and may be at street level, at sidewalk level, or at an intermediate level. If at sidewalk level, a curb or median separates them from motor traffic, while different pavement color/texture separates the cycle track from the sidewalk. If at street level, they can be separated from motor traffic by raised medians, on-street parking, or bollards. By separating cyclists from motor traffic, cycle tracks can offer a higher level of security than bike lanes and are attractive to a wider spectrum of the public.

Chicago's first cycle track on Kinzie Street between Milwaukee and Wells provides a vital connection between two of the city's major bicycle thoroughfares.

IMAGE: CHICAGO, IL

One-Way Protected Cycle Tracks

PORTLAND, OR

One-way protected cycle tracks are bikeways that are at street level and use a variety of methods for physical protection from passing traffic. A one-way protected cycle track may be combined with a parking lane or other barrier between the cycle track and the motor vehicle travel lane. When a cycle track is elevated above street level it is called a raised cycle track and different design considerations may apply.

Compared with bicycling on a reference street* ... these cycle tracks had a 28% lower injury rate.

*"Reference street" refers to a comparable street without dedicated bicycle facilities.

Lusk, A., Furth, P., Morency, P., Miranda-Moreno, L., Willett, W., Dennerlein, J. (2010). Risk of injury for bicycling on cycle tracks versus in the street. Injury Prevention.

NEW YORK, NY

Benefits

Dedicates and protects space for bicyclists in order to improve perceived comfort and safety.[16]

Eliminates risk and fear of collisions with over-taking vehicles.

Reduces risk of 'dooring' compared to a bike lane and eliminates the risk of a doored bicyclist being run over by a motor vehicle.[17]

Prevents double-parking, unlike a bike lane.

Low implementation cost by making use of existing pavement and drainage and by using parking lane as a barrier. More attractive for bicyclists of all levels and ages.[18]

LONG BEACH, CA

Typical Applications

Streets with parking lanes.

Streets on which bike lanes would cause many bicyclists to feel stress because of factors such as multiple lanes, high traffic volumes, high speed traffic, high demand for double parking, and high parking turnover. While there are no US standards for the bicyclist and motor vehicle volumes that warrant cycle tracks, several international documents provide basic guidance (see references in the appendix).

Streets for which conflicts at intersections can be effectively mitigated using parking lane setbacks, bicycle markings through the intersection, and other signalized intersection treatments.

Along streets with high bicycle volumes.

Along streets with high motor vehicle volumes and/or speeds.

Special consideration should be given at transit stops to manage bicycle and pedestrian interactions.

ADA/PROWAG Considerations

When providing accessible parking spaces alongside cycle tracks, the following general considerations are recommended to accommodate persons with disabilities in the design of one-way and two-way protected cycle tracks. Local parking regulations and roadway context may vary considerably.

- A widened buffer space may be used to accommodate a side mounted vehicle ramp or lift so that it will not protrude into the cycle track and become a hazard to bicyclists. Additional buffer space may be challenging to achieve with limited right-of-way.
- Mid-block curb ramps may be provided near marked accessible parking spaces, or curb ramps may be provided at a consistent interval along the cycle track to provide additional egress points for wheelchair users to gain access to the sidewalk. Mid-block curb ramps may also offset inconveniences in curbside freight delivery crossing the cycle track.

- Roadway cross-slopes should be considered across the cycle track during design as slopes exceeding two percent will create difficulty for bicyclists and some disabled users.
- If significant Taxi or Paratransit service exists along the cycle track, consider providing periodic loading zones to allow the vehicles to pull out of the travel lane.
- If used, consider placement of bollards in the buffer area so as not to impede access by disabled users. Individuals with sight-impairments may lack familiarity with this roadway configuration. Outreach and education for sight-impaired individuals is advised to ensure that these individuals have a better understanding of changes to the roadway alignment. Select design elements, such as tactile surfaces may help reinforce these measures.

Design Guidance

One-Way Protected Cycle Tracks

6 Desired minimum: 11 feet

Required Features

1 A cycle track, like a bike lane, is a type of preferential lane as defined by the MUTCD.[19]

2 Bicycle lane word, symbol, and/ or arrow markings (MUTCD Figure 9C-3) shall be placed at the beginning of a cycle track and at periodic intervals along the facility based on engineering judgment.

3 If pavement markings are used to separate motor vehicle parking lanes from the preferential bicycle lane, solid white lane line markings shall be used. Diagonal crosshatch markings may be placed in the neutral area for special emphasis. See MUTCD Section

3B.24. Raised medians or other barriers can also provide physical separation to the cycle track.

Recommended Features

4 The minimum desired width for a cycle track should be 5 feet. In areas with high bicyclist volumes or uphill sections, the minimum desired width should be 7 feet to allow for bicyclists passing each other.[20]

5 Three feet is the desired width for a parking buffer to allow for passenger loading and to prevent door collisions.[21]

6 When using a parking protected pavement marking buffer, desired

parking lane and buffer combined width is 11 feet to discourage motor vehicle encroachment into the cycle track.

7 In the absence of a raised median or curb, the minimum desired with of the painted buffer is 3 ft. The buffer space should be used to locate bollards, planters, signs or other forms of physical protection.[22]

8 Driveways and minor street crossings are a unique challenge to cycle track design. A review of existing facilities and design practice has shown that the following guidance may improve safety at crossings of driveways and minor intersections:

- If the cycle track is parking protected, parking should be prohibited near the intersection to improve visibility. The desirable no-parking area is 30 feet from each side of the crossing.[23]
- For motor vehicles attempting to cross the cycle track from the side street or driveway, street and sidewalk furnishings and/or other features should accommodate a sight triangle of 20 feet to the cycle track from minor street crossings, and 10 feet from driveway crossing.
- Color, yield lines, and "Yield to Bikes" signage should be used to identify the conflict area and make it clear that the cycle track has priority over entering and exiting traffic.[24]

15 At transit stops, consider wrapping the cycle track behind the transit stop zone to reduce conflicts with transit vehicles and passengers.

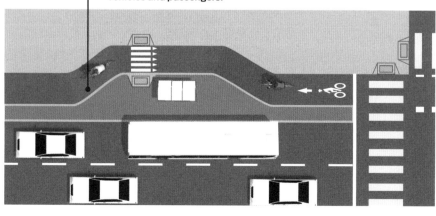

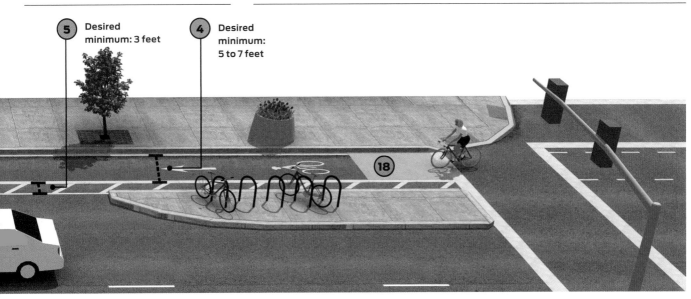

5 Desired minimum: 3 feet

4 Desired minimum: 5 to 7 feet

- Motor vehicle traffic crossing the cycle track should be constrained or channelized to make turns at sharp angles to reduce travel speed prior to the crossing.

9 Gutter seams, drainage inlets, and utility covers should be configured so as not to impede bicycle travel and to facilitate run-off.

10 Sidewalk curbs and furnishings should be used to prevent pedestrian use of the cycle zone.

11 Cycle track width should be larger in locations where the gutter seam extends more than 12 inches from the curb.[25]

Optional Features

12 Tubular markers may be used to protect the cycle track from the adjacent travel lane. The color of

the tubular markers shall be the same color as the pavement marking they supplement.[26]

13 Cycle tracks may be shifted more closely to the travel lanes on minor intersection approaches to put bicyclists clearly in the field of view of motorists. See Cycle Track Intersection Approach for other methods of transitioning a cycle track to an intersection.[27]

14 A raised median, bus bulb, or curb extension may be configured in the cycle track buffer area to accommodate transit stops. Bicyclists should yield to pedestrians crossing the roadway at these points to reach the transit stop.

15 At transit stops, consider wrapping the cycle track behind the transit stop zone to reduce conflicts with transit vehicles and passengers. Bicyclists should yield to pedestrians

in these areas. At intersection bus stops, an extended mixing zone may be provided with signage directing bicyclists to yield to buses and loading passengers. Cycle tracks may be configured on the left side of a one-way street to avoid conflicts at transit stops.

16 A "Bike Lane" sign (MUTCD R3-17) may be used to designate the portion of the street for preferential use by bicyclists. A supplemental "No Cars" selective exclusion sign may be added for further clarification.

17 "Bike Only" legend (MUTCD 3D.01) may be used to supplement the preferential lane word or symbol marking.[28]

18 Colored pavement may be used to further define the bicycle space.

Alternate Protection Strategies

12 Tubular Markers

7 Movable Planters

14 Raised Curb

CHICAGO, IL (PHOTO: STEVEN VANCE)

Maintenance

Cycle tracks should be maintained in order to be free of potholes, broken glass and other debris.

Snow removal and street sweeping may require special equipment. This is the case if the combined width of cycle track and buffer, or the cycle track width inside of the raised curb is too narrow for existing street maintenance equipment.

Street sweeping may have to be done more frequently than on streets, especially during the fall, because the lack of the sweeping effect of motor traffic, together with the canyon profile of a cycle track, tends to hold leaves and other debris.

Snow removal may be simplified by putting the cycle track at sidewalk level or by constructing a raised median between the parking lane and the cycle track. Care should be taken to make physically separated cycle tracks accessible by street maintenance equipment, otherwise street sweeping and/or snow removal will need to be done with specialized equipment.

Consider restricting parking at a regularly scheduled time of the week or day to facilitate snow removal and street cleaning.

Bollards or flexible delineators may be removed in winter to provide improved access by snow removal equipment.

If trenching is to be done in the cycle track, the entire facility should be trenched so that there is not an uneven surface or latitudinal joints.

Treatment Adoption and Professional Consensus

Commonly used in dozens of European bicycle friendly cities.

Currently used in the following US cities:
- Boulder, CO
- Cambridge, MA
- Chicago, IL
- Long Beach, CA
- Memphis, TN
- Minneapolis, MN
- Missoula, MT
- New York, NY
- Portland, OR
- San Francisco, CA
- St. Petersburg, FL
- Washington, DC

Raised Cycle Tracks

CAMBRIDGE, MA

Raised cycle tracks are bicycle facilities that are vertically separated from motor vehicle traffic. Many are paired with a furnishing zone between the cycle track and motor vehicle travel lane and/or pedestrian area. A raised cycle track may allow for one-way or two-way travel by bicyclists. Two-way cycle tracks have some different operational characteristics that merit additional consideration.

Raised cycle tracks may be at the level of the adjacent sidewalk, or set at an intermediate level between the road- way and sidewalk to segregate the cycle track from the pedestrian area. A raised cycle track may be combined with a parking lane or other barrier between the cycle track and the motor vehicle travel lane (refer to protected cycle tracks for additional guidance). At intersections, the raised cycle track can be dropped and merged onto the street

HILLSBORO, OR (PHOTO: WILL VANLUE)

(see Cycle Track Intersection Approach), or it can be maintained at side-walk level, where bicyclists cross with pedestrians, possibly with a dedicated bicycle signal.

When placed adjacent to a travel lane, one-way raised cycle tracks may be configured with a mountable curb to allow entry and exit from the bicycle lane for passing other bicyclists or to access vehicular turn lanes. This configuration has also been known as a 'raised bike lane.'

Benefits

Dedicates and protects space for bicyclists in order to improve perceived comfort and safety.[29]

More attractive to a wider range of bicyclists at all levels and ages than less separated facilities.

Keeps motorists from easily entering the cycle track.

Encourages bicyclists to ride in the bikeway rather than on the sidewalk.

Can visually reduce the width of the street when provided adjacent to a travel lane.[30]

Minimizes maintenance costs due to limited motor vehicle wear.

With new roadway construction a raised cycle track can be less expensive to construct than a wide or buffered bicycle lane.

Typical Applications

Raised cycle tracks can be considered wherever a bicycle lane would be the standard recommendation. They may be most beneficial:

- Along higher speed streets with few driveways and cross streets.

- Along streets on which bike lanes would cause many bicyclists to feel stress because of factors such as multiple lanes, high traffic volumes, high speed traffic, high demand for double parking, and high parking turnover.

- On streets for which conflicts at intersections can be effectively mitigated using parking lane setbacks, bicycle markings through the intersection, and other signalized intersection treatments.

- On streets with numerous curves where vehicle encroachment into bike lanes may be a concern.

- Along streets with high bicycle volumes.

Special consideration should be given at transit stops to manage bicycle and pedestrian interactions. See Cycle Track Intersection Approach for transitioning strategies.

PORTLAND, OR

BEND, OR

VANCOUVER, BC (PHOTO: WWW. PEDBIKEIMAGES.ORG, CARL SUNDSTROM)

MISSOULA, MT

Design Guidance

Rasied Cycle Tracks

Required Features

(1) The cycle track shall be vertically separated from the street at an intermediate or sidewalk level.

(2) Bicycle lane word, symbol, and/or arrow markings (MUTCD Figure 9C-3) shall be placed at the beginning of a cycle track and at periodic intervals along the facility based on engineering judgment.

(3) A raised cycle track shall be protected from the adjacent motor vehicle travel lane. Protection strategies may include a raised or mountable curb, street furnishings, low vegetation or a parking lane.

(4) If used, the mountable curb should have 4:1 slope edge without any seams or lips to interfere with bike tires to allow for safe entry and exit of the roadway. This curb should not be considered a ridable surface when determining cycle track width.[31]

Recommended Features

(5) Desirable one-way raised cycle track travel surface width is 6.5 feet to allow side-by-side riding or passing. Desired minimum width is 5 feet at intersections and pinch points. Additional width may be needed for protection from traffic or parking and/or shy distance to sidewalks or furnishings.[32]

(6) When configured next to a parking lane, 3 feet is the minimum desired width for a parking buffer to allow for passenger loading and to prevent dooring collisions. The buffer

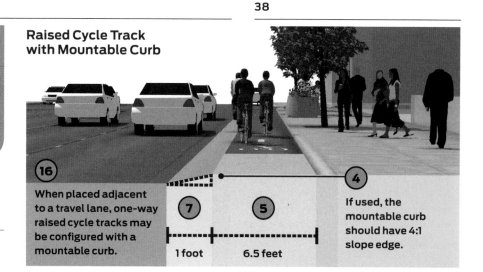

Raised Cycle Track with Mountable Curb

(16) When placed adjacent to a travel lane, one-way raised cycle tracks may be configured with a mountable curb.

(7) (5)
1 foot   6.5 feet

(4) If used, the mountable curb should have 4:1 slope edge.

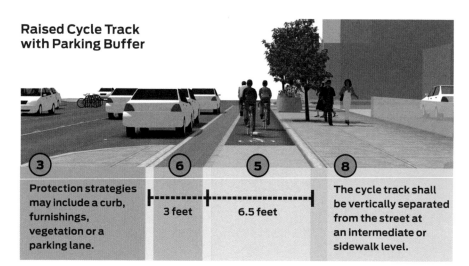

Raised Cycle Track with Parking Buffer

(3) Protection strategies may include a curb, furnishings, vegetation or a parking lane.

(6) (5)
3 feet   6.5 feet

(8) The cycle track shall be vertically separated from the street at an intermediate or sidewalk level.

can be at street level or at the level of the cycle track.[33]

(7) When configured next to a motor vehicle travel lane, the desired minimum width of a mountable curb is 1 foot, depending on elevation. Raised curbs may require additional width for added shy distance from the curb edge. Raised curb buffer minimum width should be increased to 3 feet or greater when buffer space is used to locate lamp posts, bollards, street furniture, low vegetation, and/or trees.[34]

(8) Vertical separation between the roadway and the cycle track should be between 1 and 6 inches. Higher separation values discourage illegal parking.

(9) Vertical separation between the cycle track and the sidewalk

should be between zero (flush with the sidewalk surface) and 5 inches. A separation of 3 inches or greater discourages conflicts with pedestrians.

(10) If curb or median separated, careful consideration should be given to the curb design. Curbs of 6 inches can be hazards to bicyclists by interfering with the space needed for pedaling, but can be more effective deterrents to illegal parking or loading. Consider the use of alternative bicycle-friendly curb profiles where possible.[35]

(11) Supplemental shy distance striping should be added at the entrance to curb protected cycle tracks to encourage bicyclists to keep their distance.

(12) Driveways and minor street crossings are a unique challenge

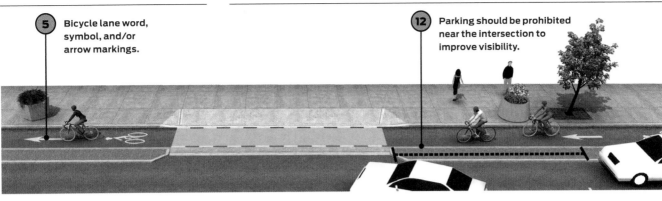

5 Bicycle lane word, symbol, and/or arrow markings.

12 Parking should be prohibited near the intersection to improve visibility.

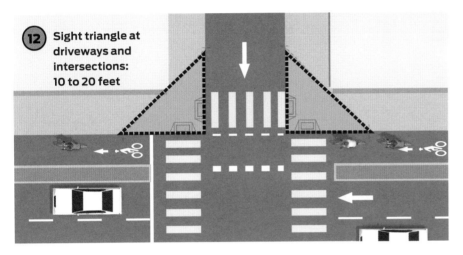

12 Sight triangle at driveways and intersections: 10 to 20 feet

to cycle track design. A review of existing facilities and design practice has shown that the following guidance may improve safety at crossings of driveways and minor intersections:

- If the cycle track is parking protected, parking should be prohibited near the intersection to improve visibility. The desirable no-parking area is 30 feet from each side of the crossing.[36]

- For motor vehicles attempting to cross the cycle track from the side street or driveway, street and sidewalk furnishings and/or other features should accommodate a sight triangle of 20 feet to the cycle track from minor street crossings, and 10 feet from driveway crossings.

- Color, yield lines, and "Yield to Bikes" signage should be used to identify the conflict area and make it clear that the cycle track has priority over entering and exiting traffic.[37]

- Motor vehicle traffic crossing the cycle track should be constrained or channelized to make turns at sharp angles to reduce travel speed prior to the crossing.

- The crossing should be raised, in which the sidewalk and cycle track maintain their elevation through the crossing. Sharp inclines on either side from road to sidewalk level serve as a speed hump for motor vehicles.[38]

- If configured at a height flush with the sidewalk, color, pavement markings, textured surfaces, landscaping, or other furnishings should be used to discourage pedestrian use of the cycle zone.

13 Drainage should slope to the street. Drainage grates should be in adjacent travel or parking lane.

14 Two-stage turn boxes should be provided to assist in making turns from the cycle track facility.

Optional Features

15 Cycle tracks may be shifted more closely to the travel lanes on minor intersection approaches to put bicyclists clearly in the field of view of motorists.[39]

16 When placed adjacent to a travel lane, one-way raised cycle tracks may be configured with a mountable curb to allow entry and exit from the bicycle lane for passing other bicyclists or to access vehicular turn lanes. This configuration has also been known as a "raised bike lane."

17 If the cycle track is not already at sidewalk level, consider raising the cycle track to sidewalk level and wrapping the cycle track around the transit stop zone to reduce conflicts with transit vehicles at midblock or signal protected intersections. Bicyclists should yield to pedestrians in these areas.

18 Contra-flow bike lanes may be raised in a cycle track configuration to offer further physical protection for contra-flow riders.

19 Cycle tracks may be configured on the left side of a one-way street to avoid conflicts at transit stops.

20 Color may be used to contrast with the adjacent pedestrian area or to increase the visibility of the cycle track in conflict areas.

DENVER, CO

PORTLAND, OR

Maintenance

Raised cycle tracks should be maintained to be free of pavement damage, broken glass, and other debris.

Raised cycle tracks may be incompatible with conventional street sweeping equipment and snow plow equipment, depending on their configuration. There should be enough shy distance on the adjacent roadway so that snow is not stored on the raised cycle track.

Raised cycle tracks receive less wear and tear than travel lanes.

ADA/PROWAG Considerations

Raised cycle tracks may function better for persons with mobility disabilities than street level cycle tracks. If accessible parking spaces are to be provided adjacent to the raised cycle track, a widened buffer may be provided to accommodate a side mounted ramp or lift that will not protrude into the cycle track and become a hazard to bicyclists. At these locations, the raised cycle track may be flush with the buffer and adjacent sidewalk with street furnishings placed to minimize conflict.

Treatment Adoption and Professional Consensus

Commonly used in dozens of European bicycle friendly cities.

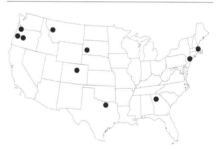

Currently used in the following US cities:
- Atlanta, GA
- Bend, OR
- Cambridge, MA
- Denton, TX
- Denver, CO
- Eugene, OR
- Missoula, MT
- New York, NY
- Portland, OR
- Rapid City, SD

Two-Way Cycle Tracks

NEW YORK, NY

Two-way cycle tracks (also known as protected bike lanes, separated bikeways, and on-street bike paths) are physically separated cycle tracks that allow bicycle movement in both directions on one side of the road. Two-way cycle tracks share some of the same design characteristics as one-way tracks, but may require additional considerations at driveway and side-street crossings.

A two-way cycle track may be configured as a protected cycle track at street level with a parking lane or other barrier between the cycle track and the motor vehicle travel lane and/or as a raised cycle track to provide vertical separation from the adjacent motor vehicle lane.

PORTLAND, OR

Benefits

Dedicates and protects space for bicyclists by improving perceived comfort and safety. Eliminates risk and fear of collisions with over-taking vehicles.[40]

Reduces risk of 'dooring' compared to a bike lane, and eliminates the risk of a doored bicyclist being run over by a motor vehicle.

On one-way streets, reduces out of direction travel by providing contra-flow movement.

Low implementation cost when making use of existing pavement and drainage and using parking lane or other barrier for protection from traffic.

More attractive to a wide range of bicyclists at all levels and ages.[41]

VANCOUVER, BC

Typical Applications

On streets with few conflicts such as driveways or cross-streets on one side of the street.

On streets where there is not enough room for a one-way cycle track on both sides of the street.

On one-way streets where contra-flow bicycle travel is desired.

On streets where more destinations are on one side thereby reducing the need to cross the street.

On streets with extra right-of-way on one side.

To connect with another bicycle facility, such as a second cycle track on one side of the street.

Along streets on which bike lanes would cause many bicyclists to feel stress because of factors such as multiple lanes, high traffic volumes, high speed traffic, high incidence of double parking, and high parking turnover.

On streets for which conflicts at intersections can be effectively mitigated using parking lane setbacks, bicycle markings through the intersection, and other signalized intersection treatments.

Along streets with high bicycle volumes. Along streets with high motor vehicle volumes and/or speeds.

Special consideration should be given at transit stops to manage bicycle and pedestrian interactions.

Design Guidance

Two-Way Cycle Track

Required Features

(1) Bicycle lane word, symbol, and/or arrow markings (MUTCD Figure 9C-3) shall be placed at the beginning of a cycle track and at periodic intervals along the facility to define the bike lane direction and designate that portion of the street for preferential use by bicyclists.

(2) If configured on a one-way street, a "ONE WAY" sign (MUTCD R6-1, R6-2) with "Except Bikes" plaque shall be posted along the facility and at intersecting streets, alleys, and driveways informing motorists to expect two-way traffic.

(3) A "DO NOT ENTER" sign (MUTCD R5-1) with "EXCEPT BIKES" plaque shall be posted along the facility to only permit use by bicycles.

(4) Intersection traffic controls along the street (e.g., stop signs and traffic signals) shall also be installed and oriented toward bicyclists traveling in the contra-flow direction.

Recommended Features

(5) The desirable two-way cycle track width is 12 feet. Minimum width in constrained locations is 8 feet.[42]

(6) When protected by a parking lane, 3 feet is the desired width for a parking buffer to allow for passenger loading and to prevent dooring collisions.[43]

(7) A dashed yellow centerline should be used to separate two-way bicycle traffic and to help distinguish the cycle track from any adjacent pedestrian area.

(8) Driveways and minor street crossings are a unique challenge to cycle track design. A review of existing facilities and design practice has shown that the following guidance may improve safety at crossings of driveways and minor intersections:

- If the cycle track is parking protected, parking should be prohibited near the intersection to improve visibility. The desirable no-parking area is 30 feet from each side of the crossing.[44]

- For motor vehicles attempting to cross the cycle track from the side street or driveway, street and sidewalk furnishings and/or other features should accommodate a sight triangle of 20 feet to the cycle track from minor street crossings, and 10 feet from driveway crossing.

- Color, yield lines, and "Yield to Bikes" signage should be used to identify the conflict area and make it clear that the cycle track has priority over entering and exiting traffic.[45]

- Motor vehicle traffic crossing the cycle track should be constrained or channelized to make turns at sharp angles to reduce travel speed prior to the crossing.

- If configured as a raised cycle track, the crossing should be raised, in which the sidewalk and cycle track maintain their elevation through the crossing. Sharp inclines on either side from road to sidewalk level serve as a speed hump for motor vehicles.[46]

(9) Two-stage turn queue boxes should be provided to assist in making turns from the cycle track facility.

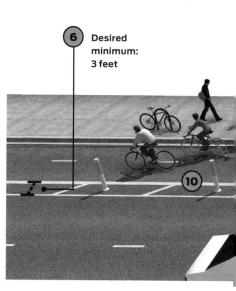

6 Desired minimum: 3 feet

6 Desired minimum: 3 feet

Optional Features

(10) Tubular markers may be used to protect the cycle track from the adjacent travel lane. The color of the tubular markers shall be the same color as the pavement marking they supplement.[47]

(11) Cycle tracks may be shifted more closely to the travel lanes on minor intersection approaches to put bicyclists clearly in the field of view of motorists.[48]

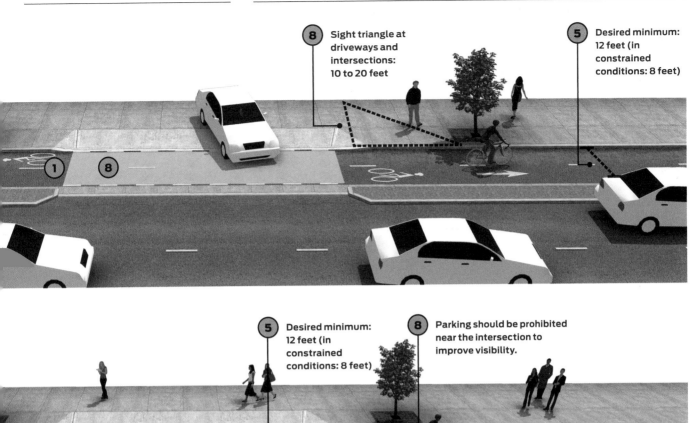

8 Sight triangle at driveways and intersections: 10 to 20 feet

5 Desired minimum: 12 feet (in constrained conditions: 8 feet)

5 Desired minimum: 12 feet (in constrained conditions: 8 feet)

8 Parking should be prohibited near the intersection to improve visibility.

Intersection Configuration Alternatives

12 A raised median, bus bulb or curb extension may be configured in the cycle track buffer area to accommodate transit stops. Cyclists should yield to pedestrians crossing the roadway at these points to reach the bus stop. A two-way cycle tracks may be configured on the left side of a one-way street to avoid conflicts at transit stops.

13 May be configured as a raised cycle track.

See the Cycle Track Intersection Approach and Bicycle Signals sections for details on design strategies at intersections.

Bicycle Signal Phase
A dedicated bicycle signal phase can eliminate conflict between turning automobiles and bicyclists.

"Bend In" Crossing
Using a curb extension or painted buffer, the cycle track may be bent-in to promote visibility of bicyclists in advance of the intersection.

NEW YORK, NY

The results show that the paths with raised crossings attracted more than 50 percent more bicyclists and that the safety per bicyclist was improved by approximately 20 percent due to the increase in bicycle flow, and with an additional 10 to 50 percent due to the improved layout.

Garder, P., Leden, L., Pulkkinen, U. (1998). Measuring the Safety Effect of Raised Bicycle Crossings Using a New Research Methodology. Transportation Research Record, 1636.

ADA/PROWAG Considerations

Two-way cycle tracks have similar ADA/PROWAG considerations as one-way protected cycle tracks and raised cycle tracks depending on the configuration. The wider overall facility width of two-way cycle tracks may simplify accommodating disabled users.

Maintenance

Two-way cycle tracks should be maintained to be free of pavement damage, broken glass, and other debris. Two-way cycle tracks have similar maintenance requirements to one-way protected cycle tracks and raised cycle tracks depending on the configuration.

Treatment Adoption and Professional Consensus

Commonly used in dozens of European bicycle friendly cities.

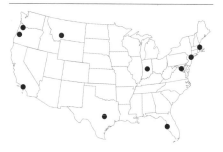

Currently used in the following US cities:
· Austin, TX
· Cambridge, MA
· Eugene, OR
· New York, NY
· Indianapolis, IN
· Portland, OR
· San Juan Capistrano, CA
· St. Petersburg, FL
· Washington, DC

Intersections

Bike Boxes   49

Intersection Crossing Markings   55

Two-Stage Turn Queue Boxes   61

Median Refuge Island   67

Through Bike Lanes   73

Combined Bike Lane/Turn Lane   79

Cycle Track Intersection Approach   85

Designs for intersections with bicycle facilities should reduce conflict between bicyclists (and other vulnerable road users) and vehicles by heightening the level of visibility, denoting a clear right-of-way, and facilitating eye contact and awareness with competing modes. Intersection treatments can resolve both queuing and merging maneuvers for bicyclists, and are often coordinated with timed or specialized signals.

The configuration of a safe intersection for bicyclists may include elements such as color, signage, medians, signal detection, and pavement markings. Intersection design should take into consideration existing and anticipated bicyclist, pedestrian and motorist movements. In all cases, the degree of mixing or separation between bicyclists and other modes is intended to reduce the risk of crashes and increase bicyclist comfort. The level of treatment required for bicyclists at an intersection will depend on the bicycle facility type used, whether bicycle facilities are intersecting, the adjacent street function and land use.

Broadway now forms a critical south-bound bicycle network link, with protected bicycle facilities for over 40 blocks through the heart of Midtown Manhattan.

IMAGE: NEW YORK, NY

Bike Boxes

PORTLAND, OR

A bike box is a designated area at the head of a traffic lane at a signalized intersection that provides bicyclists with a safe and visible way to get ahead of queuing traffic during the red signal phase.

AUSTIN, TX

77% of cyclists felt bicycling through the intersections was safer with the bike boxes.

Monsere, C., & Dill, J. (2010). Evaluation of Bike Boxes at Signalized Intersections. Final Draft. Oregon Transportation Research and Education Consortium.

NEW YORK, NY

Benefits

Increases visibility of bicyclists.

Reduces signal delay for bicyclists.

Facilitates bicyclist left turn positioning at intersections during red signal indication. This only applies to bike boxes that extend across the entire intersection.

Facilitates the transition from a right-side bike lane to a left-side bike lane during red signal indication. This only applies to bike boxes that extend across the entire intersection.

Helps prevent 'right-hook' conflicts with turning vehicles at the start of the green indication.[49]

Provides priority for bicyclists at signalized bicycle boulevard crossings of major streets.

Groups bicyclists together to clear an intersection quickly, minimizing impediment to transit or other traffic.

Pedestrians benefit from reduced vehicle encroachment into the crosswalk.[50]

Despite positioning themselves further from the intersection, motorists were observed to give bicyclists the right-of-way more often with the presence of the bicycle box.

Brady, J., Mills, A., Loskorn, J., Duthie, J., Machemehl, R., Center for Transportation Research. (2010). Effects of Bicycle Boxes on Bicyclist and Motorist Behavior at Intersections. The City of Austin.

NEW YORK, NY

CHICAGO, IL

PORTLAND, OR

TUCSON,AZ (PHOTO: TUCSON DEPARTMENT OF TRANSPORTATION)

Typical Applications

At signalized intersections with high volumes of bicycles and/or motor vehicles, especially those with frequent bicyclist left-turns and/or motorist right-turns.

Where there may be right or left-turning conflicts between bicyclists and motorists.

Where there is a desire to better accommodate left turning bicycle traffic.

Where a left turn is required to follow a designated bike route, access a shared-use path, or when the bicycle lane moves to the left side of the street.

When the dominant motor vehicle traffic flows right and bicycle traffic continues through (such as a Y intersection or access ramp).

Design Guidance

Bike Boxes

NO TURN ON RED

MUTCD R10-11

Required Features

1 A box formed by transverse lines shall be used to hold queuing bicyclists, typically 10 to 16 feet deep. Deeper boxes show less encroachment by motor vehicles.[51]

2 Stop lines shall be used to indicate the point behind which motor vehicles are required to stop in compliance with a traffic control signal. See MUTCD 3B.16.[52]

3 Pavement markings shall be used and centered between the crosswalk line and the stop line to designate the space as a bike box. The marking may be a Bike Symbol (MUTCD 9C-3A) or Helmeted Bicyclist Symbol (MUTCD 9C-3B.)

4 In cities that permit right turns on red signal indications, a "No Turn on Red" sign shall be installed overhead to prevent vehicles from entering the Bike Box.

Recommended Features

5 A "Stop Here on Red" sign should be post-mounted at the stop line to reinforce observance of the stop line. Additional signs may be used to clarify signal control. Among the legends that may be used for this purpose are "Bikes Stop Here on Red" or a supplemental "Except Bicycles" plaque in conjunction with R10-6 to indicate the bicyclist stop line.

6 Colored pavement should be used as a background color within the bike box to encourage compliance by motorists.[53]

7 An ingress lane should be used to define the bicycle space. Colored pavement may be used. When color is used, length shall be 25 to 50 feet to guarantee bicycle access to the box.[54]

8 An egress lane should be used to clearly define the potential area of conflict between motorists and bicyclists in the intersection when intersection is operating on a green signal indication. Refer to intersection crossing markings in this guide. Colored pavement or other markings may be used to define the potential area of conflict. An egress lane should not be used when there is no complimentary bicycle facility or lane on the far side of the intersection.[55]

9 A "Yield to Bikes" sign should be post-mounted in advance of and in conjunction with an egress lane to reinforce that bicyclists have the right-of-way going through the intersection.[56]

Optional Features

10 A "Wait Here" legend marking may be used to supplement the stop line and "Stop Here on Red" sign at a bike box.[57]

11 Stop lines may be placed up to 7 feet in advance of the bike box space to limit encroachment by motor vehicles.

12 The box may be setback from the pedestrian crossing to minimize encroachment by cyclists into the pedestrian crossing.

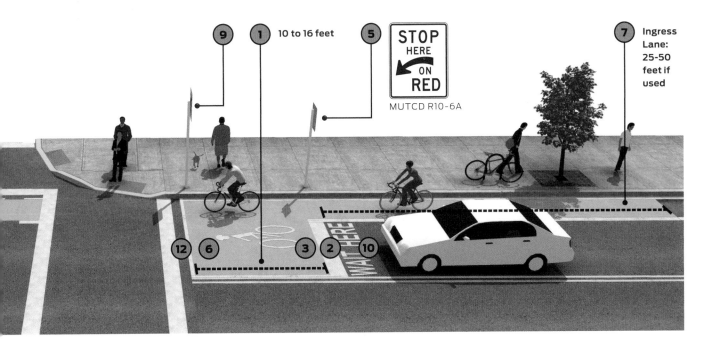

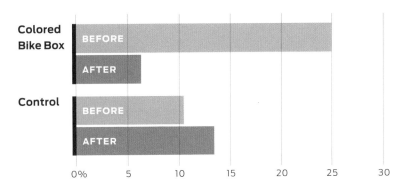

13 Bike boxes may extend across multiple travel lanes to facilitate bicyclist left turn positioning. A two-stage turn queue box may be an alternative approach to facilitating left turns where there are multiple vehicle through lanes.[58]

14 Bike boxes may be combined with an exclusive bicycle signal phase or leading bicycle interval through the use of bicycle signal heads to allow clearance of the bicycle queue prior to the green indication for motorists.[59]

15 At areas with high volumes of right turning vehicles, an active display sign may be used to further alert drivers to the potential of conflict movements with bicyclists. This sign should use signal detection and actuation to activate only in the presence of bicyclists. At areas with high volumes of right turning vehicles, or low levels of motorist yielding compliance, an active display sign may be used to further alert drivers to the potential of conflict movements with bicyclists. This sign should use signal detection and actuation to activate only in the presence of bicyclists.

Proportion of Motor Vehicle Encroachment in Crosswalk

Adapted from: Dill, J., Monsere, C., McNeil, N. (2011). Evaluation of Bike Boxes at Signalized Intersections.

NEW YORK, NY

VANCOUVER, BC (PHOTO: WWW.
PEDBIKEIMAGES.ORG, CARL SUNDSTROM)

Maintenance

Colored pavement surface may
be costly to maintain, especially in
climates prone to snow/ice.

Placement of markings between tire
tracks will reduce wear.

Treatment Adoption and
Professional Consensus

Commonly used in dozens of European
bicycle friendly cities.

Currently used in the following
US cities:

- Alexandria, VA
- Austin, TX
- Baltimore, MD
- Boston, MA
- Cambridge, MA
- Chicago, IL
- Columbus, OH
- Decatur, GA
- Madison, WI
- Minneapolis, MN
- New York, NY
- Phoenix, AZ
- Portland, OR
- Roswell, GA
- San Francisco, CA
- San Luis Obispo, CA
- Seattle, WA
- Tucson, AZ
- Washington, DC

Intersection Crossing Markings

VANCOUVER, BC (PHOTO: WWW.PEDBIKEIMAGES.ORG, CARL SUNDSTROM)

Intersection crossing markings indicate the intended path of bicyclists. They guide bicyclists on a safe and direct path through intersections, including driveways and ramps. They provide a clear boundary between the paths of through bicyclists and either through or crossing motor vehicles in the adjacent lane.

This guidance covers a number of different marking strategies currently in use in the United States and Canada. Cities considering implementing markings through intersections should consider standardizing future designs to avoid confusion.

CHICAGO, IL

Benefits

Raises awareness for both bicyclists and motorists to potential conflict areas.[60]

Reinforces that through bicyclists have priority over turning vehicles or vehicles entering the roadway (from driveways or cross streets).[61]

Guides bicyclists through the intersection in a straight and direct path.

Reduces bicyclist stress by delineating the bicycling zone.[62]

Makes bicycle movements more predictable.

Increases the visibility of bicyclists. Reduces conflicts between bicyclists and turning motorists.[63]

NEW YORK, NY

AUSTIN, TX (PHOTO: AUSTIN TRANSPORTATION DEPARTMENT)

MISSOULA, MT

Best estimates for safety effects of one blue cycle crossing in a junction are a reduction of 10% in accidents and 19% in injuries.

Jensen, S. U. (2008). Safety effects of blue cycle crossings: A before-after study. Accident Analysis & Prevention, 40(2), 742-750.

Typical Applications

Across signalized intersections, particularly through wide or complex intersections where the bicycle path may be unclear.

Along roadways with bike lanes or cycle tracks.

Across driveways and Stop or Yield-controlled cross-streets.

Where typical vehicle movements frequently encroach into bicycle space, such as across ramp-style exits and entries where the prevailing speed of ramp traffic at the conflict point is low enough that motorist yielding behavior can be expected.

May not be applicable for crossings in which bicycles are expected to yield priority, such as when the street with the bicycle route has Stop or Yield control at an intersection.

Design Guidance

Intersection Crossing Markings

Required Features

① Dotted lines shall bind the bicycle crossing space. See MUTCD Section 3B.08 for dotted line extensions through intersections.[64]

② Striping width shall be a minimum of 6 inches adjacent to motor vehicle travel lanes and shall otherwise match the width and lateral positioning of leading bike lane striping, except when using elephant's feet markings.[65]

Recommended Features

③ Dotted lines should be 2 foot lines with 2 to 6 foot spacing. Markings should be white, skid resistant and retro-reflective.

④ Crossing lane width should match width and positioning of the leading bike lane.

⑤ On crossings of two-way paths and cycle tracks, markings should indicate that there is two-way traffic either by marking the path center line through the intersection, or by marking bicycle silhouettes and/or chevrons in opposite directions in the two lanes. See Two-Way Cycle Tracks.

Optional Features

⑥ Chevrons may be used for increased visibility within conflict areas or across entire intersections. Placement shall be in the middle of the moving lanes, and close to crosswalks.

⑦ Shared lane markings (MUTCD Figure 9C-9) may be used for increased visibility within conflict areas or across entire intersections. Placement shall be in the middle of the moving lanes, and close to crosswalks.[66]

⑧ Helmeted rider or bicycle symbol pavement markings may be used for increased visibility within conflict areas or across entire intersections. Placement should consider a rotated symbol facing cross-traffic in the middle of the bicycle lane.[67]

④ **Crossing lane width should match width and positioning of the leading bike lane.**

Dotted Line Extensions

Shared Lane Markings

Colored Conflict Area

Elephant's Feet

9 Colored pavement may be used for increased visibility within conflict areas or across entire intersections.[68]

10 Elephant's feet markings may be used as an alternative to dotted line extensions to offer increased visibility. If used, the markings should be 14 to 20 inches square, with equal distance spacing between markings. Markings should be positioned on outside of lane.[69]

11 Combinations of several of the listed strategies may be considered to increase visibility.

12 Yield Lines, also known as "Sharks Teeth" may be used when crossing driveways and alleyways to mark the edge of the bike lane.[70]

10 **Elephant's feet markings may be used as an alternative to dotted line extensions to offer increased visibility.**

14 to 20 inch square | Equal distance spacing

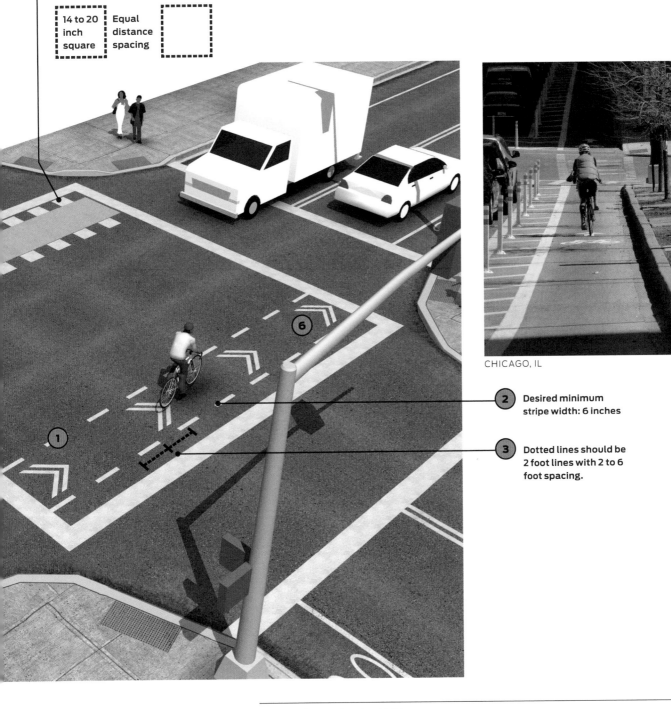

CHICAGO, IL

2 Desired minimum stripe width: 6 inches

3 Dotted lines should be 2 foot lines with 2 to 6 foot spacing.

CHICAGO, IL

SEATTLE, WA

Maintenance

Routine roadway/utility maintenance.

Because the effectiveness of marked crossings depends entirely on their visibility, maintaining marked crossings should be a high priority.

Treatment Adoption and Professional Consensus

Commonly used in dozens of European bicycle friendly cities.

Seen in the form of dotted line extensions in most US bicycle-friendly cities.

- Austin, TX
- Boston, MA
- Cambridge, MA
- Chicago, IL
- Decatur, GA
- Denver, CO
- Eugene, OR
- Long Beach, CA
- Memphis, TN
- Missoula, MT
- New York, NY
- Portland, OR
- San Francisco, CA
- Seattle, WA
- Washington, DC

Two-Stage Turn Queue Boxes

CHICAGO, IL

Two-stage turn queue boxes offer bicyclists a safe way to make left turns at multi-lane signalized intersections from a right side cycle track or bike lane (or right turns from a left side cycle track or bike lane). Two-stage turn queue boxes may also be used at unsignalized intersections to simplify turns from a bicycle lane or cycle track, as for example onto a bicycle boulevard. At midblock crossing locations, a two-stage turn queue box may be used to orient bicyclists properly for safe crossings. Multiple positions are available for queuing boxes, depending on intersection configuration.

Cycle track design often prevents bicyclists from merging into traffic to turn. This makes the provision of two-stage turns critical for basic transportation function. The same principles for two-stage turns apply to bike lanes as well.

OTTAWA, CANADA

PORTLAND, OR

While two stage turns may increase bicyclist comfort in many locations, this configuration typically results in increases delay for bicyclists. Bicyclists now need to receive two separate green signal indications (one for the through street, followed by one for the cross street) to turn. At unsignalized intersections this configuration may also increase delay for bicyclists due to the need to wait for appropriate gaps in crossing motor vehicle traffic.

PORTLAND, OR

Benefits

Improves bicyclist ability to safely and comfortably make left turns.

Provides a formal queuing space for bicyclists making a two-stage turn.

Reduces turning conflicts between bicyclists and motor vehicles.

Prevents conflicts arising from bicyclists queuing in a bike lane or crosswalk.

Separates turning bicyclists from through bicyclists.

Typical Applications

At signalized intersections.

Along multi-lane roadways.

Along roadways with high traffic speeds and/or traffic volumes.

Where a significant number of bicyclists turn left from a right side facility.

Along cycle tracks.

To safely navigate streetcar tracks.

Design Guidance

Two-Stage Turn Queue Box

Required Features

(1) An area shall be designated to hold queuing bicyclists and formalize two-stage turn maneuvers.[71]

(2) Pavement markings shall include a bicycle stencil and a turn arrow to clearly indicate proper bicycle direction and positioning.

SALT LAKE CITY, UT (PHOTO: SALT LAKE CITY PUBLIC WORKS)

VANCOUVER, CANADA (PHOTO: WILL VANLUE)

(3) The queue box shall be placed in a protected area. Typically this is within an on-street parking lane or between the bicycle lane and the pedestrian crossing.

(4) In cities that permit right turns on red signal indications, a "No Turn on Red" sign shall be installed overhead to prevent vehicles from entering the queuing area. (MUTCD Section 2B.54)

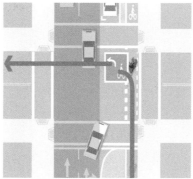

Cycle Track Buffer Configuration

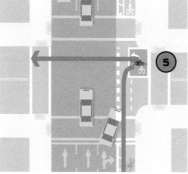

Crosswalk Setback Configuration
Wider corner radii, set back pedestrian crossing, and/or narrowed bikeway space, provides opportunity for queue box.

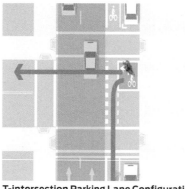

T-intersection Parking Lane Configuration

Recommended Features

(5) In cases where a constrained roadway geometry or right of way prevents the creation of a dedicated two stage turn queue box in a protected location:

- The pedestrian crosswalk may be adjusted or realigned to enable space for a queue box.

- A bike box may be provided behind the pedestrian crossing to serve the same purpose. This configuration

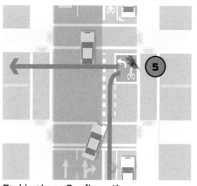

Parking Lane Configuration

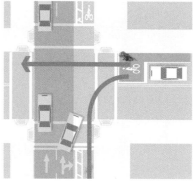

Bike Box Configuration
Bicyclists yield to pedestrians. Not recommended in areas with high pedestrian volumes.

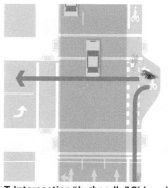

T-Intersection "Jughandle" Sidewalk Configuration

should only be considered if pedestrian volumes are low, as bicyclists must yield to pedestrians in the crosswalk before entering the queue.

(6) The queue box should be positioned laterally in the cross-street, to promote visibility of bicyclists.

(7) Colored paving inside of the queuing area should be used to further define the bicycle space.

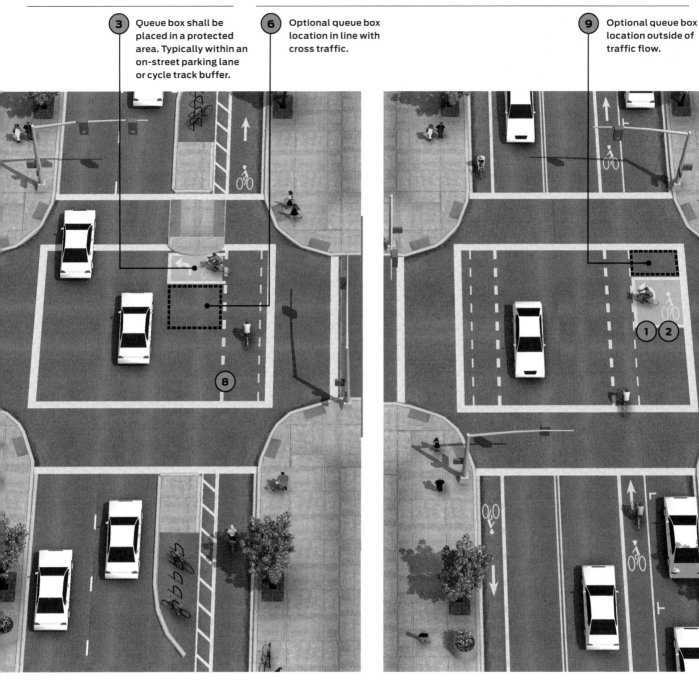

3 Queue box shall be placed in a protected area. Typically within an on-street parking lane or cycle track buffer.

6 Optional queue box location in line with cross traffic.

9 Optional queue box location outside of traffic flow.

8 Markings across intersections should be used to define through bicyclist positioning.

Optional Features

9 The queue box may be positioned laterally in the cross street parking lane rather than in front of the travel lane. This may require bicyclists to weave into the travel lane to resume through movement if no dedicated

bicycle facility is present since the parking lane ahead will be occupied.

10 At midblock turning locations, the queue box may be integrated into the sidewalk space. This configuration is also known as a "jughandle." Consider the use of some form of signalization at these locations.

11 Signage may be used to define proper positioning and improve visibility of the queue box.

12 A bicycle signal, with leading bicycle interval, may be installed in conjunction with the two-stage turn queue box.[72]

13 Guide lines, pavement symbols, and/or colored pavement may be used to lead bicyclists into the queue box.

PHOTO: RICHARD DRUDL

Other innovative bicycle treatments are starting to gain popularity that also encourage a safer crossing angle at tracks, including the two-stage turn for bicyclists.

Boorse, J., Hill, M., Danaher, A. (2011). General Design and Engineering Principles of Streetcar Transit. ITE Journal, 81(1), 38.

Maintenance

Colored pavement, if used, may be difficult to maintain in climates prone to snow and ice.

Treatment Adoption and Professional Consensus

Commonly used in dozens of European bicycle friendly cities.

Currently used in the following US cities:
- Atlanta, GA
- Cambridge, MA
- Chicago, IL
- New York, NY
- Philadelphia, PA
- Portland, OR
- Salt Lake City, UT

Median Refuge Island

SAN LUIS OBISPO, CA (PHOTO: WWW.PEDBIKEIMAGES.ORG, ADAM FUKUSHIMA)

Median refuge islands are protected spaces placed in the center of the street to facilitate bicycle and pedestrian crossings. Crossings of two-way streets are facilitated by allowing bicyclists and pedestrians to navigate only one direction of traffic at a time. Medians configured to protect cycle tracks can both facilitate crossings and also function as two-stage turn queue boxes. See Two-Stage Turn Queue Boxes for guidance details.

For bicycle facility crossings of higher volume or multi-lane streets, increased levels of treatment may be desired including bicycle signals, hybrid beacons, or active warning beacons.

TUCSON, AZ (PHOTO: MICHAEL MCKISSON, TUCSONVELO.COM)

Benefits

By simplifying crossings, allows bicyclists to more comfortably cross streets.

Provides a protected space for bicyclists to wait for an acceptable gap in traffic.

On two-way streets allows bicyclists to take advantage of gaps in one direction of traffic at a time.

Reduces the overall crossing length and exposure to vehicle traffic for a bicyclist or pedestrian.

Decreases the amount of delay that a bicyclist will experience to cross a street.

Calms traffic on a street by physically narrowing the roadway and potentially restricts motor vehicle left turn movements.

Establishes and reinforces bicycle priority on bicycle boulevards by restricting vehicle through movements.

When used with a protected cycle track, raised medians can be installed at each side of the block to give structure to the floating parking lane.

When used to protect a cycle track, raised medians can provide crossing pedestrians with a refuge area and/or provide shelter for a bicyclist making a two-stage turn across traffic.

PORTLAND, OR

NEW YORK, NY

Typical Applications

Where a bikeway crosses a moderate to high volume or high speed street.

Along streets with high bicycle and pedestrian volumes.

Along streets with few acceptable gaps to cross both directions of traffic.

At signalized or unsignalized intersections.

Where it is desirable to restrict vehicle through movements, a median can double as a diverter to prevent cut-through traffic on a bicycle route.

With protected cycle tracks.

Design Guidance

Median Refuge Island

Required Features

1 The desirable width of the median refuge is 10 feet or greater. The absolute minimum width is 6 feet.[73]

2 When applied on a two-way street, the median refuge shall be placed along the centerline of the roadway between the opposing directions of travel.

3 Pavement markings on the approach to the refuge island shall follow the guidance provided in Section 31.02 of the MUTCD.[74]

4 The approach edge of the raised median shall be outlined in retroreflective white or yellow material.[75]

5 In areas with snow accumulation, reflective delineators shall be used to mark the island for increased visibility to snow plow crews.

Recommended Features

6 The length of the refuge island should be greater than 6 feet.[76]

7 Reflective markers should be used on the approach to the nose of the island's curb.[77]

8 The height of the island should be curb level, 6 inches high. When used as an exclusive bicycle facility it may be desirable to keep the refuge area at street level.[78]

9 An angled cut-through (45 degrees) should be provided to position bicyclists to face oncoming traffic. If the cut-through is to be shared with pedestrians, the 45-degree angle of the curb should transition back to being perpendicular to the street to provide proper directional cues for the blind.

10 The refuge area should be wide enough to accommodate two-way bicycle traffic.

Optional Features

11 "Advanced Stop" signs and markings for motorists may be included.[78]

12 Landscaping may be provided in the median, but it should not compromise visibility.[80]

13 Lighting may be installed for improving visibility of the facility at night.

14 At signalized intersections, push buttons or other detection methods may be provided to actuate the signal head.

15 The median refuge can be carried across the entire cross street approach to act as a diverter to prevent cut-through traffic on a bicycle route.

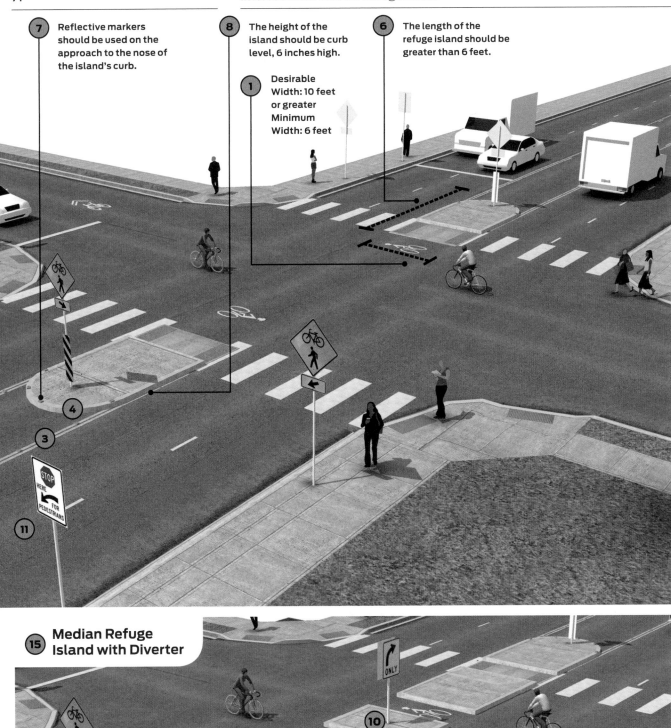

7 Reflective markers should be used on the approach to the nose of the island's curb.

8 The height of the island should be curb level, 6 inches high.

6 The length of the refuge island should be greater than 6 feet.

1 Desirable Width: 10 feet or greater Minimum Width: 6 feet

4

3

11

15 Median Refuge Island with Diverter

10

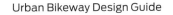

VANCOUVER, BC

VANCOUVER, BC (PHOTO: WWW.PEDBIKEIMAGES.ORG, CARL SUNDSTROM)

Maintenance

Refuge islands may collect road debris and may require somewhat frequent maintenance.

Refuge islands should be visible to snow plow crews and should be kept free of snow berms that block access.

Treatment Adoption and Professional Consensus

Commonly used in dozens of European bicycle friendly cities.

Currently used in the following US cities:
- Austin, TX
- Bellevue, WA
- Los Angeles, CA
- Minneapolis, MN
- New York, NY
- Portland, OR
- San Francisco, CA
- San Luis Obispo, CA

Through Bike Lanes

SANTA ROSA BEACH, FL

For bicyclists traveling in a conventional bike lane or from a truncated cycle track, the approach to an intersection with vehicular turn lanes can present a significant challenge. For this reason it is vital that bicyclists are provided with an opportunity to correctly position themselves to avoid conflicts with turning vehicles. This treatment specifically covers the application of a through bicycle lane or 'bicycle pocket' at the intersection. For other potential approaches to provide accommodations for bicyclists at intersections with turn lanes, please see bike box, combined bike lane/turn lane, bicycle signals, and colored bike facilities.

PORTLAND, OR

ST. PETERSBURG, FL

Benefits

Enables bicyclists to correctly position themselves to the left of right turn lanes or to the right of left turn lanes.

Reduces conflicts between turning motorists and bicycle through traffic.

Provides bicyclists with guidance to follow the preferred travel path.

Leads to more predictable bicyclist and motorist travel movements.

Alerts motorists to expect and yield to merging bicycle traffic.

Signifies an appropriate location for motorists to safely merge across the bike lane into the turn lane.

BOULDER, CO

CHICAGO, IL

Typical Applications

On streets with right-side bike lanes and right-turn only lanes at intersections.

On streets with left-side bike lanes and left-turn only lanes at intersections.

On streets with bike lanes and an auxiliary right-turn-only lane added in advance of the intersection.

On streets with bike lanes and a parking lane that transition into a turn lane at intersections.

Design Guidance

Through Bike Lanes

Required Features

1 The desired width of a dashed bike transition lane and through bike lane is 6 feet with a minimum width of 4 feet.

2 Bicycle lane word and/or symbol and arrow markings (MUTCD Figure 9C-3) shall be used to define the bike lane and designate that portion of the street for preferential use by bicyclists.

3 The through bike lane shall be placed to the left of the right-turn only lane.

4 Dotted lines signifying the merge area shall begin a minimum of 50 feet before the intersection (MUTCD). Dotted lines should begin 100 feet before the intersection if along a high speed/volume roadway.

5 Dotted lane line transition areas to through bike lanes shall not be used on streets with double right turn lanes. Double right turn lanes are extremely difficult for bicyclists to negotiate. Shared lane markings may be used in the center of the inside turn lane to designate the preferred path of through bicycle travel.

Recommended Features

6 Accompanying signage should include R3-7R "Right Lane Must Turn Right" and R4-4 "Begin Right Turn Yield to Bikes" (MUTCD).

7 Dotted white lines should be 6 inches wide and 2 feet long with a 2- to 6-foot gap between dashes (MUTCD).

8 Through bike lanes should be provided at any intersection approach where a right turn only auxiliary lane is created (also known as a right turn add lane). It is desirable for bicyclists to travel straight through the merging area to reinforce right-of-way.

9 Dotted lane line transition areas to through bike lanes should not be provided at any intersection approach where a through travel lane transitions into a right turn only lane (also known as a right turn drop or trap lane). In such instances consider utilizing an exclusive bicycle signal phase with the bike lane remaining to the right, or not delineating the merging area connecting to the through lane. Shared lane markings may be used to provide additional guidance.

10 At intersections with high right turning vehicle volumes, high bicyclist volumes, or along priority bicycle corridors, treatments beyond dotted white lines such as coloring and increased signing should be provided.

11 Right-turn only lanes should be as short as possible in order to limit the speed of cars in the right turn lane. Fast moving traffic on both sides can be uncomfortable for bicyclists.

12 Terminating the bike lane in advance of the intersection is discouraged.

13 For intersections that lack the physical width to install a bicycle pocket, a combined bike/turn lane should be used.

14 Vehicle turn lane width should not be reduced to less than 9 feet.

15 Bicycle detection should be provided within the through bike lane.

Optional Features

16 On streets with a combined turn and through lane, shared lane markings may be used in the center of the lane.

17 A bike box may be used in lieu of a designated through bike lane.

18 Bicycle warning signs may be used in advance of the merge/transition area.

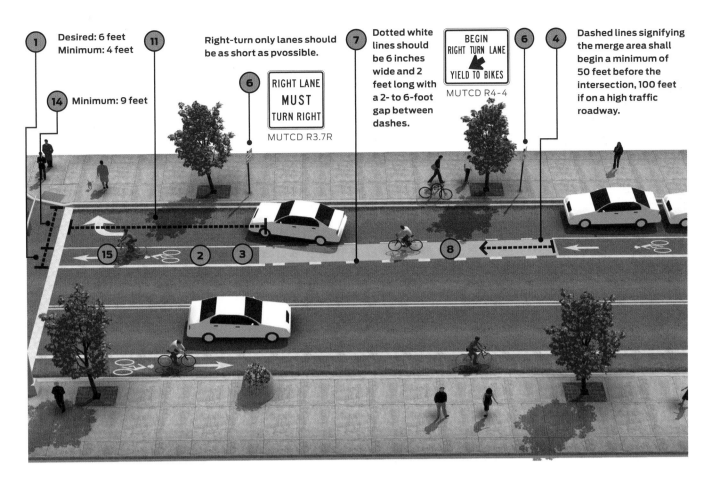

1 Desired: 6 feet
Minimum: 4 feet

14 Minimum: 9 feet

11 Right-turn only lanes should be as short as pvossible.

6 RIGHT LANE
MUST
TURN RIGHT
MUTCD R3.7R

7 Dotted white lines should be 6 inches wide and 2 feet long with a 2- to 6-foot gap between dashes.

BEGIN
RIGHT TURN LANE
YIELD TO BIKES
MUTCD R4-4

6

4 Dashed lines signifying the merge area shall begin a minimum of 50 feet before the intersection, 100 feet if on a high traffic roadway.

Auxiliary Right-Turn-Only Lane Added

These are appropriate conditions for use of through bike lanes.

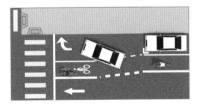

Parking lane into right-turn-only lane.
Through bike lanes provide bicycle priority within weaving area

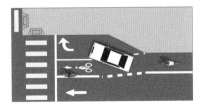

Right-turn-only lane added at intersection with throat widening.
Through bike lanes provide bicycle priority within weaving area.

Through Travel Lane Transitions into Right-Turn-Only Lane

These are generally inappropriate conditions for use of through bike lanes. Consider alternate treatments.

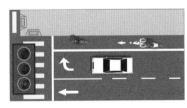

Exclusive bicycle signal phase used to separate conflicting movements.

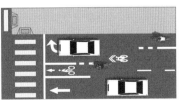

Bicycle lane dropped in advance of the intersection encourages bicyclists to merge across as gaps permit. Shared lane markings may be used to provide additional guidance.

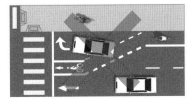

Bicyclists are not provided priority in weaving area and must use caution to merge across potentially high-speed motor vehicle traffic. Dotted lane line transition areas to through bike lanes should not be provided at these locations.

PORTLAND, OR

Maintenance

Routine roadway maintenance is needed.

Dashed lines should be installed with thermoplastic to increase durability and resist tire wear.

Because the effectiveness of markings depends entirely on their visibility, maintaining markings should be a high priority.

Treatment Adoption and Professional Consensus

Bicycle lanes are the most common bicycle facility in use in the US, and most jurisdictions are familiar with their design and application as described in the MUTCD and AASHTO Guide for the Development of Bicycle Facilities. Many US cities offer through bicycle lanes at intersections; some offer increased levels of comfort and security to bicyclists through the application of some of the recommended and optional elements noted within this guide.

Combined Bike Lane/ Turn Lane

EUGENE, OR (PHOTO: CITY OF EUGENE)

A combined bike lane/turn lane places a suggested bike lane within the inside portion of a dedicated motor vehicle turn lane. Shared Lane Markings or conventional bicycle stencils with a dashed line can delineate the space for bicyclists and motorists within the shared lane or indicate the intended path for through bicyclists. This treatment includes signage advising motorists and bicyclists of proper positioning within the lane.

When configured on a cycle track corridor, the combined lane is commonly called a mixing zone, and is intended to minimize conflicts with turning vehicles at intersections as an alternative to an exclusive bike signal phase.

BEND, OR

More than 17 percent of the surveyed bicyclists using the narrow-lane intersection felt that it was safer than the comparison location with a standard-width right-turn lane, and another 55 percent felt that the narrow-lane site was no different safety-wise than the standard-width location.

Hunter, W.W. (2000). Evaluation of a Combined Bicycle Lane/Right-Turn Lane in Eugene, Oregon. Publication No. FHWA-RD-00-151, Federal Highway Administration, Washington, DC.

Benefits

Preserves positive guidance for bicyclists in a situation where the bicycle lane would otherwise be dropped prior to an intersection.

Maintains bicyclist comfort and priority in the absence of a dedicated bicycle through lane.

Guides bicyclists to ride in part of the turning lane, which tends to have lower speed traffic than the adjacent through lane, allowing higher speed through traffic to pass unimpeded.

Encourages motorists to yield to bicyclists when crossing into the narrow right-turn lane.

Reduces motor vehicle speed within the right turn lane.

Reduces the risk of 'right hook' collisions at intersections.

Typical Applications

On streets where there is a right turn lane but not enough space to maintain a standard-width bicycle lane at the intersection.

On streets where there is no dedicated right turn lane, but on which high volumes of right turning traffic may cause conflicts between motorists and bicyclists.

On cycle track corridors where there is a dedicated turn lane on the side of the street with the cycle track, but where a separate bike signal phase is not appropriate or feasible.

May not be appropriate at intersections with very high peak automobile right turn demand.

NEW YORK, NY

Design Guidance

Combined Bike Lane/ Turn Lane

Guidance for conventional bicycle lanes and intersection crossing markings may also apply. When configured as a mixing zone for a cycle track, additional guidance for a cycle track intersection approach may also apply.

Required Features

(1) Some form of bicycle marking shall be used to clarify bicyclist positioning within the combined lane.

Recommended Features

(2) Within the combined lane, the bicycle area width should be 4 feet minimum.

(3) Width of combined lane should be 9 feet minimum, 13 feet maximum. A full bicycle through lane can be accommodated if the vehicle right turn only lane can be made 14 feet or wider.

(4) A dotted 4 inch line and bicycle lane marking should be used to bicyclist positioning within the combined lane without excluding cars from the suggested bicycle area.

(5) If the right lane is signed for "Right Turn Only," or if a sign is otherwise needed to make it legal for through bicyclists to use a right turn lane, signage should be installed in advance alerting the start of the combined turn lane.

(6) If configured as a mixing zone on a cycle track corridor, the following features are recommended:

- A Turning Vehicles Yield to Bikes (modified R10-15) sign should be used in advance of the mixing zone.

- A yield line should be used in advance of the mixing zone.

- The transition to the mixing zone should begin a minimum of 70 feet in advance of the intersection. Mixing zones that are shorter in length and begin abruptly encourage slower vehicle speed.

Optional Features

(7) A shared lane marking (MUTCD figure 9C-9) may be used as an alternative to dotted striping to clarify bicyclist position within the combined lane.

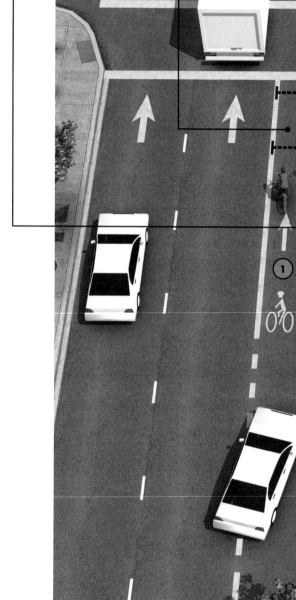

(4) A dotted 4 inch line and bicycle lane marking should be used to clarify bicyclist positioning within the combined lane.

(2) Minimum width: 4 feet

(3) Width of combined lane should be 9 feet minimum, 13 feet maximum

7 A shared lane marking (MUTCD figure 9C-9) may be used as an alternative to dotted striping to clarify bicyclist position within the combined lane.

6 A yield line should be used in advance of the intersection

1 Shared lane marking

6 The transition to the mixing zone should begin a minimum of 70 feet in advance of the intersection.

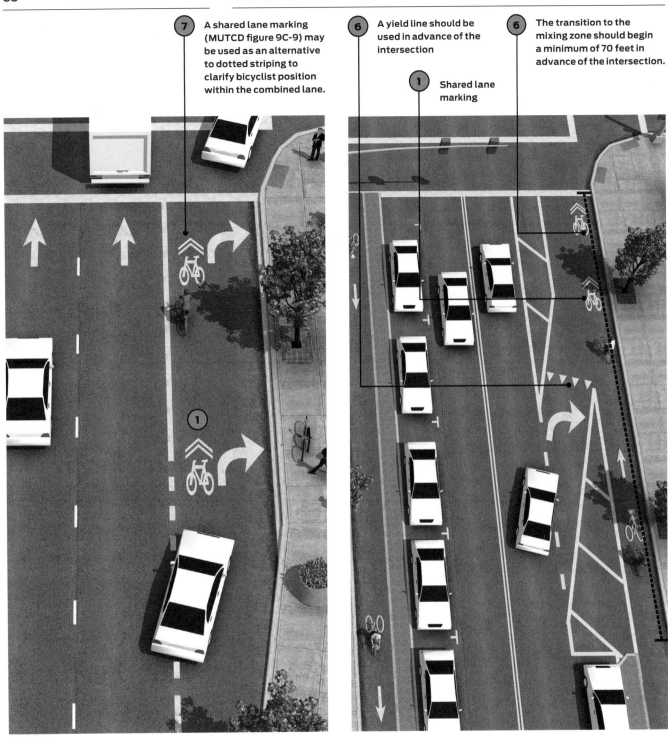

EUGENE, OR

BILLINGS, MT

Maintenance

Markings within the shared lane will require regular maintenance and marking repairs due to frequent wear from motor vehicle use. Inlaid thermoplastic application is recommended for increased durability.

Treatment Adoption and Professional Consensus

Currently used in the following US Cities:

- Austin, TX
- Bend, OR
- Billings, MT
- Bozeman, MT
- Colorado Springs, CO
- Eugene, OR
- Kona, HI
- New York, NY
- Portland, OR
- Provo, UT
- San Francisco, CA
- Washington, DC

Cycle Track Intersection Approach

NEW YORK, NY

The approach to an intersection from a cycle track should be designed to reduce turn conflicts for bicyclists and/or to provide connections to intersecting bicycle facility types. This is typically achieved by removing the protected cycle track barrier or parking lane (or lowering a raised cycle track to street level), and shifting the bicycle lane to be closer to or shared with the adjacent motor vehicle lane. At these intersections, the experience is similar to a conventional bike lane and may involve similar applications of merging area treatments and markings across intersections. At the intersection, the cycle track may transition to a conventional bike lane or a combined bike lane/turn lane. Cycle track crossings of signalized intersections can also be accomplished through the use of a bicycle signal phase that reduces conflicts with motor vehicles by separating in time potentially conflicting bicycle and motor vehicle movements.

CAMBRIDGE, MA

Benefits

Increases visibility of bicyclists and motorists in advance of the intersection.

Mitigates the risk of "left or right hook" crashes with turning motorists.

May be less expensive than using full bicycle signals.

Encourages motorists to yield to bicyclists when crossing into the narrow right-turn lane.

Reduces motor vehicle speed within the right turn lane.

Typical Applications

Where cycle tracks approach intersections where turning movements across the path of the bicyclist (either left or right) is allowed.

At intersections with a single dedicated right turn lane for motor vehicles.

On cycle tracks protected by on street parking or otherwise removed from the travel lane.

NEW YORK, NY

Design Guidance

Cycle Track Intersection Approach

Required Features

1 When the cycle track is dropped on an intersection approach, the intersection shall provide some type of bicycle facility to receive cycle track users. This may be a conventional bike lane, bike box, or combined bike lane/turn lane.

Recommended Features

2 For a transition to a bike lane, minimum desirable width is 6 feet, with an absolute minimum of 4 feet. At constrained intersections with right turn lanes, consider transitioning to a mixing zone (combined bike lane/right turn lane.).

3 The desirable distance to drop a cycle track prior to an intersection varies by the specific treatment and lane configuration. More space is required when bicyclists and motorists will be mixing or merging.[81]

4 Parking should be prohibited 30 to 50 feet in advance of where the cycle track buffer ends to promote visibility between bicyclists and motorists.

5 Tactile warnings or pavement markings should be used on slopes from raised cycle tracks to slow bicyclist speed prior to the transition out of the cycle track, and to warn users of potential conflicts with motor vehicles.[82]

6 Cycle tracks should be shifted more closely to the travel lanes on intersection approaches to put bicyclists clearly in the field of view of motorists.

7 When transitioning from a raised cycle track to street level, the grade should be smooth and comfortable, without significant longitudinal pavement joints or sharp changes in direction. Maximum slope should be 1:8.

8 Intersection crossing markings should be used with truncated cycle tracks to indicate the intended path of bicyclists through the intersection.

9 Two-stage turn queue boxes should be provided to assist in making turns from the cycle track facility.

Optional Features

10 Color may be used to mark conflict areas at intersections with turn lanes, or to extend color applied to the cycle track facility. See Colored Bicycle Facilities for more guidance.

11 At intersections with heavy right turn movements, the facility may be combined with a bike box or an advanced stop bar to position bicyclists ahead of motorists.

12 At intersection transit stop locations where separate signal control for the cycle track is possible, consider raising the cycle track to sidewalk level and wrapping the cycle track behind the transit stop zone to reduce conflicts with transit vehicles and passengers. Bicyclists should yield to pedestrians in these areas.

13 Where separate bicycle signal phase is not possible, an extended mixing zone may be provided with signage directing bicyclists to yield to buses and loading passengers.

14 Cycle tracks may be configured on the left side of a one-way street to avoid conflicts at transit stops.

15 A bicycle exclusive signal phase may be used to segregate conflicting movements between bicyclists and motorists.

Adjacent to Right Turn Only Lane

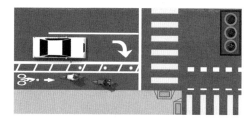

Bicycle Signal Phase
A dedicated bicycle signal phase can eliminate conflict between turning automobiles and bicyclists.

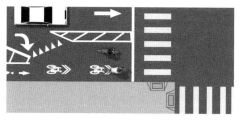

Mixing Zone
A combined bike lane/turn lane encourages motor vehicles and bicyclists to negotiate the space within the travel lane in advance of the intersection.

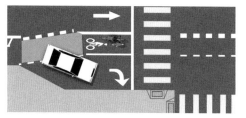

Through Bike Lane
Maintaining the bike lane to the left of a right turn-only-lane positions road users to avoid right-hook collisions.

Lane transitions show here are for illustration purposes only and are not meant to reflect actual design dimensions.

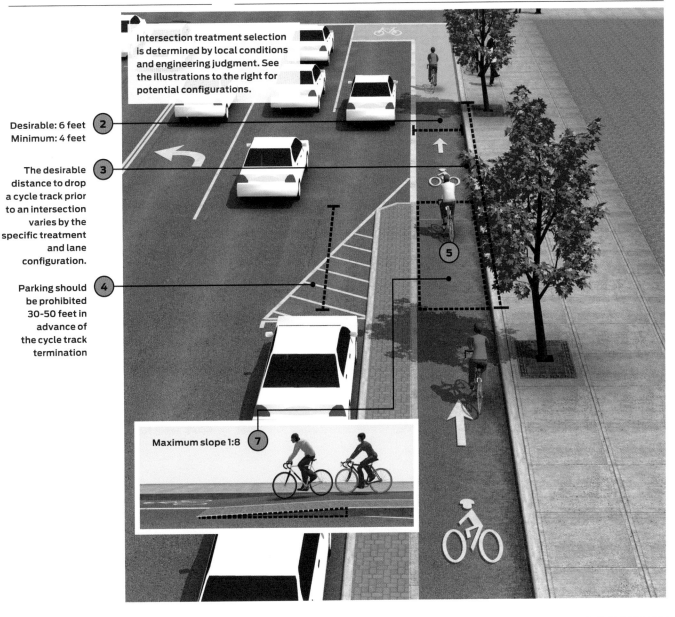

Intersection treatment selection is determined by local conditions and engineering judgment. See the illustrations to the right for potential configurations.

2 Desirable: 6 feet
Minimum: 4 feet

3 The desirable distance to drop a cycle track prior to an intersection varies by the specific treatment and lane configuration.

4 Parking should be prohibited 30-50 feet in advance of the cycle track termination

7 Maximum slope 1:8

Adjacent to Through/Right Turn Lane

Bike Lane/Bike Box
Positioning bicyclists ahead of automobiles helps prevent right-hook conflicts with turning vehicles at the start of the green indication.

"Bend In" Crossing
Using a curb extension or painted buffer, the cycle track should be bent-in toward the roadway promote visibility of bicyclists in advance of the intersection.

VANCOUVER, BC (WWW.PEDBIKEIMAGES.ORG, CARL SUNDSTROM)

WASHINGTON, DC

MISSOULA, MT

VANCOUVER, BC

Maintenance

Routine roadway/utility maintenance.

Maintaining markings should be a high priority.

Treatment Adoption and Professional Consensus

Commonly used in dozens of European bicycle friendly cities.

Currently used in the following

US cities:

· Cambridge, MA
· Denver, CO
· Long Beach, CA
· Missoula, MT
· New York, NY
· Portland, OR
· San Francisco, CA
· Washington, DC

Signals

Bicycle Signal Heads 93

Signal Detection and Actuation 99

Active Warning Beacon for Bike Route at Unsignalized Intersection 105

Hybrid Beacon for Bike Route Crossing of Major Street 111

Bicycle signals and beacons facilitate bicyclist crossings of roadways. Bicycle signals make crossing intersections safer for bicyclists by clarifying when to enter an intersection and by restricting conflicting vehicle movements. Bicycle signals are traditional three lens signal heads with green-yellow and red bicycle stenciled lenses that can be employed at standard signalized intersections and Hybrid Beacon crossings. Flashing amber warning beacons are utilized at unsignalized intersection crossings. Push buttons, signage, and pavement markings may be used to highlight these facilities for both bicyclists and motorists.

Determining which type of signal or beacon to use for a particular intersection depends on a variety of factors. These include speed limits, average daily traffic (ADT), anticipated bicycle crossing traffic, and the configuration of planned or existing bicycle facilities. Signals may be required as part of the construction of a protected bicycle facility such as a cycle track with potential turning conflicts, or to decrease vehicle or pedestrian conflicts at major crossings. An intersection with bicycle signals may reduce stress and delays for a crossing bicyclist, and discourage illegal and unsafe crossing maneuvers.

Bicycle signal heads in New York City are placed near side and far side at intersections along city's protected bike lanes. The signals prevent right-hook collisions and give bicycles a dedicated time to cross through busy traffic.

NEW YORK, NY

Bicycle Signal Heads

PORTLAND, OR

A bicycle signal is an electrically powered traffic control device that should only be used in combination with an existing conventional traffic signal or hybrid beacon. Bicycle signals are typically used to improve identified safety or operational problems involving bicycle facilities or to provide guidance for bicyclists at intersections where they may have different needs from other road users (e.g., bicycle only movements, leading bicycle intervals). Bicycle signal heads may be installed at signalized intersections to indicate bicycle signal phases and other bicycle-specific timing strategies. In the United States, bicycle signal heads typically use standard three-lens signal heads in green, yellow, and red lenses.

LONG BEACH, CA

Benefits

Separates bicycle movements from conflicting motor vehicle, streetcar, light rail, or pedestrian movements.

Provides priority to bicycle movements at intersections
(e.g., a leading bicycle interval).

Accommodates bicycle-only movements within signalized intersections (e.g., providing a phase for a contra-flow bike lane that otherwise would not have a phase). Though bicycle travel may also occur simultaneously with parallel auto movement if conflicting automobile turns are restricted.

Protects bicyclists in the intersection, which may improve real and perceived safety at high-conflict areas.

Improves operation and provides appropriate information for bicyclists (as compared to pedestrian signals).

Helps to simplify bicycle movements through complex intersections and potentially improve operations or reduce conflicts for all modes.[83]

NEW YORK, NY

Typical Applications

Where a stand-alone bike path or multi-use path crosses a street, especially where the needed bicycle clearance time differs substantially from the needed pedestrian clearance time.

To split signal phases at intersections where a predominant bicycle movement conflicts with a main motor vehicle movement during the same green phase.

At intersections where a bicycle facility transitions from a cycle track to a bicycle lane, if turning movements are significant.

At intersections with contra-flow bicycle movements that otherwise would have no signal indication and where a normal traffic signal head may encourage wrong-way driving by motorists.

To give bicyclists an advanced green (like a leading pedestrian interval), or to indicate an "all-bike" phase where bicyclist turning movements are high.

To make it legal for bicyclists to enter an intersection during an all-pedestrian phase (may not be appropriate in some cities).

At complex intersections that may otherwise be difficult for bicyclists to navigate.

At intersections with high numbers of bicycle and motor vehicle crashes.

At intersections near schools (primary, secondary, and university).

Design Guidance

Bicycle Signal Heads

Required Features

1 The bicycle signal head shall be placed in a location clearly visible to oncoming bicycles.

2 If the bicycle phase is not set to recall each cycle, bicycle signals shall be installed with appropriate detection and actuation.

3 An adequate clearance interval (i.e., the movement's combined time for the yellow and all-red phases) shall be provided to ensure that bicyclists entering the intersection during the green phase have sufficient time to safely clear the intersection before conflicting movements receive a green indication.[84]

4 If the bicycle signal is used to separate through bicycle movements from right turning vehicles, then right turn on red shall be prohibited when the bicycle signal is active. This can be accomplished with the provision of a traffic signal with red, yellow, and green arrow displays. An active display to help emphasize this restriction is recommended.

5 Bicycle signal heads are generally the preferred option over installing a sign instructing bicycles to use pedestrian signals. While instructing bicyclists to use pedestrian signals is a low-cost option, the length of the pedestrian clearance interval (typically timed at 3.5 feet per second) is usually inappropriate for bicyclists. The result is that approaching bicyclists have poor information about when it is safe and legal to enter the intersection.

Recommended Features

6 A supplemental "Bicycle Signal" sign plaque should be added below the bicycle signal head to increase comprehension.

7 Signal timing with bicycle-only indications should consider activating the signal with each cycle prior to implementation with detection. This will increase awareness of the interval for motorists and bicyclists. In a close network of signals, the timing should consider how often a bicyclist will be stopped in the system to insure that undue delay is not a result of the bicycle-only signal.

8 Intersection crossing markings should be used where the bicycle travel path through the intersection is unusual (e.g., diagonal crossing) or needed to separate conflicts.

9 Passive actuation of bicycle signals through loops or another detection method is preferred to the use of push-buttons for actuation where practical. Passive actuation is more convenient for bicyclists. If push buttons are used, they should be mounted such that bicyclists do not have to dismount to actuate the signal.

10 There are currently no national standards for determining the appropriate clearance intervals for bicycle signals. However, the primary factors in choosing an appropriate clearance interval are bicyclist travel speed and intersection width. At most signalized intersections, vehicular clearance intervals will likely function well for bicyclists. Exceptions requiring consideration include signals along cycle tracks or bicycle facilities that may be likely to serve significant levels of novice cyclists. See guidance for selecting clearance intervals at left.

11 Bicyclists typically need longer minimum green times than motor vehicles due to slower acceleration speeds. This time is usually more critical for bicyclists on minor-road approaches, since crossing distance of major roads is typically greater than that of minor roads, and crossings from minor roads are often subject to short green intervals. Bicycle minimum green time is determined using the bicycle crossing time for standing bicycles.[85]

12 Design and operation of bicycle signal heads should consider general MUTCD guidance on standards for traffic signals where applicable (e.g., positions of signal indications; visibility, aiming, and shielding of signal faces). Many of the MUTCD considerations for traffic signals will not apply to bicycle signals. Existing experience with bicycle signal installations in some cities has resulted in post mounted signals being utilized adjacent to the bikeway with a lower overall height. Some existing designs use shields and louvers to limit the driver's visibility of the bicycle signal to avoid potential confusion. Engineering judgment should be used to ensure that the positioning of bicycle signal heads is optimal for each installation. It is recommended that bicycle signal heads be separated from motor vehicle signal heads by at least two feet to increase comprehension.

Optional Features

13 For improved visibility, near-sided bicycle signals may be used to supplement far-side signals. Smaller, half-sized signal heads with 4 inch lenses may be more appropriate in scale for near side installations.

14 Visual variation in signal head housing for the bicycle signal when compared to adjacent traffic signals may increase contrast and awareness.

13 For improved visibility, near-sided bicycle signals may be used to supplement far-side signals.

1

1 The bicycle signal head shall be placed in a location clearly visible to oncoming bicycles.

6

14

4 If the bicycle signal is used to separate through bicycle movements from right turning vehicles, then right turn on red shall be prohibited if it is normally allowed.

A supplemental "Bicycle Signal" sign plaque should be added below the bicycle signal head to increase comprehension.

9

8

2

3 The following provides general guidance for selecting clearance intervals. This guidance should be tailored to local conditions using engineering judgment.

· At a minimum, the bicycle clearance interval should be sufficient to accommodate the 15th percentile biking speed (i.e., it should accommodate 85 percent of bicyclists at their normal travel speed). This is consistent with MUTCD guidance on pedestrian clearance intervals.

· Ideally, typical bicyclist speeds (V) should be measured in the field to determine a clearance interval appropriate for local conditions. However, at intersections with level approaches, 14 feet per second (9.5 miles per hour) may be used as a default speed in the absence of local data.[86]

· Intersection width (W) should be calculated from the intersection entry

(i.e., stop-line or crosswalk in the absence of a stop-line) to half-way across the last lane carrying through traffic.

Calculate the total clearance interval (Ci) based on the following equation:

$$C_i = 3 + \frac{W}{V}$$

· Yellow intervals for automobiles will typically be longer than those needed for bicycles, because of slower bicycle travel speeds. The intersection clearance time needed for bicyclists can be met partly through the automobile yellow interval, as well as through the all-red phase.

The above guidance should be supplemented with engineering judgment as some wider intersections could be left with extremely long all-red signal phases.

15 If signal controlled bicycle turning movements are desired, consider pairing the bicycle signal head with a turn signal head to clarify protected, permissive, or restricted turning movements.

16 Near-side bicycle signals may incorporate a "countdown to green" display to provide information about when a green bicycle indication will be provided. This treatment has proved popular in Europe, but there are currently no known installations in the United States.

MADISON, WI

SALT LAKE CITY, UT

Maintenance

Bicycle signal heads require the same maintenance as standard traffic signal heads, such as replacing bulbs and responding to power outages.

Treatment Adoption and Professional Consensus

Bicycle signal heads are widely used in Europe and China, as well as the following US cities:

- Alexandria, VA
- Austin, TX
- Davis, CA
- Denver, CO
- Long Beach, CA
- Madison, WI
- Minneapolis, MN
- New York, NY
- Portland, OR
- Salt Lake City, UT
- San Francisco, CA
- San Luis Obispo, CA
- Tucson, AZ
- Washington, DC

Note that while bicycle signal heads are not currently included in the MUTCD, the National Committee on Uniform Traffic Control Devices has formed a Task Force that is considering adding guidance to the MUTCD on the use of bicycle signals. The State of California has added them to its own version of the MUTCD-Section 4D.104(CA), and the State of Oregon is considering similar legislation.

Signal Detection and Actuation

PHOTO: RICHARD DRUDL

Bicycle detection is used at actuated signals to alert the signal controller of bicycle crossing demand on a particular approach. Bicycle detection occurs either through the use of push-buttons or by automated means (e.g., in-pavement loops, video, microwave, etc). Inductive loop vehicle detection at many signalized intersections is calibrated to the size or metallic mass of a vehicle. For bicycles to be detected, the loop must be adjusted for bicycle metallic mass. Otherwise, undetected bicyclists must either wait for a vehicle to arrive, dismount and push the pedestrian button (if available), or cross illegally.

PORTLAND, OR

Proper bicycle detection meets two primary criteria:
1) accurately detects bicyclists; and
2) provides clear guidance to bicyclists on how to actuate detection (e.g., what button to push, where to stand).

This section covers four primary types of bicycle signal detection:

Loop
Induction loop embedded in the pavement

Video
Video detection aimed at bicyclist approaches and calibrated to detect bicyclists

Push-button
User-activated button mounted on a pole facing the street

Microwave
Miniature microwave radar that picks up non-background targets

Benefits

Improves efficiency and reduces delay for bicycle travel.

Increases convenience and safety of bicycling and helps establish bicycling as a legitimate mode of transportation on streets.

Discourages red light running by bicyclists without causing excessive delay to motorists.

Can be used to prolong the green phase to provide adequate time for bicyclists to clear the intersection.

Signals: Detection and Actuation

SAN LUIS OBISPO, CA

SAN LUIS OBISPO, CA

PHOTO: RICHARD DRUDL

Typical Applications

In the travel lane on intersection approaches without bike lanes where actuation is required.

At intersections with bicycle signal heads and/or bicycle-specific phasing that are actuated.

In bike lanes on intersection approaches that are actuated.

In left turn lanes with actuated left-turn signals where bicyclists may also turn left.

To increase the green signal phase on intersection approaches whose combined minimum green plus yellow plus all-red is insufficient for bicyclists to clear the intersection when starting on a green signal. Advanced bicyclist detection can be applied to extend the green phase or to call the signal.

At clearly marked locations to designate where a bicyclist should wait.

Design Guidance

Bicycle Detection

Required Features

(1) The sensitivity of standard video, microwave and in-pavement loop detectors shall be adjusted to ensure that they detect bicyclists.

(2) Due to magnetic field symmetry, the center of inductive loops is the most sensitive location for detection for both diagonal slashed detectors and quadrupole loop detectors. Square and unmodified circle detectors are most sensitive at their edge.

(3) If not provided within a dedicated bike lane, shoulder, or cycle track, bicycle signal detection shall be visible to bicyclists through signs and/or stencils so that bicyclists know that the intersection has detection and where to position their bicycle to activate the signal.

(4) If provided, push-button activation shall be located so bicyclists can activate the signal without dismounting. If used, push buttons should have a supplemental sign facing the bicyclist's approach to increase visibility.

(5) On streets with bike lanes or bikeable shoulders, bicycle detectors shall be located in the bike lane or shoulder. Detection shall be located where bicycles are intended to travel and/or wait. If leading signal detection is provided, it shall be located along a bike lane or in the outside travel lane. Detection at signals shall be placed where bicyclists wait, either in the center of a bike box or immediately behind the stop bar in the bike lane. Intersections without painted bicycle infrastructure shall provide detection in the center of the outside lane.

(5) If leading signal detection is provided, it should be located along a bike lane.

(3) Detection shall be located where bicycles are intended to travel and/or wait.

(3) Bicycle detection shall be located in the bike lane.

Recommended Features

(6) The MUTCD provides guidance on stencil markings and signage related to signal detection.

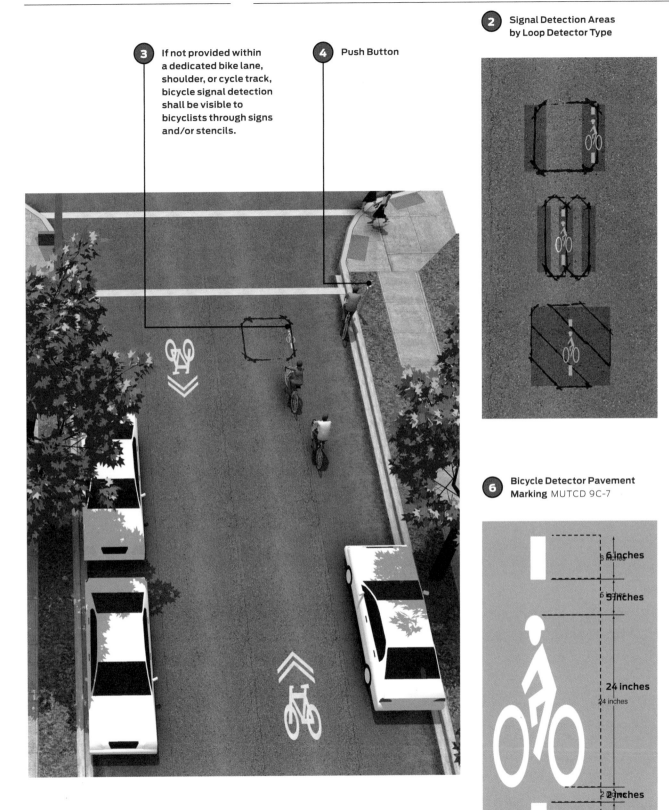

3 If not provided within a dedicated bike lane, shoulder, or cycle track, bicycle signal detection shall be visible to bicyclists through signs and/or stencils.

4 Push Button

2 Signal Detection Areas by Loop Detector Type

6 Bicycle Detector Pavement Marking MUTCD 9C-7

6 inches

5 inches

24 inches

2 inches

6 inches

2 inches

MILPITAS, CA

ANN ARBOR, MI

SIMULATED VIDEO DETECTION TARGET AREAS FOR BICYCLE SIGNAL DETECTION

Maintenance

Inductive loop detector sensitivity settings need to be monitored and adjusted over time.

Treatment Adoption and Professional Consensus

Bicycle signal detection is widely used in North American and European cities, both at standard signalized intersections and those with bicycle signal phases. Some US examples include:

· Ann Arbor, MI
· Arlington, VA
· Austin, TX
· Berkeley, CA
· Denver, CO
· Eugene, OR
· Madison, WI
· Marin County, CA
· Milpitas, CA
· Portland, OR
· San Luis Obispo, CA
· Santa Clara Valley, CA

Active Warning Beacon for Bike Route at Unsignalized Intersection

BILLINGS, MT

Active warning beacons are user-actuated amber flashing lights that supplement warning signs at unsignalized intersections or mid-block crosswalks. Beacons can be actuated either manually by a push-button or passively through detection. Rectangular Rapid Flash Beacons (RRFBs), a type of active warning beacon, use an irregular flash pattern similar to emergency flashers on police vehicles and can be installed on either two-lane or multi-lane roadways. Active warning beacons should be used to alert drivers to yield where bicyclists have the right-of-way crossing a road.

The RRFB offers significant potential safety and cost benefits, because it achieves very high rates of compliance at a very low relative cost in comparison to other more restrictive devices that provide comparable results, such as full midblock signalization.

Federal Highway Administration. (2008). Interim Approval for Optional Use of Rectangular Rapid Flashing Beacons (IA-11).

ALEXANDRIA, VA

BEND, OR

ST. PETERSBURG, FL (PHOTO: WWW.PEDBIKEIMAGES.ORG, DAN BURDEN)

Benefits

Offers lower cost alternative to traffic signals and hybrid signals.

Significantly increases driver yielding behavior at crossings when supplementing standard crossing warning signs and markings.

The unique nature of the stutter flash (RRFBs) elicits a greater response from drivers than traditional methods.

ST. PETERSBURG, FL

Overall, motorist yielding increased from 2% before to 35% after. When the flasher was activated, motorist yielding was 54%.

Hunter, W. W., Srinivasan, R., Martell, C. (2009). Evaluation of the Rectangular Rapid Flash Beacon at a Pinellas Trail Crossing in St. Petersburg, Florida. Florida Department of Transportation.

Typical Applications

Usually implemented at high-volume pedestrian crossings, but may also be considered for priority bicycle route crossings.

At locations where bike facilities cross roads at mid-block locations or at intersections where signals are not warranted or desired.

At locations where driver compliance at bicycle crossings is low.

Design Guidance

**Active Warning Beacon
for Bike Route at
Unsignalized Intersection**

Required Features

1 Active warning beacons shall be installed on the side of the road. If center islands or medians exist, providing secondary installations in these locations marginally improves driver yielding behavior.

2 Beacons shall be unlit when not activated.

Recommended Features

3 If intended for use by bicyclists, push button actuation shall be provided, and should be located so bicyclists can activate the signal without dismounting. Push buttons should have a supplemental sign facing the bicyclist's approach to increase visibility.

4 The MUTCD provides additional guidance on use of Rectangular Rapid Flash Beacons (RRFBs):

- RRFBs shall be used to supplement standard pedestrian and bicycle crossing signs and markings.
- RRFBs should not be used where the crosswalk approach is controlled by a yield sign, stop sign, or traffic-control signal.
- RRFBs can be used at a crosswalk at a roundabout.

Federal Highway Administration. (2009). Manual on Uniform Traffic Control Devices.

Motor Vehicle Yielding Compliance

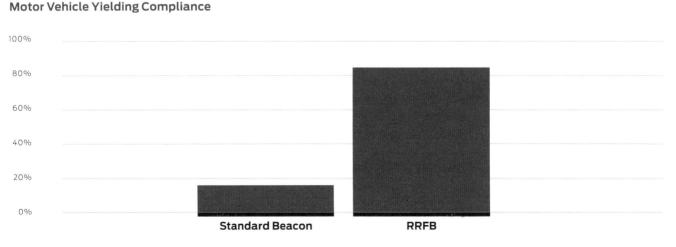

Modified from: Van Houten, R., Malenfant, J.E. L. (2008).
An Analysis of the Efficacy of Rectangular-shaped Rapid-Flash LED Beacons
to Increase Yielding to Pedestrians Using Crosswalks on
Multilane Roadways in the City of St. Petersburg, FL

1 If center islands or medians exist, providing secondary installations in these locations marginally improve driver yielding behavior

4 RRFBs shall be used to supplement standard pedestrian and bicycle crossing signs and markings

ST. PETERSBURG, FL

With the introduction of a two- and four-beacon system came increases of 70.6% and 77.8% increases over baseline, respectively, and increases of 66% and 73.2% over the standard-beacon efficacy.

Houten, R. V., Malenfant, L. (Undated). Efficacy of Rectangular-shaped Rapid Flash LED Beacons.

Maintenance

Depending on power supply, maintenance can be minimal. If solar power is used, RRFBs should run for years without issue.

Treatment Adoption and Professional Consensus

Several municipalities and counties in the United States have experimented with and evaluated RRFBs for bicycles (as well as pedestrians), including the following:

· Alexandria, VA
· Billings, MT
· Boulder, CO
· Las Cruces, NM
· Miami-Dade, FL
· Portland, OR
· Roswell, NM
· St. Petersburg, FL
· Teton County, ID
· Washington, DC
· Wilmington, NC

Hybrid Beacon for Bike Route Crossing of Major Street

TUCSON, AZ (PHOTO: TOM THIVENER)

A hybrid beacon, also known as a High-intensity Activated CrossWalk (HAWK), consists of a signal-head with two red lenses over a single yellow lens on the major street, and pedestrian and/ or bicycle signal heads for the minor street. There are no signal indications for motor vehicles on the minor street approaches. Hybrid beacons were developed specifically to enhance pedestrian crossings of major streets. However, several cities have installed modified hybrid beacons that explicitly incorporate bicycle movements. The information provided here focuses on the application of hybrid beacons for bicyclists.

Hybrid beacons are used to improve non-motorized crossings of major streets in locations where side-street volumes do not support installation of a conventional traffic signal (or where there are concerns that a conventional signal will encourage additional motor vehicle traffic on the minor street). Hybrid beacons may also be used at mid-block crossing locations (e.g., trail crossings).

PHOENIX, AZ (PHOTO: WWW.PEDBIKEIMAGES.COM, MIKE CYNECKI)

The hybrid beacon can significantly improve the operations of a bicycle route, particularly along bicycle boulevards. Because of the low traffic volumes on these facilities, intersections with major roadways are often unsignalized, creating difficult and potentially unsafe crossing conditions for bicyclists. Hybrid beacons may be supplemented with a bike signal and signal detection for the minor street approaches to facilitate bicycle crossings.

Benefits

Can be implemented when a conventional signal warrant is not met or where a conventional traffic signal is not desired due to the potential to increase traffic volumes on minor street approaches.

Creates gaps for bicyclists to cross busy streets.

Is more flexible for bicyclists than a full signal as bicyclists do not have to actuate it if they find ample crossing opportunities during off-peak conditions.[87]

Associated with very high driver compliance (studies show greater than 95% driver compliance with red indications).[88]

Improves street crossing safety.

Typical Applications

Where bike routes intersect major streets without existing signalized crossings.

Where off-street bicycle or pedestrian facilities intersect major streets without existing signalized crossings.

At mid-block crossings of major roadways with high bicycle or pedestrian volumes.

Suggested signal phasing to serve bicyclists and pedestrians at a minor street crossing of a major street.

	Major Street		Minor Street	
Interval	Motor Vehicle		Bicyclist	Pedestrian
1			Flashing Red	
2	Flashing Yellow			
3				
4				
4				
5				15
6				10
7				5
8	Alternating Flashing Red			
1			Flashing Red	

Design Guidance

Hybrid Beacon for Bike Route Crossing of Major Street

Required Features

(1) The MUTCD provides warrants for the use of hybrid beacons based on motor vehicle speed, crossing length, motor vehicle volumes, and pedestrian volumes. These warrants do not explicitly consider bicyclists; however bicyclist crossing volumes may be added to pedestrian crossing volumes for the purposes of evaluating the warrant.[89]

(2) Engineering judgment and best practices should be used to ensure safe and appropriate signal timing for all phases. Appropriate yellow and red clearance intervals for bicycles should be calculated using the guidance provided for bike signals.

(3) The MUTCD provides standards related to the design and location of hybrid beacons (e.g., mounting location, height, etc.).

Recommended Features

(4) When hybrid beacons are installed to facilitate bicycle movements, a bicycle signal head should be installed in addition to pedestrian signal heads. This allows for safer and more efficient operations that effectively account for the different clearance requirements for pedestrians and bicycles. When used, a bicycle signal head should display a flashing red indication to bicyclists when the hybrid beacon is dark (i.e., the bicycle signal should not rest in dark). This allows bicyclists to treat the intersection as a "Stop" and proceed without the requirement of activating the hybrid signal.

(5) The 2009 MUTCD provides general guidance on establishing the length of flashing yellow and steady yellow phases; this guidance remains the same regardless of whether the hybrid beacon is used for a pedestrian crossing or bicycle crossing.

(6) The operations associated with the clearance intervals for the minor street approaches differ considerably when a hybrid beacon is used to facilitate bicycle crossings as opposed to pedestrian crossings. The MUTCD specifies that the corresponding phase on the major street for the pedestrian clearance interval is alternating flashing red, which allows vehicle to stop and proceed if

there is no pedestrian. In particular, because of the speed at which bicyclists can enter the intersection and because many bicyclists will actually speed up when presented with a flashing "Don't Walk" indication, hybrid beacons should maintain the solid red indication for motorists throughout the full bicycle clearance interval (yellow plus all-red).

(7) The minimum length of the main street "rest in dark" interval should be set as short as possible to minimize bicyclist and pedestrian waiting time. Consider using a shorter minimum main street interval during off-peak periods than during peak periods.

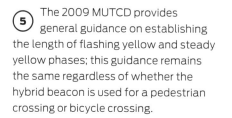

(4) When used to facilitate bicycle movements, a bicycle signal head should be installed in addition to pedestrian signal heads.

8 Parking and other sight obstructions should be prohibited for at lease 100 feet in adcance of and at least 20 feet beyond the marked crosswalk.

Operations

Hybrid beacon operations are significantly different from the operations of standard traffic control signals. The figure here on the reverse side illustrates the general sequence of phases for a hybrid beacon as applied for pedestrian crossings. The primary difference compared to a standard signal is that a hybrid beacon displays no indication (i.e., it is dark) when it is not actuated. Upon actuation (by a pedestrian or bicyclist on the minor street), the beacon begins flashing yellow, changes to steady yellow, then displays a solid red indication with both red lenses. During the solid red phase, drivers must stop and remain stopped, as with a standard traffic signal.

Prior to returning to no indication, the beacon displays an alternating flashing "wig-wag" red that allows drivers to stop and proceed when clear, as they would with a stop sign. To maximize safety when used for bicycle crossings, this phase should be very short and occur after the pedestrian signal head has changed to a solid "Don't Walk" indication as bicyclists can enter an intersection quickly.

8 Parking and other sight obstructions should be prohibited for at least 100 feet in advance of and at least 20 feet beyond the marked crosswalk, or site accommodations should be made through curb extensions or other techniques to provide adequate sight distance.[90]

9 The installation should include suitable standard signs and pavement markings.[91]

10 If installed within a signal system, signal engineers should evaluate the need for the hybrid beacon to be coordinated with other signals.

Optional Features

11 Due to the unique operational features of hybrid beacons, communities that are installing hybrid beacons for the first time may wish to coordinate installation with a public information campaign to educate roadway users on the operations and legal requirements associated with hybrid beacons.[92]

PORTLAND, OR

SALT LAKE CITY, UT

This application provides a pedestrian crossing without signal control for the side street because signal control on the side street can encourage unwanted additional traffic through the neighborhood.

Fitzpatrick, K. and Park, E.S. (2010). Safety Effectiveness of the HAWK Pedestrian Crossing Treatment. Federal Highway Administration. Publication No. FHWA-HRT-10-042.

Maintenance

Hybrid signals are subject to the same maintenance needs and requirements as standard traffic signals.

Signing and striping need to be maintained to help users understand the relatively unfamiliar traffic control.

Treatment Adoption and Professional Consensus

Hybrid beacons have been implemented in several US cities, including the following:

· Alexandria, VA
· Bloomington, IN
· Fort Collins, CO
· Madison, WI
· Miami, FL
· Phoenix, AZ
· Portland, OR
· Salt Lake City, UT
· Tucson, AZ
· Washington, DC
· West Bloomfield Township, MI

Signing and Marking

Colored Bike Facilities 119

Colored Pavement Material Guidance 125

Shared Lane Markings 133

Bike Route Wayfinding 139

Bikeway Signing and Marking encompasses any treatment or piece of infrastructure whose primary purpose is either to indicate the presence of a bicycle facility or to distinguish that facility for bicyclists, motorists, and pedestrians. Bicycle signage includes several sub-categories. These include way-finding and route signage, regulatory signage, and warning signage. Some bicycle specific signage exists to provide motorized traffic with information and instruction.

Bikeway markings represent any device applied onto the pavement surface and intended to designate a specific right-of-way, direction, potential conflict area, or route option. These markings must take into consideration the use of particular colors, materials, and designs, as well as the legibility of these elements for motorists and pedestrians. Markings may be used to augment a particular lane, intersection, or signal treatment. In all cases, markings must strive for a high level of visibility, instant identification, and take into account both motorist and bicyclist movements in relation to the marking placement.

On Kent Avenue in New York City, green colored pavement denotes the main bikeway corridor, while chevron and shared lane markings distinguish intersections and driveways.

NEW YORK, NY

Colored Bike Facilities

SAN FRANCISCO, CA

Colored pavement within a bicycle lane increases the visibility of the facility, identifies potential areas of conflict, and reinforces priority to bicyclists in conflict areas and in areas with pressure for illegal parking. Colored pavement can be utilized either as a corridor treatment along the length of a bike lane or cycle track, or as a spot treatment, such as a bike box, conflict area, or intersection crossing marking. Color can be applied along the entire length of bike lane or cycle track to increase the overall visibility of the facility. Consistent application of color across a bikeway corridor is important to promote clear understanding for all users.

Benefits

Promotes the multi-modal nature of a corridor.

Increases the visibility of bicyclists. Discourages illegal parking in the bike lane.

When used in conflict areas, raises motorist and bicyclist awareness to potential areas of conflict.

Increases bicyclist comfort though clearly delineated space.[93]

Increases motorist yielding behavior.[94]

Helps reduce bicycle conflicts with turning motorists.

BOSTON, MA

Anecdotally, most cyclists like the green paint treatment and believe that it is more effective at keeping cars from parking in bike lanes than regular striping. In particular, cyclists cite the conspicuousness of cars parked in green painted lanes as a deterrent to drivers parking there.

New York City Department of Transportation. (2011). Evaluation of Solid Green Bicycle Lanes, to Increase Compliance and Bicycle Safety.

SEATTLE, WA

Typical Applications

Within bike lanes or cycle tracks.

Across turning conflict areas such as vehicle right turn lanes.

Across intersections, particularly through wide or complex intersections where the bicycle path may be unclear.[95]

Across driveways and Stop or Yield-controlled cross-streets.

Where typical vehicle movements frequently encroach into bicycle space, such as across ramp-style exits and entries where the prevailing speed of turning traffic at the conflict point is low enough that motorist yielding behavior can be expected.

Color may be applied along an entire corridor, with gaps in coloring to denote crossing areas.[96]

Facility designers should match coloring strategy to desired design outcomes of projects.

May not be applicable for crossings in which bicycles are expected to yield right of way, such as when the street with the bicycle route has Stop or Yield control at an intersection.

Bicyclists familiar with more traditional sharrows have noted that the additional emphasis resulting from the green pavement paint appears to be creating an heightened awareness by the motorists in the lane.

City of Long Beach. (2010). Final Report: Second Street Sharrows and Green Lane in the City of Long Beach, California (RTE 9-113E).

LONG BEACH, CA

Design Guidance

Colored Bike Facilities

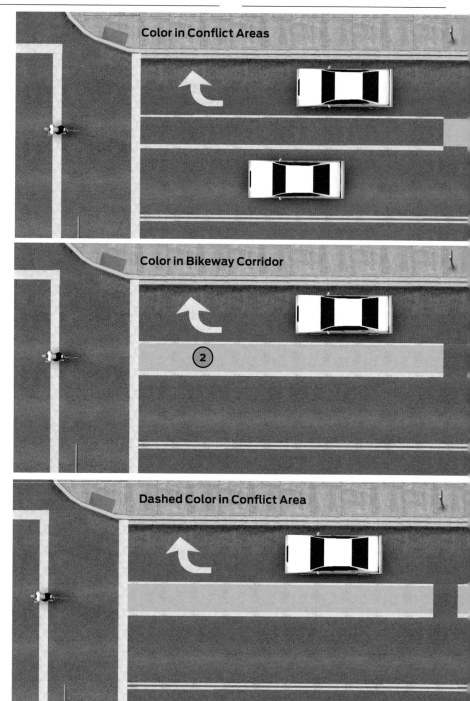

Color in Conflict Areas

Color in Bikeway Corridor

②

Dashed Color in Conflict Area

Required Features

① The color green shall be used to minimize confusion with other standard traffic control markings.[97]

② Color shall be applied to the road surface to delineate space, increase visibility, and emphasize proper vehicle priority.[98]

③ Normal white bike lane lines shall be provided along the edges of the colored lane to provide consistency with other facilities and to enhance nighttime visibility.

Recommended Features

④ The colored surface should be skid resistant and retro-reflective.

⑤ A "Yield to Bikes" sign should be used at intersections or driveway crossings to reinforce that bicyclists have the right-of-way at colored bike lane areas.[99]

⑥ The configuration of color should be consistently applied throughout the corridor.

Optional Features

⑦ Color may be applied within conflict areas for increased visibility of bicyclists.

⑧ Color may be applied along a dashed pattern within a dashed bicycle lane to indicate merging areas. Dashed application of colored pavement mimics typical traffic striping layouts, where dashed markings indicate areas where merging maneuvers are permitted.[100]

⑨ Color may be applied along a corridor, with gaps in coloring to denote crossing areas. When used in this fashion, color can distinguish the bicycle facility along its entire length.

This is particularly useful in high traffic situations or areas where traffic may encroach into the bike facility.[101]

⑩ Color may be used to supplement shared lane markings for added visibility.[102]

Best estimates for safety effects of one blue cycle crossing in a junction are a reduction of 10% in accidents and 19% in injuries.

Jensen, S. U. (2008). Safety effects of blue cycle crossings: A before-after study. Accident Analysis & Prevention, 40(2): 742-750.

TUSCON, AZ

SAN FRANCISCO, CA (PHOTO: SFSTREETSBLOG)

CHICAGO, IL

NEW YORK, NY

SEATTLE, WA

AUSTIN, TX

Treatment Adoption and Professional Consensus

Application of colored pavement is seen in the following US cities:

- Austin, TX
- Boston, MA
- Cambridge, MA
- Chicago, IL
- Columbia, MO
- Columbus, OH
- Eugene, OR
- Indianapolis, IN
- Long Beach, CA
- Madison, WI
- Minneapolis, MN
- Missoula, MT
- New York, NY
- Portland, OR
- Salt Lake City, UT
- San Francisco, CA
- Seattle, WA
- Washington, DC

Maintenance

Colored pavement requires varying levels of maintenance depending on materials.

Because the effectiveness of markings depends entirely on their visibility, maintaining markings should be a high priority.

Colored facilities should be maintained to be free of potholes, broken glass, and other debris.

Colored Pavement Material Guidance

Colored pavement can be utilized either as a corridor treatment along the length of a bike lane or cycle track, or in limited locations as a spot treatment, such as a bike box, conflict area, or intersection crossing marking. Colored pavement for use within bikeways treatments may take the form of an overlay, when the colored material is placed on top of the pavement or embedded, when the colored material is mixed into the pavement.

Overlay

Paint, sometimes with additives such as reflective glass beads for retro reflectivity and sand for skid resistance, is the most widely used method to mark road surfaces. Paint is considered a non-durable pavement marking, is easily worn by vehicle tires and the elements in snowy winter climates, and often requires annual reapplication. Paint is the least expensive of the overlay materials.

Durable Liquid Pavement Markings (DLPM) include **epoxy** and **Methyl Methacrylate (MMA). Epoxies** are adhesive, waterborne acrylics that are typically applied as a paint or spray. **MMA** are 2-part liquids comprised of a resin and activator. While both coatings can be skid resistant, retro reflective and can adhere to concrete or asphalt surfaces, epoxies are sensitive to moisture and temperature and may require long dry times. MMA may be installed at any temperature, is durable and dries quickly, but is more expensive than epoxy.

Thermoplastic, another type of durable pavement marking, is a type of plastic made from polymer resins that becomes a homogenized liquid when heated and hard when cooled. Thermoplastic can be pre-formed in specific shapes, such as tiles that can be assembled like a puzzle to color bicycle facilities. Thermoplastic can also be used for bicycle lane symbols, arrows, pavement legends and shared lane markings.

Thermoplastic tends to last longer than epoxy and is easier to apply then MMA. Retro reflective and anti-skid materials can be applied or mixed throughout the plastic.

Embedded

Colored asphalt is composed of the same material as standard asphalt, but has a colored pigment added. The colored asphalt may be installed as a thin layer over conventional asphalt to reduce cost. One well-known use of colored asphalt is Bend, Oregon's red bike lanes, which utilize a localized red pigment in the colored asphalt. The tinted asphalt was applied over fresh black asphalt before the year 2000 and has worn well with regular street sweeping and maintenance, but has faded over time. Green pigment options are available.

Spot Treatments	Pros & Cons
Paint · Recommended for temporary, pilot, or experimental spot treatments.	+ Easy application and moderate dry time. − Proven to wear quickly in areas with moderate to heavy motor vehicle traffic.
DLPM · MMA is more appropriate for spot treatments than epoxy.	+ Material is durable if installed according to manufacturer specifications. + MMA has quick dry times and good durability. − Epoxy can have long dry times, causing increased disruption to roadway traffic. − Requires special installation equipment.
Thermoplastic · Recommended for spot treatments. · Ideal for intersection treatments and other high-traffic conflict areas.	+ Quick cure time minimizes traffic impact. + Relatively low-cost equipment investment. + Easy spot maintenance. + Shown to wear well in conflict areas. − May be cost-prohibitive for large scale applications.
Colored Asphalt · Recommended for corridor treatments.	+ Not recommended due to complexity of paving operations. − Spot maintenance is difficult and may result in color loss when trenching occurs. − Requires equipment and expertise to install.

OTTAWA, CANADA

What has led to successful installation?

Staff training and expertise as well as careful design of the treatment have resulted in successful installations in North America cities and abroad. Where pavement quality was good, most cases of failed installation reported were due to poor surface preparation and/or a desire to expedite the installation.

Corridor Treatments	Pros & Cons
Paint · Recommended for corridor treatments. · Ideal for protected bicycle facilities like cycle tracks.	+ Cost-effective along corridors with low or no motor vehicle traffic impacts. – Can be slick when wet. – Not durable in high wear locations.
DLPM · Recommended for corridor treatment.	+ Materials are long-lasting and can be cheaper than thermoplastic. – Requires special installation equipment.
Thermoplastic · Not recommended for long corridors due to cost.	+ Material is known to have long life and good performance qualities in the US and Europe. – Cost-prohibitive in corridor applications.
Colored Asphalt · Recommended for corridor treatments.	+ Long lasting treatment. + Should be coupled with initial construction or repaving for cost savings. + Has same lifespan of standard asphalt. + Proven long-term use as an effective treatment in Europe. + Requires little maintenance. – Requires cleaning of machinery or maintenance of special machinery for colored applications. – Colored asphalt is not retroreflective by itself; in the Netherlands a white thermoplastic stripe is used for visibility. – Can require special attention at joints between colored and standard asphalt.

What are the benefits of installation by a contractor vs. city crew?

Many cities prefer to have a city crew install coloration to reduce cost when possible though a contractor may be cheaper when installation requires special equipment. Some cities used a contractor when colored pavement was installed as part of a larger capital project, when city staff do not have the training, or when liability may be a concern.

PHILADELPHIA, PA

Paint

Composition	Pigment and binder, glass beads and/or a fine aggregate can be added for retroreflectivity and skid resistance.
Surface Preparation	Pavement should be free of dirt, dust and moisture.
Installation Temperature	Pavement and air temperature should be at least 40 degrees Fahrenheit.
Installation Considerations	Most paints can be applied immediately to new asphalt or concrete. Primer is not required on concrete roadways. Paint dry time depends on ambient temperature.
Maintenance Considerations	Spot maintenance requires a simple reapplication of paint
Material Cost*	$0.6 Sq. Ft. for raw materials, $1.20 – $1.60 Sq. Ft. installed.
Longevity	Six months to two years based on weather, motor vehicle traffic and snow removal operations (if applicable).
Availability	Widely available in the US.
Skid resistance and Retroreflectivity	Glass beads may be added to paint for retroreflectivity and sand added for skid resistance.
Peer City Experience	Several cities have reported satisfactory performance in corridors without motor vehicle wear.

SAN FRANCISCO, CA

*Installation costs vary depending on size of application, and whether city crews or contractors perform.

Durable Liquid Pavement Markings (Epoxy and MMA)

Composition	Epoxy — epoxy/resin. MMA — acrylic-based resin.
Surface Preparation	Pavement should be free of dirt, old pavement markings, dust, and moisture. Poor asphalt quality can significantly shorten the lifetime of a treatment. Presence of oil may result in failure to bond to roadway surface. Installation of MMA on concrete requires shot blasting and priming.
Installation Temperature	Most epoxies require air and substrate temperatures of at least 40 degrees Fahrenheit. MMAs may be installed at almost any temperature.
Installation Considerations	Installation generally requires special equipment. Epoxy dry time increases as temperature decreases. Dry time is measured in hours. MMA dries in about one hour.
Maintenance Considerations	Some cities have reported that epoxy color intensity fades over time due to color instability under ultraviolet lighting (sunlight) exposure. Pooling water can reduce material longevity.
Material Cost*	Epoxy: $1 – $3 Sq. Ft. for raw materials. $8 – 11 Sq. Ft. installed. MMA: $3 – 4 Sq. Ft. for raw materials. $8 – 11 Sq. Ft. installed.
Longevity	Similar to thermoplastic. Poor pavement quality impacts treatment longevity.
Availability	Epoxy currently has wider US availability than MMA.
Skid resistance and Retroreflectivity	Material can be skid resistant and retro reflective.
Peer City Experience	Epoxy paint used in peer cities has proven skid resistance and longevity of 3 – 5 years. MMA may last as long as 3 – 6 years.

SALT LAKE CITY, UT

Thermoplastic

Composition	Polymer resin, pigment, glass beads, and filler.
Surface Preparation	Pavement should be free of dirt, dust, and moisture. Typical preparation consists of street sweeping and then brushing.
Installation Temperature	Some (but not all) thermoplastic requires that pavement and air temperature be 50 to 55 degrees Fahrenheit for most materials to bond properly. Most thermoplastics should be heated to 400 – 450 degrees Fahrenheit.
Installation Considerations	Many thermoplastics can be applied immediately to new asphalt, but new concrete must cure at least 30 or longer days prior to installation. Primer is typically required for application to concrete roadways and may assist with adherence on older asphalt surfaces. Cure time is measured in minutes.
Maintenance Considerations	Spot fixes are simple: a small piece of plastic is torched into place. Thermoplastic can be recessed to make edge flush with pavement or tamped down to form a seal with the roadway to reduce likelihood of snow plow impact.
Material Cost*	$3 – $6 Sq. Ft. for raw materials, $10 – $14 Sq. Ft installed.
Longevity	Six months to two years based on weather, motor vehicle traffic and snow removal operations (if applicable).
Availability	Average of 5 years, or 3 times the lifetime of paint under the same conditions. Many installations have lasted significantly longer. Poor initial pavement quality shortens lifespan.
Skid resistance and Retroreflectivity	Material can be skid resistant and retroreflective. Most effective materials will mix corundum and beads throughout materials rather than top coating material.
Peer City Experience	Most common material used for colored bikeways in North America. Many treatments are too new to report long-term results. Cities with a longer history of use (such as Portland) report positively on durability, skid resistance, and maintenance.

AUSTIN, TX

Colored Pavement

Composition	Bituminous pitch, sand/gravel, and pigment.
Surface Preparation	Preparation for installation is the same for colored and standard asphalt. A base course is placed on an aggregate base heated to insure adhesion between layers.
Installation Temperature	Standard paving considerations apply.
Installation Considerations	Standard paving considerations apply.
Maintenance Considerations	It is expected that colored asphalt at least 1 cm thick will last for the life of the pavement.
Material Cost*	More expensive than standard asphalt installation based on cost of pigment. When applied as a thin top layer within new construction, pigmented asphalt costs between 30 and 50 percent more than a non-colored structural asphalt section. For thin overlay applications, the difference in cost will be greater.
Longevity	Based on motor vehicle traffic, but typically similar to conventional asphalt.
Availability	Available in the US.
Skid resistance and Retroreflectivity	Skid resistance equal to uncolored asphalt. Asphalt is not retroreflective.
Peer City Experience	Embedded colored pavement is used in few North American cities but many have expressed interest for longer corridor installations.

BEND, OR

European Experience

Many European countries commonly use color in bikeways, but the color chosen and the material used varies widely. European countries with the most extensive bikeway color tradition are the Netherlands and Denmark. In the Netherlands, colored asphalt or colored concrete pavers are used for most applications. Colored asphalt is an economical treatment that provides permanent color, durability, skid resistance and is well-suited to the Dutch practice of coloring bikeways along their entire length. It should be noted that the Dutch choice of red for bikeways lends itself to the use of colored asphalt for two reasons:

1) the coloring agent can be successfully applied to either black bitumen or clear bitumen (as opposed to other colors, which can only be implemented with the more expensive clear bitumen), and 2) naturally red-colored rock can be used for the aggregate agent. In Denmark, France, Luxembourg and Germany, bikeway coloring strategies vary, but are generally applied as spot treatments (as opposed to coloring the entire facility). Thermoplastic and epoxy (also known as cold plastic in Europe) are the preferred medium for applying intersection spot treatment bikeway color in many European countries.

Peer City Experience

Twenty-one North American peer cities where colored pavement is in use, or where installations are planned for the near future, were interviewed to determine the state of the practice.

Interviewees represented a range of regions, climates, sizes, and levels of experiences with colored pavement. The interviews resulted in several common themes, including:

· Generally positive response to colored pavement from both bicyclists and motor vehicle drivers.

· There is a need to further improve technical expertise for installing and maintaining colored pavement.

· Thermoplastic is the most commonly used material and spot applications are the most frequent type of installation.

· Green will be brighter at installation and material should be allowed to settle and wear prior to judging color satisfaction.

Shared Lane Markings

NEW YORK, NY

Shared Lane Markings (SLMs), or "sharrows," are road markings used to indicate a shared lane environment for bicycles and automobiles. Among other benefits, shared lane markings reinforce the legitimacy of bicycle traffic on the street, recommend proper bicyclist positioning, and may be configured to offer directional and wayfinding guidance. The shared lane marking is not a facility type, it is a pavement marking with a variety of uses to support a complete bikeway network. The MUTCD outlines guidance for shared lane markings in section 9C.07.

Benefits

Encourages bicyclists to position themselves safely in lanes too narrow for a motor vehicle and a bicycle to comfortably travel side by side within the same traffic lane.[103]

Alerts motor vehicle drivers to the potential presence of bicyclists.

Alerts road users of the lateral position bicyclists are expected to occupy within the travel lane.

Indicates a proper path for bicyclists through difficult or potentially hazardous situations, such as railroad tracks.

Advertises the presence of bikeway routes to all users.

Provides a wayfinding element along bike routes.

Demonstrated to increase the distance between bicyclists and parked cars, keeping bicyclists out of the "door zone."[104]

Encourages safe passing by motorists.[105]

Requires no additional street space. Reduces the incidence of sidewalk riding.[106]

Reduces the incidence of wrong-way bicycling.[107]

SALT LAKE CITY, UT

Typical Applications

Shared lane markings should not be considered a substitute for bike lanes, cycle tracks, or other separation treatments where these types of facilities are otherwise warranted or space permits. Shared lane markings can be used as a standard element in the development of bicycle boulevards to identify streets as bikeways and to provide wayfinding along the route.

BROOKLINE, MA

Desirable shared lane marking applications:

To indicate a shared lane situation where the speed differential between bicyclist and motorist travel speeds is very low, such as:

· On bicycle boulevards or similar low volume, traffic calmed, shared streets with a designed speed of < 25 mph.

· On downhill segments, preferably paired with an uphill bike lane. If space permits, consider a wide downhill bike lane.

· On streets where the traffic signals are timed for a bicycling travel speed of 12 to 15 miles per hour.

As a reasonable alternative to a bike lane:

· Where street width can only accommodate a bicycle lane in one direction. On hills, lanes should be provided in the uphill direction.

· Within single or multi-lane roundabouts.[108]

· Along front-in angled parking, where a bike lane is undesirable.

To strengthen connections in a bikeway network:

· To fill a gap in an otherwise continuous bike path or bike lane, generally for a short distance.

· To transition bicyclists across traffic lanes or from conventional bike lanes or cycle tracks to a shared lane environment.

· To direct bicyclists along circuitous routes.

To clarify bicyclist movement and positioning in challenging environments:

· To designate movement and positioning of bicycles through intersections.

· To designate movement and positioning of bicyclists through a combined bike lane/turn lane.

· To assist bicyclists in taking the lane in the presence of a double turn lanes. Double turn lanes are undesirable for bicyclists.

· In the street alongside separated bikeway facilities such as cycle tracks, to permit continued use of the street by bicyclists who prefer to ride in the street.

· Generally, not appropriate on streets that have a speed limit above 35 mph.[109]

Design Guidance

Shared Lane Markings

Required Features

(1) The Shared Lane Marking in use within the United States is the bike-and-chevron "sharrow," illustrated in MUTCD figure 9C-9.

(2) Shared Lane Markings shall not be used on shoulders, in designated bicycle lanes, or to designate bicycle detection at signalized intersections. (MUTCD 9C.07 03)

Recommended Features

(3) Frequent, visible placement of markings is essential. The number of markings along a street should correspond to the difficulty bicyclists experience taking the proper travel path or position. SLMs used to bridge discontinuous bicycle facilities or along busier streets should be placed more frequently (50 to 100 feet) than along low traffic bicycle routes (up to 250 feet or more). SLMs used along low volume routes can be staggered by direction to provide markings closer together.[110]

(4) Lateral placement is critical to encourage riders to avoid the "door zone," and to encourage safe passing behavior. MUTCD guidance recommends minimum placement when a parking lane is present at 11 feet from the curb face.[111]

(5) On streets with posted 25 mph speeds or slower, preferred placement is in the center of the travel lane to minimize wear and encourage bicyclists to occupy the full travel lane.

(6) On streets with posted 35 mph speeds or faster and motor vehicle volumes higher than 3,000 vpd shared lane markings are not a preferred

Optional Shared Lane Marking Applications

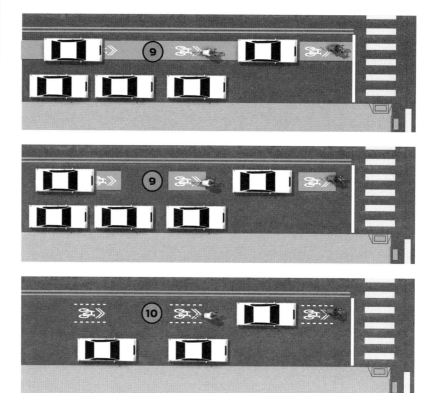

(8) Modified Shared Lane Markings as seen in Portland, OR

treatment. On these streets other bikeway types are preferred.

(7) If on-street vehicle parking is not present, SLMs should be placed far enough from the curb to direct bicyclists away from gutters, seams, and other obstacles. On streets with posted 25 mph speeds or slower, preferred placement is in the center of the travel lane to minimize wear and encourage bicyclists to occupy the full travel lane. MUTCD guidance recommends minimum placement with no parking at 4 feet from the curb face.[112]

Optional Features

(8) For wayfinding purposes the orientation of the chevron marking may be adjusted to direct bicyclists along discontinuous routes.

(9) Color may be used to enhance the visibility of the shared lane marking and to further encourage desired lane positioning.[113]

(10) Dotted line markings may accompany the shared lane marking to further encourage desired lane positioning.[114]

 7

Minimum placement: 4 feet

 4

Lateral placement is critical to encourage riders to avoid the "door zone."

The door zone represents an area where bicyclists must be especially aware of hazards that could be presented by the driver side door. Dedicated

bicycle facilities can be designed to heighten this awareness. See guidance for Bike Lanes and Cycle tracks for more information.

4

Minimum placement: 11 feet

 5

Preferred placement on 25 mph streets: center of travel lane

PORTLAND, OR (PHOTO: DAVE ROTH)

MISSOULA, MT

In an evaluation of a lane-within-a-lane treatment in Salt Lake City, researches found that "Eleven months after implementation, the fraction of in street cyclists riding in the preferred zone, at least 4 ft from the curb, had risen from 17% to 92%."

Furth, P., Dulaski, D. M., Bergenthal, D., Brown, S. (2011). More Than Sharrows: Lane-Within-A-Lane Bicycle Priority Treatments in Three U.S. Cities. Presented at the 2011 Annual Meeting of the Transportation Research Board.

Maintenance

Frequent, visible placement of markings is essential.

Lateral placement is critical to encourage riders to avoid the "door zone."

The shared lane marking may be placed in the center of the lane between wheel treads to minimize wear.

Treatment Adoption and Professional Consensus

Used by at least 76 jurisdictions in 26 States, including most NACTO member cities.

Bike Route Wayfinding

Benefits

Familiarizes users with the bicycle network.

Identifies the best routes to destinations.

Overcomes a "barrier to entry" for infrequent bicyclists.

Signage that includes mileage and travel time to destinations may help minimize the tendency to overestimate the amount of time it takes to travel by bicycle.

Visually indicates to motorists that they are driving along a bicycle route and should use caution.

Passively markets the bicycle network by providing unique and consistent imagery throughout the jurisdiction.

Typical Applications

Along all streets and/or bicycle facility types that are part of the bicycle network.

Along corridors with circuitous bikeway facility routes to guide bicyclists to their intended destination.

BALTIMORE, MD

A bicycle wayfinding system consists of comprehensive signing and/or pavement markings to guide bicyclists to their destinations along preferred bicycle routes. Signs are typically placed at decision points along bicycle routes—typically at the intersection of two or more bikeways and at other key locations leading to and along bicycle routes.

Types of Signs

Confirmation Signs

PURPOSE: Indicate to bicyclists that they are on a designated bikeway. Make motorists aware of the bicycle route.

INFORMATION: Can include destinations and distance/time. Do not include arrows.

PLACEMENT: Every 1/4 to 1/2 mile on off-street facilities and every 2 to 3 blocks along bicycle facilities, unless another type of sign is used (e.g., within 150 ft of a turn or decision sign). Should be placed soon after turns to confirm destination(s). Pavement markings can also act as confirmation that a bicyclist is on a preferred route.

BERKELEY, CA

OAKLAND, CA

CHICAGO, IL

Turn Signs

PURPOSE: Indicate where a bikeway turns from one street onto another street. Can be used with pavement markings.

INFORMATION: Include destinations and arrows.

PLACEMENT: Near-side of intersections where bike routes turn (e.g., where the street ceases to be a bicycle route or does not go through). Pavement markings can also indicate the need to turn to the bicyclist.

MUTCD D1-1

CHICAGO, IL

Decision Signs

PURPOSE: Mark the junction of two or more bikeways. Inform bicyclists of the designated bike route to access key destinations.

INFORMATION: Destinations and arrows, distances, and travel times are optional but recommended.

PLACEMENT: Near-side of intersections in advance of a junction with another bicycle route. Along a route to indicate a nearby destination.

BERKELEY, CA

OAKLAND, CA

PORTLAND, OR

Types of Destinations

Wayfinding signs can direct users to a number of different types of destinations, including the following:
- On-street bikeways
- Commercial centers
- Public transit centers and stations
- Schools
- Civic/community destinations
- Local or regional parks and trails
- Hospitals
- Bridges

Prior to developing the wayfinding signage, it can be useful to classify a list of destinations for inclusion on the signs based on their relative importance to users throughout the area. A particular destination's ranking in the hierarchy can be used to determine the physical distance from which the locations are signed. For example, primary destinations (such as the downtown area) may be included on signage up to five miles away. Secondary destinations (such as a transit station) may be included on signage up to two miles away. Tertiary destinations (such as a park) are more local in nature and may be included on signage up to one mile away.[115]

Design Guidance

Bike Route Wayfinding

Required Features

(1) Follow MUTCD standards (Section 9B.01—Application and Placement of Signs), including mounting height and lateral placement from edge of path or roadway. Additional standards and guidance are found in Section 9B.20—Bicycle Guide Signs.

Recommended Features

(2) Decision signs should be placed in advance of all turns (near side of the intersection) or decision points along the bicycle route.[116]

(3) Decision signs should include destinations, directional arrows, and distance. Travel time required to reach the destination provides bicyclists with additional information and may also be included. It is recommended that a 10 mph bicycle speed be used for travel time calculations.[117]

(4) Place the closest destination to each sign in the top slot. Destinations that are further away can be placed in slots two and three. This allows the nearest destination to "fall off" the sign and subsequent destinations to move up the sign as the bicyclist approaches. For longer routes, show intermediate destinations rather than include all destinations on a single sign.

(5) Turn signs should be placed on the near-side of the intersection to indicate where the bike route turns.[118]

Library

B — BIKE ROUTE — B

(6) Confirmation signs should be placed every 1/4 to 1/2 mile along off-street bicycle routes or every 2 to 3 blocks along on-street routes, as well as on the far side of major street intersections.

(7) Clearview Hwy font is recommended, as it is commonly used for guide signs in the United States.[119]

Optional Features

(8) Signs may be placed on "feeder" streets between the bicycle route and nearby destinations.

(9) Bicycle route map signs may be periodically placed along bike routes to provide additional wayfinding benefits to users.

(10) Conventional street name signs along bicycle routes may be redesigned to incorporate the street's identity as a bicycle route.

(11) The placement of wayfinding signs may be limited specifically to the designated bicycle network, as other streets may be difficult or dangerous for bicyclists.

(12) Pavement markings may be used to help reinforce routes and

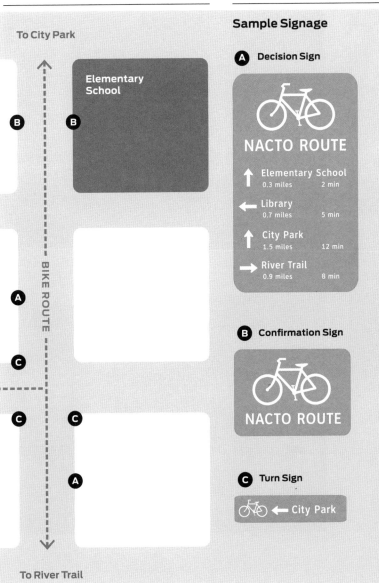

To City Park

Elementary School

B

B

BIKE ROUTE

A

C

C C

A

To River Trail

Sample Signage

A Decision Sign

NACTO ROUTE

↑ Elementary School
0.3 miles   2 min

← Library
0.7 miles   5 min

↑ City Park
1.5 miles   12 min

→ River Trail
0.9 miles   8 min

B Confirmation Sign

NACTO ROUTE

C Turn Sign

← City Park

Pavement Markings

Pavement markings can be installed to help reinforce routes and directional signage and to provide bicyclist positioning and route branding benefits. Under urban conditions, pavement markings may often be more visible than signs to users of the route. Pavement markings may be especially useful where signs are difficult to see (due to vegetation or parked cars). They can also help bicyclists navigate difficult turns. In the United States, Portland OR, Berkeley CA and Minneapolis MN have experimented with pavement markings. Berkeley and Minneapolis have applied a large stencil taking up nearly the entire travel lane designating the street as a 'bicycle boulevard.' In Portland, smaller markings including a small circle and arrow system were initially used; however, since the adoption and wide spread use of the shared lane marking, most bicycle boulevards are being retrofitted with these larger markings. Portland has also applied the shared lane marking as a wayfinding device by turning the chevrons of the marking in the direction of intended travel.

NEW YORK, NY

directional signage. Pavement markings may be useful where signs are difficult to see (due to vegetation or parked cars) and can help bicyclists navigate difficult turns and provide route reinforcement. Pavement markings may also be a standard component of bicycle routes.

13 Some wayfinding signage networks, such as those in San Francisco and Denver, utilize a route numbering system. Refer to MUTCD Section 9B.21—Bicycle Route Signs for standards and options. Route numbering systems may not be intuitive for bicyclists without a map or directory.

14 There is no standard color for bicycle wayfinding signage. Section 1A.12 of the MUTCD establishes the general meaning for signage colors. Green is the color used for directional guidance and is the most common color of bicycle wayfinding signage in the US, including those included in the MUTCD. Signed bicycle routes may be partnered with a printed or on-line bicycle route map. Many online services, such as Google, now offer bicycle route mapping that may differ from signed routes. Cities may wish to consider such advancements in technology when planning wayfinding programs.[120]

VANCOUVER, CANADA

BERKELEY, CA

NEW YORK, NY

Maintenance

Maintenance needs for bicycle wayfinding signs are similar to other signs, and will need periodic replacement due to wear. Cities should maintain comprehensive inventories of the location and age of bicycle wayfinding signs to allow incorporation of bicycle wayfinding signs into any asset management activities. Maintenance for pavement markings are covered under shared lane markings.

Treatment Adoption and Professional Consensus

In the United States, the use of pavement markings to identify bikeways has been experimented with in Portland OR and Berkeley, CA. American cities with some implementation of advanced wayfinding and signing systems include the following:

- Albuquerque, NM
- Austin, TX
- Baltimore, MD
- Berkeley, CA
- Cambridge, MA
- Chicago, IL
- Davis, CA
- Emeryville, CA
- New York, NY
- Oakland, CA
- Portland, OR
- San Francisco, CA
- Seattle, WA
- Washington, DC
- Wilmington, NC

Bicycle Boulevards

Route Planning   149

Signs and Pavement Markings   161

Speed Management   167

Volume Management   177

Minor Street Crossings   185

Major Street Crossings   191

Offset Intersections   201

Green Infrastructure   209

Bicycle boulevards are streets with low motorized traffic volumes and speeds, designated and designed to give bicycle travel priority. Bicycle Boulevards use signs, pavement markings, and speed and volume management measures to discourage through trips by motor vehicles and create safe, convenient bicycle crossings of busy arterial streets.

Berkeley, California established one of the first networks of bicycle boulevards in the early 2000s with the enhancement of seven corridors. This initial network totaled 15 miles and cost approximately $330,000. Today the city considers the bicycle boulevards the 'backbone' of the bicycle network.

BERKELEY, CA

MADISON, WI

Design Elements

Many local streets with low existing speeds and volumes offer the basic components of a safe bicycling environment. These streets can be enhanced using a range of design treatments, tailored to existing conditions and desired outcomes, to create bicycle boulevards. Design treatments are grouped into measures that provide the following benefits.

1. **Route Planning:** Direct access to destinations
2. **Signs and Pavement Markings:** Easy to find and to follow
3. **Speed Management:** Slow motor vehicle speeds
4. **Volume Management:** Low or reduced motor vehicle volumes
5. **Minor Street Crossings:** Minimal bicyclist delay
6. **Major Street Crossings:** Safe and convenient crossings
7. **Offset Crossings:** Clear and safe navigation
8. **Green Infrastructure:** Enhancing environments

Many of the treatments presented in this section not only benefit people on bicycles, but they also help create and maintain "quiet" streets that benefit residents and improve safety for all road users.

NAMPA, ID (PHOTO: CHARLIE LITCHFIELD/IDAHO PRESS-TRIBUNE)

Naming and Branding

Many cities around the United States have chosen to brand their bicycle boulevards using different names. Names used throughout the U.S. and Canada include:

- Neighborhood greenways
- Bicycle priority streets
- Quiet streets
- Neighborhood connectors
- Neighborhood byways
- Bicycle friendly streets/corridors
- Bicycle/neighborhood parkways
- Bike/walk streets
- Local bicycle streets

Many factors should be taken into consideration when branding a bicycle boulevard. These include existing bikeway definitions used by the state or city, citizen ideas and input, and specific features and activities expected to take place along the route (jogging, green infrastructure, etc.).

Route Planning

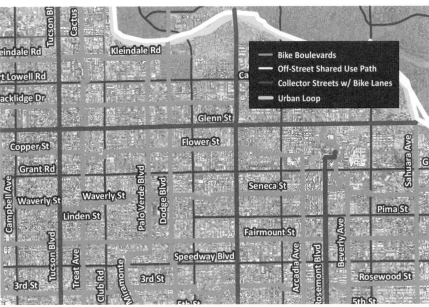

TUCSON, AZ

Route selection for bicycle boulevards is critical. Bicycle boulevards will not work if routed in illogical ways, require frequent or unnecessary stopping, or follow higher traffic speed and volume roadways. Bicycle boulevards have the potential to play a key role in a low-stress bikeway network, as they can complement, and provide strategic connections between, off-street paths, cycle tracks and bike lanes.[121]

A bicycle boulevard should be considered where local streets offer a continuous and direct route along low-traffic streets (or a route interspersed with bicycle/pedestrian-only connections). A candidate route can be enhanced by treatments described elsewhere in this section: speed management to reduce traffic speeds, volume management to lessen traffic volumes, minor street crossing treatments to reduce bicyclist delay, and major street crossing treatments where a route crosses a major street.

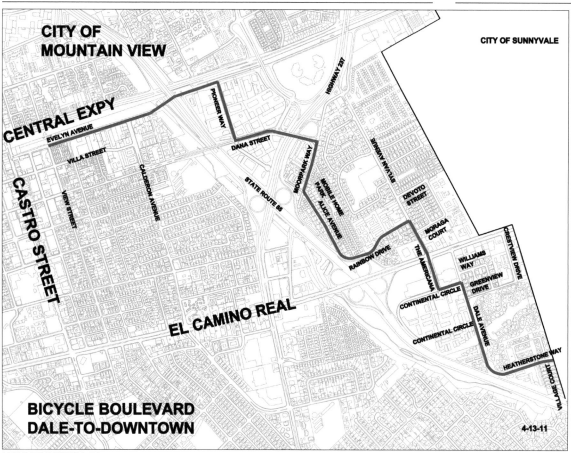

MOUNTAIN VIEW, CA

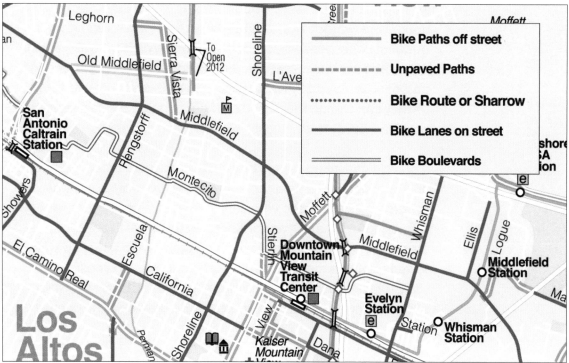

SANTA CLARA VALLEY, CA

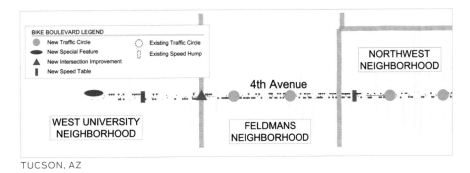

TUCSON, AZ

Connectivity

Potential routes for bicycle boulevards should closely follow a desire line for bicycle travel that are ideally long and relatively continuous (2-5 miles, or the length of a typical urban bicycle trip). While a given route may already have low motor vehicle speeds and volumes and provide continuous travel with safe major street crossings, most corridors will present at least a few sections that call for intervention to achieve the desired low speed/volume conditions and adequate crossings.

A bicycle boulevard running parallel to a major roadway can provide access to commercial destinations for people who do not feel safe riding along the main street particularly in cases where the main roadway lacks a low-stress or protected facility. It is important to note that low-stress bikeways should be provided wherever possible along major roads, even where a parallel bicycle boulevard exists. Similarly, bike lanes along a commercial corridor are not an equivalent substitute for bicycle boulevards; many people are uncomfortable riding on higher-speed streets and should be provided an alternative route to access commercial areas.

Though many practitioners begin defining a bicycle boulevard route by locating key opportunities, especially at crossings of barriers, such as a existing bicycle/pedestrian-only crossings of parks, highways and rivers, as well as existing or potential at-grade crossings (such as traffic signals) of major streets. In many areas, local streets are discontinuous or not in a grid pattern, and the route between key crossings may require significant diversion. In some cases, the addition of a bicycle/pedestrian-only link, such as a path through a park, a footbridge over a river or highway, or a short connection between two cul-de-sacs, can overcome a major barrier to connectivity and become the keystone of a bicycle boulevard route. Routes that require significant diversion are inappropriate for bicycle boulevards. Bicyclists are typically willing to deviate from the most direct route for only very short distances (two to three short blocks), to overcome a barrier, access a continuous bicycle route, or access a specific land use.

Depending on the length of the diversion (and steepness of the hill) bicyclists also tend to be willing to travel out of direction to avoid steep grades. Though generally undesirable, if a direct connection uses an existing staircase to cross an obstacle (such as at an overcrossing), a ramp or a stair channel should be provided. A climbing bike lane (see shared lane markings) may be appropriate on steep bicycle boulevards, although bicyclists' ability to traverse the hill by using the full lane should be weighed with the motor vehicle volumes on the road.

ALBUQUERQUE, NM

MINNEAPOLIS, MN

Identification

The advantage of the bicycle boulevard—bicycling on a quiet, safe, and residential roadway—can also be its downside, as these routes may be less visible and intuitive than major parallel streets. Thus one goal of marking a bicycle boulevard route is to make it as clearly visible to people as a bicycle route as are streets striped with bicycle lanes or developed with cycle tracks. A second goal is to encourage people to bicycle along the route and to alert drivers that they should expect to encounter people bicycling. A third goal of marking the route is to communicated that bicycle travel has priority on the roadway. This visibility can be accomplished through wayfinding signs and pavement markings. Additional elements, such as art, public spaces, and landscaping, further increase the visibility of the corridor.

The bicycle boulevard should also be actively marketed through events, activities, and maps to help reach its potential. Facilitating awareness of and education regarding the many benefits of bicycle boulevards for all types of roadway users can improve public perception, build support for additional treatments and provide confidence to new bicyclists.

Motor Vehicle Speeds and Volumes

Streets formally designated as bicycle boulevards should meet strict targets of fewer than 3,000 motor vehicles per day (1,500 preferred) and an 85th percentile speed of no more than 25 mph (20 mph preferred). Traffic conditions, including motor vehicle speeds and volumes and bicyclist delay, should be monitored before implementation and on a regular basis after implementation. Should conditions exceed the target thresholds, additional speed and/or volume management treatments should be implemented.[122]

While most bicycle boulevards are located on residential streets, they can also be designated along commercial or industrial streets with low vehicular speeds and volumes. Because of the greater intensity of access demand on commercial streets compared to residential streets, volumes up to 3,000 vehicles per day (vpd) can be acceptable, though below 1,500 vpd is always preferred. However, due to the higher number of vehicles, which often include more heavy vehicles, motor vehicle speeds should be reduced to 20 mph or less. Additional signs and markings are encouraged to improve the visibility of the corridor as a bicycle boulevard.

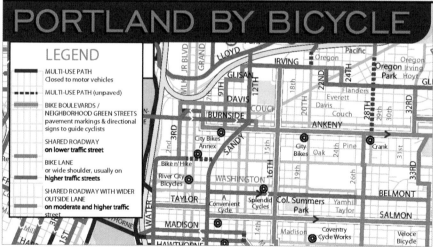

PORTLAND, OR

LA HABRA, CA

Bicycle Boulevards and Emergency Vehicle Routes

Bicycle boulevards can be compatible with emergency vehicle routes. While not all speed and volume management treatments are appropriate on emergency routes, several treatments that lower general traffic speeds and volumes while minimizing constraints to emergency vehicles can be applied. When identifying the bicycle boulevard network, communities should develop an emergency response route classification map designating primary or major emergency response routes, which focuses the bulk of emergency response activity along major roads.

Emergency vehicle routes should form a regular grid of streets that concentrate emergency responses on streets that are wider and provide mobility across a jurisdiction.

PORTLAND, OR

MADISON, WI

Such streets will often have signals that can be pre-empted to facilitate emergency response. The wider streets also permit auto traffic to move aside more easily, clearing a pathway for emergency vehicles. Such streets rarely coincide with bicycle boulevard streets, which can prevent the need for trade-offs between speed/volume management and emergency response delay.[123]

It should be clear from the beginning of a bicycle boulevard implementation process that not only are volume and speed control measures allowed on the route in question, but that emergency-vehicle-friendly access will be provided through the closure. Emergency response maps must be updated to reflect any volume control measures implemented.

Similarly, bicycle boulevards can be designated on lightly-traveled corridors that also serve as minor transit routes. Bicycle boulevards are incompatible with routes with a significant amount of heavy vehicle traffic.

Benefits

Provides comfortable and attractive places to bicycle, attracting people of all ages and abilities.[124]

Can make cost-effective use of existing roadways and connections with a series of relatively minor treatments that substantially improve bicycling conditions on local streets.

Can benefit residents with reduced vehicle speeds and less through traffic.[125]

Can benefit pedestrians and other users through crossing improvements, wayfinding, landscaping, and reduced motor vehicle speeds and volumes.

The majority of respondents felt that the SE Salmon Street bicycle boulevard has had a positive impact on home values, quality of life, sense of community, noise, air quality, and convenience for bicyclists.

VanZerr, M. (2009). Resident Perceptions of Bicycle Boulevards: A Portland, Oregon Case Study.

Typical Applications

Streets with 85th percentile speeds at 25 mph or less (20 mph or less preferred) and with traffic volumes of fewer than 3,000 vehicles per day (below 1,500 vehicles per day preferred). These conditions should either exist or be established with speed and volume management techniques.[126]

Lower motor vehicle volume and speed streets that are parallel and in close proximity to major thoroughfares, which also provide a similar level of land use connectivity and travel demand function.

Note: Bicycle Boulevards and other low-stress parallel routes should complement, but not substitute, cycle tracks or buffered bike lanes along main roads and retail corridors. Bicycle facilities on major streets provide direct access to businesses, jobs, and key destinations and often serve as the most direct and intuitive route.

Streets where a relatively continuous route for bicyclists exists and/or where treatments can provide wayfinding and improve crossing opportunities at offset intersections (often streets where people are already bicycling).

Streets where bicyclists have right-of-way at intersections or where right-of-way can be established.

Design Guidance

Route Planning

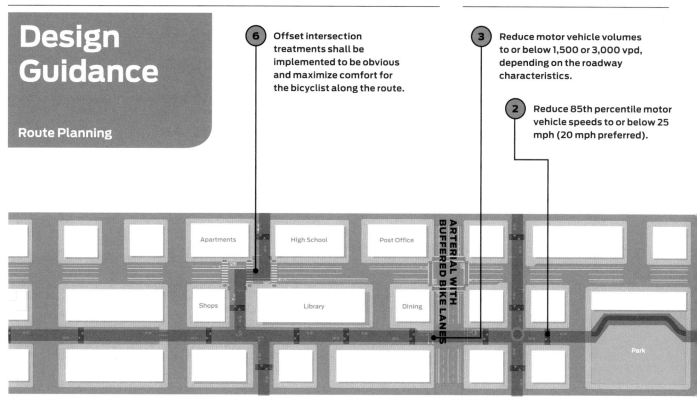

6 Offset intersection treatments shall be implemented to be obvious and maximize comfort for the bicyclist along the route.

3 Reduce motor vehicle volumes to or below 1,500 or 3,000 vpd, depending on the roadway characteristics.

2 Reduce 85th percentile motor vehicle speeds to or below 25 mph (20 mph preferred).

Apartments

High School

Post Office

ARTERIAL WITH BUFFERED BIKE LANES

Shops

Library

Dining

Park

Required Features

1 Signs and pavement markings shall be utilized to identify the corridor as a bicycle boulevard, make the facility as visible as streets with bicycle lanes, cycle tracks, or other bicycle facilities.

2 Speed management techniques shall be implemented, if needed, to reduce 85th percentile motor vehicle speeds to or below 25 mph (20 mph or less always preferred and required where motor vehicle volumes exceed 1,500 vpd).

3 Volume management techniques shall be implemented, if needed, to reduce motor vehicle volumes to or below 1,500 or 3,000 vpd, depending on the roadway characteristics.

4 Minor street crossing treatments shall be implemented to minimize bicyclist delay along the route.

5 Major street crossing treatments shall be implemented to maximize bicyclist safety and comfort at crossings.

6 Offset intersection treatments shall be implemented to be obvious and maximize comfort for the bicyclist along the route.

Recommended Features

7 Wayfinding signs and pavement markings should be used to tie the bicycle boulevard to nearby land uses and to direct users through turns and jogs.

8 Pavement quality should be fair to good and the street should be prioritized for repaving and other maintenance activities over other local streets.

9 Green infrastructure, including bioswales and other storm management techniques, street trees, and pocket parks, may be provided where opportunities present themselves.

10 Enhanced signage beyond simple identification or wayfinding signs may be used to improve visibility and awareness of the route.

11 Art work may be used to enhance the user experience.

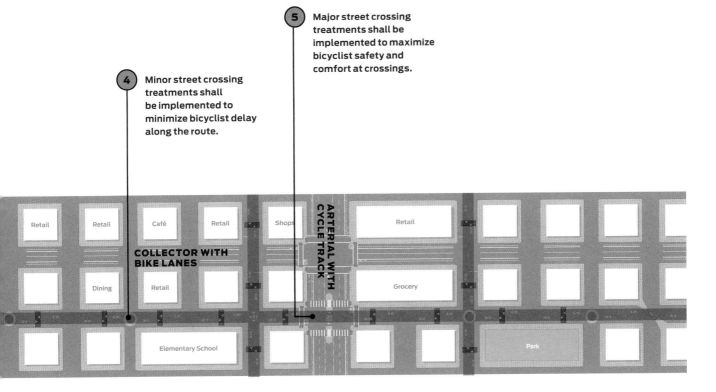

④ Minor street crossing treatments shall be implemented to minimize bicyclist delay along the route.

⑤ Major street crossing treatments shall be implemented to maximize bicyclist safety and comfort at crossings.

Intersection Crossings

All intersections along bicycle boulevards should minimize delay and improve safety for bicyclists on the bicycle boulevard. These two goals can be accomplished with a variety of treatments, including supplemental signs and markings, geometric design features, and traffic control devices. While all crossing treatments should provide both benefits, there are trade-offs between these goals, which vary based on the operational characteristics of the cross street. In some cases, local streets intersect either minor or major streets at a "dog-leg" intersection. See Offset Intersections for guidance on providing comfortable and direct bicycle access through such intersections.

At minor street crossings or intersections with other local streets, crossing treatments primarily reduce delay for users on the bicycle boulevard. If stop signs require people on bikes to stop repeatedly, they may be more likely to seek other routes, disregard the stops signs or not bicycle at all. Improved safety at these minor intersections

should include appropriate traffic control for cross traffic with optional supplemental warning signs and other treatments that improve the visibility of the bicycle boulevard.

Bicyclists can expect some delay at crossings of major streets that have more motor vehicle traffic than the bicycle boulevard and therefore have right-of-way priority. As the complexity of the cross street increases, bicyclists are willing to trade off delay for increased safety and comfort at the crossing. However, bicyclists will not

and should not be expected to tolerate excessive delay, which can result in poor compliance or lower bicyclist volume than desired. On larger streets with three or more travel lanes and/or posted speeds of 35 mph or higher, bicycle boulevard crossings should be accommodated with median refuge islands, beacons, or signals.

Engineers should employ techniques that seek to both maximize safety and reduce delay, especially at signalized crossings.

Minimize Delay   **Maximize Safety**

- **Uncontrolled intersections**
- **Traffic circles**
- **Stop-control the cross-street**
  - **Supplemental signs and markings**
  - **Geometric design**
- **Medians**
- **Beacons**
- **Signals**

Increasing Cross Street Complexity →

Increasing speed, volume, number of lanes and decreasing number of crossing gaps.

Maintenance

Bicycle boulevards should be kept in good condition, with a smooth riding surface. Many cities have maintenance schedules for resurfacing and rehabilitating road surfaces. Local streets are typically the lowest priority for repaving, but bicycle boulevards should have a higher priority for repaving or spot improvements than other residential streets. If no budget is available for repaving, the candidate bicycle boulevard route should have good pavement conditions, or an alternative route may be considered.

Bicycle boulevards can incorporate sidewalk maintenance, including curb ramps and painted crossings. These corridors are often branded as neighborhood greenways to emphasize the benefits to all road users.

Where used, green street treatments and other landscaping must be maintained to preserve visibility.

Treatment Adoption and Professional Consensus

Bicycle boulevards are implemented as Local Street Bikeways and Neighborhood Greenways in Vancouver, British Columbia.

Currently used in the following U.S. cities:

- Albuquerque, NM
- Arcata, CA (planned)
- Austin, TX (planned)
- Berkeley, CA
- Columbia, MO
- Denver, CO (planned)
- Emeryville, CA
- Eugene, OR
- Long Beach, CA
- Madison,WI
- Minneapolis, MN
- Nampa, ID
- Ocean City, NJ
- Palo Alto, CA
- Pasadena, CA (planned)
- Portland, OR
- Salt Lake City, UT (planned)
- San Luis Obispo, CA
- Seattle, WA
- Syracuse, NY (planned)
- Tacoma, WA (planned)
- Tucson, AZ
- Wilmington, NC

Signs and Pavement Markings

BERKELEY, CA

Signs and pavement markings create the basic elements of a bicycle boulevard. They indicate that a roadway is intended as a shared, slow street, and reinforce the intention of priority for bicyclists along a given route. Signs and pavement markings alone do not create a safe and effective bicycle boulevard, but act as reinforcements to other traffic calming and operational changes made to the roadway.

There are three applications for signing and markings on bicycle boulevards:

Modified street signs identify and brand the route without introducing a new sign. A bicycle symbol can be placed on a standard road sign, along with the coloration associated with the bicycle boulevard network. These are commonly used in tandem with pavement markings.

Pavement markings identify the route as a bicycle boulevard and can guide users through jogs. These vary throughout North America from small dots about a foot across to stencils that take up nearly a full lane at 30 feet by 6 feet. Several jurisdictions are using MUTCD-approved shared lane markings on bicycle boulevards for consistency with the rest of the bicycle network and because they are visible and proven to impact desired lane positioning by bicyclists.[127]

Wayfinding signs also guide users through jogs, help brand the network, and include information about the route by identifying intersecting bikeways and providing distance/time information to nearby or popular destinations. Since few businesses or services are typically located along local streets, wayfinding signs inform users of the direction and distance to key destinations, including neighborhoods, commercial districts, transit hubs, schools and universities, and connecting bikeways.

BALTIMORE, MD

Benefits

Signs and pavement markings help users remain on the designated route as it turns.

Signs and markings differentiate bicycle boulevards from other local streets, indicating good routes for people bicycling and reminding people driving to watch for bicyclists.

Signs and markings brand the bicycle boulevard to raise awareness of the designated routes and to encourage new users.

Pavement markings encourage people on bicycles to properly position themselves in the roadway and reinforce to all users where bicyclists should be riding, promoting a more comfortable shared use environment for all users.

Wayfinding signs provide information about nearby destinations and route finding, improving confidence for people bicycling in a new area.

Typical Applications

Along all bicycle boulevards.

At intersections where the bicycle boulevard crosses another bikeway or 'jogs' (turns onto another street).

Design Guidance

Signs and Pavement Markings

2 Where the bicycle boulevard turns or jogs onto another street, signs and/or markings shall be provided to indicate how users can remain on the route.

5 Decision and turn signs should include destinations with arrows and distance and/or bicycling times.

Required Features

1 Bicycle wayfinding signage and pavement markings shall be included on bicycle boulevards. Pavement markings and identification/wayfinding signs provide a strong visual identity for the street and designate the corridor as a bicycle route.

2 Where the bicycle boulevard turns or jogs onto another street, signs and/or markings shall be provided to indicate how users can remain on the route.

3 Center line stripes (if present) shall be removed or not repainted, except for short sections on intersection approaches that have a stop line or traffic circle. Drivers have an easier time passing bicyclists on roads that do not have centerline stripes. If vehicles cannot easily pass each other using the full width of the street, it is likely that there is too much traffic for the street to be a successful bicycle boulevard.[128]

Recommended Features

4 Pavement markings should be large enough to be visible to all road users; 112 inches by 40 inches (the standard size of a shared lane marking) is the minimum recommended size.

5 Decision and turn signs should include destinations with arrows and distance and/or bicycling times. Bicycling time should assume a typical speed of 10 mph.

6 Advanced crossing warning signs such as MUTCD sign W11-1 (bicycle crossing; may be supplemented with AHEAD plaque) should be placed on intersecting streets with more than 5,000 vpd. A non-standard sign using the coloration and style of other bicycle boulevard signs may be used with an arrow showing bi-directional cross traffic.

7 On narrow local streets where it can be difficult for cars traveling in opposite directions to pass, pavement markings should be applied in closer intervals near the center of the travel lane.

Optional Features

8 Signs may differ from those outlined in the MUTCD to highlight or brand the bicycle boulevard network. If used, signs shall be consistent in content, design, and intent; colors reserved by the MUTCD Section 1A.12 for regulatory and warning road signs (red, yellow, orange, etc.) are not recommended. Green, blue and purple are commonly used.

9 Confirmation signs may include destinations and distance and/or bicycling times.

10 To minimize sign clutter, a bicycle symbol may be placed on a standard street name sign, along with distinctive coloration.[129]

11 Either shared lane markings or non-standard markings may be used along bicycle boulevards.

12 On particularly narrow streets (approximately 25 feet wide with parking), shared lane marking stencils may be placed either in the center of the lane facing each other, or with the

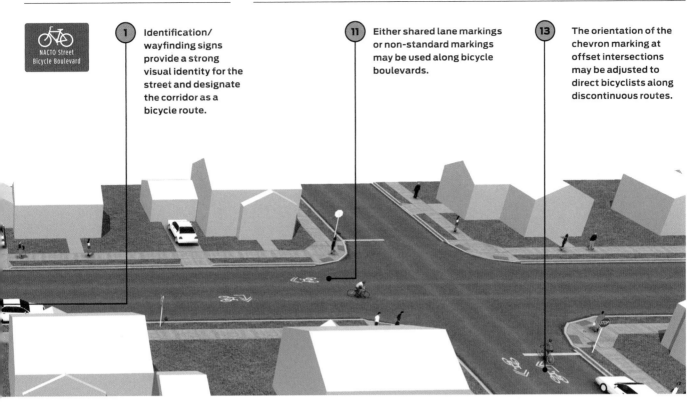

1 Identification/ wayfinding signs provide a strong visual identity for the street and designate the corridor as a bicycle route.

11 Either shared lane markings or non-standard markings may be used along bicycle boulevards.

13 The orientation of the chevron marking at offset intersections may be adjusted to direct bicyclists along discontinuous routes.

bicycle marking in the center of the roadway and two sets of chevrons offset 1 foot in each direction or travel.

13 For wayfinding purposes, the orientation of the chevron marking at offset intersections may be adjusted to direct bicyclists along discontinuous routes. Alternately, an arrow may be used with the chevrons to indicate the direction of the turn.

14 On-street parking spaces may be delineated with paint or other materials to clearly indicate where a vehicle should be parked and to discourage motorists from parking their vehicles too far into the adjacent travel lane.[130]

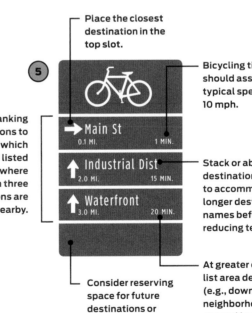

Place the closest destination in the top slot.

5

Bicycling time should assume a typical speed of 10 mph.

Consider ranking destinations to determine which should be listed on a sign where more than three destinations are nearby.

Stack or abbreviate destination names to accommodate longer destination names before reducing text size.

Consider reserving space for future destinations or bikeways.

At greater distances, list area destinations (e.g., downtown and neighborhoods) as a general location.

MADISON, WI

BERKELEY, CA

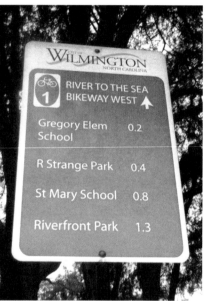

WILMINGTON, NC (PHOTO: NATE EVANS)

Maintenance

Maintenance needs for bicycle signs are similar to other signs. Signs will need periodic replacement due to wear.

The shared lane marking may be placed in the center of the lane between wheel treads to minimize wear.

Treatment Adoption and Professional Consensus

Shared lane markings and bicycle wayfinding signs were adopted as part of the 2009 MUTCD.

The use of pavement markings to indicate turns and jogs is being tested in Columbus, MO and is used in Portland, OR.

Minneapolis, MN, Berkeley, CA, and Vancouver, BC, use a modified street name sign with distinctive coloration and a bicycle symbol to indicate bicycle boulevards.

Speed Management

PORTLAND, OR

Speed Management measures for bicycle boulevards bring motor vehicle speeds closer to those of bicyclists. Reducing speeds along the bicycle boulevard improves the bicycling environment by reducing overtaking events, enhancing drivers' ability to see and react, and diminishing the severity of crashes if they occur. Speed management is critical to creating a comfortable and effective bicycle boulevard.

Streets developed as bicycle boulevards should have 85th percentile speeds at 25 mph or less (20 mph preferred). Speed management (traffic calming) measures can be divided into vertical or horizontal features. These measures can be implemented individually or in combination to increase their efficacy. Common combinations include raised crosswalks with pinchpoints, raised intersections with pinchpoints, and speed humps with center island narrowings, chicanes, or pinchpoints.[131]

Reduced Speed Limits

Bicycle boulevards should have a maximum posted speed of 25 mph. Some jurisdictions are starting to sign residential speed limits below 25 mph. Simply changing the speed limit is unlikely to reduce speeds; speed management and street design techniques are necessary. Once actual speeds decrease, lower speed limit signs can reinforce the desired speed with regulatory control. Targeted enforcement is also recommended.

Reduced speed limits may require authorizing legislation. The MUTCD designates that speed limits shall be in increments of 5 mph and requires an engineering study to reduce the speed below the statutory speed for the type of roadway. In some jurisdictions, speed limits may be reduced beyond the statutory residential speed limit. State statutory limits might restrict the maximum speed limit that can be established on a particular road.[132]

ALBUQUERQUE, NM

Vertical Deflection

Vertical speed control measures are composed of wide, slight pavement elevations that self-enforce a slower speed for motorists. Note: the type of narrow, abrupt speed bumps used in private driveways or parking lots are not recommended for public streets and are a hazard to bicyclists.

Some examples of recommended speed management treatments include the following:

Speed humps are 3 to 4 inches high and 12 to 14 feet long, such that speeds are reduced to 15 to 20 mph. They are often referred to as "bumps" on signage and by the general public.[133]

Speed cushions or speed lumps are either speed humps or speed tables that include wheel cutouts to allow large vehicles to pass unaffected, while reducing passenger car speeds. They can be offset to allow unimpeded passage by emergency vehicles and are typically used on key emergency response routes. They should be used with caution, however, as people driving sometimes seek out the space between the lumps, reducing the traffic calming effect and causing unpredictable driving.[134]

Speed tables are longer than speed humps and flat-topped, with a height of 3 to 3.5 inches and a length of 22 feet. Vehicle operating speeds range from 25 to 35 mph, depending on the spacing, and speed tables may be used on collector streets and/or transit and emergency response routes.

Split speed tables are also 22 feet long and extend across one direction of travel lanes from the centerline. A longitudinal gap is provided to allow emergency vehicles to weave around the treatment. While studies have indicated that this treatment does not reduce speeds below 25 mph, it has been found to deter cut-through traffic, particularly by large trucks.[135]

A raised crosswalk is a speed table that is marked and signed for pedestrian crossing. It extends fully across the street, can be longer than a typical speed table, and is typically 3 inches high. An entire minor intersection can be raised to reduce motor vehicle speeds in all directions.[136]

Horizontal Deflection

Horizontal speed control measures cause motorists to slow down in response to either a visually narrower roadway or a need to navigate a curving travel lane. Where traffic calming features do not extend beyond the parking lane, they visually narrow the road and improve the approaching bicyclists' view of cross traffic, but do not act as speed management. "When motor vehicle speeds are already below target thresholds, elements can either extend into the travel lane or narrow a bi-directional street to a single lane. Under these conditions bicyclists are comfortable taking the lane and overtaking cars do not encroach on bicyclists' space. Where possible, provide sufficient space for bicyclists to pass around the outside of the elements.

Examples of horizontal deflection include the following:

Curb extensions or bulb-outs extend the sidewalk or curb face into the parking lane at an intersection. When placed on the bicycle boulevard, they visually narrow the roadway. Curb extensions on the cross street act as a minor street crossing. All curb extensions reduce the crossing distance for pedestrians, can increase the amount of space available for street furniture and trees, and can act as stormwater management features.

Edge islands are curb extensions that leave a 1- to 2-foot gap by the curb to improve drainage.

Neighborhood traffic circles are minor street crossing treatments that also provide speed management. They are raised or delineated islands placed at intersections that reduce vehicle speeds by narrowing turning radii, narrowing the travel lane, and, if planted, obscure the visual corridor along the roadway. It should be noted that the City of Portland has found such circles to be less effective than frequently spaced speed humps, and many people on bicycles complain that motorists overtake them when approaching the circles, creating a hazardous condition.[137]

Chicanes are a series of raised or delineated curb extensions, edge islands, or parking bays on alternating sides of a street forming an S-shaped travel way. This reduces vehicle speeds by requiring drivers to shift laterally through narrowed travel lanes.[138]

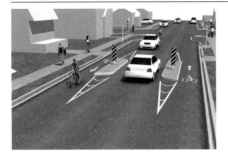

A pinchpoint or choker narrowing includes curb extensions or edge islands placed on either side of the street to narrow the center of the lane such that two drivers have difficulty passing through simultaneously. Pinchpoints should only be used where traffic speeds are already low. Cut-through passageways should be provided to the outside of the pinchpoint to accommodate bicyclists.[139]

Neckdowns are pinchpoints at intersections; they are minor street crossing treatments that narrow at least one side of an intersection using curb extensions or edge islands on both sides of the street. They are often combined with parking bays on side streets off of commercial main streets.[140]

A short center island narrowing is a median parallel to the bicycle boulevard that causes a small amount of deflection without blocking driveway access (such treatments can also act as median refuge islands for pedestrians crossing the bicycle boulevard, but in this configuration it is not a crossing treatment for the bicycle boulevard). Medians can be used for volume management and to assist in bicycle turns at offset intersections.[141]

Skinny streets or queuing streets are narrow residential streets that require low motor vehicle speeds and accommodate travel in a bi-directional lane. These types of streets act as traffic calming as drivers must yield to each other to allow one direction of travel at a time to pass.[142]

BERKELEY, CA

Benefits

Decreases motor vehicle speeds.[143]

Decreases the likelihood that crashes will occur, by increasing drivers' response time and minimizing motor vehicles overtaking movements.

Decreases the likelihood of an injury resulting from a crash.[144]

Improves bicyclist comfort and benefits pedestrians and residents by reducing traffic speeds along the corridor.

Establishes and reinforces bicycle priority on bicycle boulevards by discouraging through vehicle travel.

Provides opportunities for landscaping and other community features such as benches, message boards, and colored pavement in the intersection, benefiting all roadway users and residents.

Typical Applications

Bicycle boulevards where motor vehicle speeds are at or above posted speed or established target speed.[145]

Streets where the neighborhood feels traffic speeds are too high and are supportive of speed management treatments.

Streets where minor street crossing improvements to reduce bicycle delay (e.g., flipping stop signs to favor the bicycle boulevard) may otherwise encourage higher motor vehicle volumes and/or speeds.

At high-use pedestrian crossings of a bicycle boulevard (raised crosswalk or intersection).

Anywhere green infrastructure or sewer improvements are desired; bioswales can be integrated into the design of curb extensions, chicanes, pinchpoints, and narrowings.

Design Guidance

Speed Management

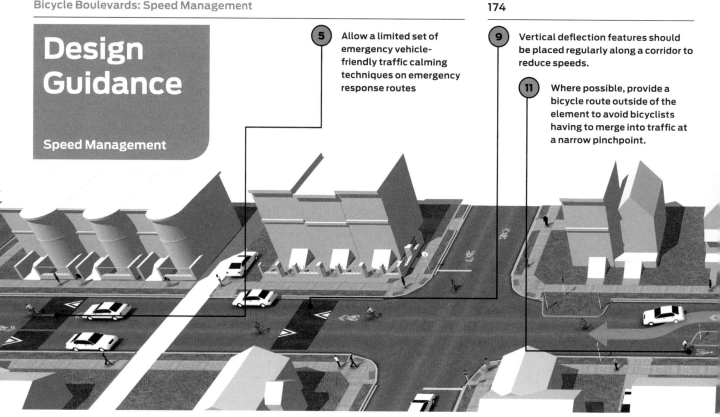

5 Allow a limited set of emergency vehicle-friendly traffic calming techniques on emergency response routes

9 Vertical deflection features should be placed regularly along a corridor to reduce speeds.

11 Where possible, provide a bicycle route outside of the element to avoid bicyclists having to merge into traffic at a narrow pinchpoint.

Speed Lump   Speed Hump   Chicane

Required Features

1 When using horizontal speed management treatments, a minimum clear width of 12 feet for travel shall be maintained.

2 Speed limits shall comply with local restrictions.

3 Speed zones (other than statutory speed limits) shall only be established on the basis of an engineering study that has been performed in accordance with traffic engineering practices (MUTCD 2B.13).

4 Speed limits shall be in multiples of 5 mph and signs shall be located at the points of change from one speed limit to another (MUTCD 2B.13).Recommended Features

Recommended Features

5 Emergency services should be in sync with transportation departments in recognizing that reducing speed and volume on local roadways, in addition to getting more people on foot and bike and out of cars, benefits their overall safety goals by reducing crash frequency and severity. The primary way of doing this is to develop an emergency response route classification map at the onset of the planning process, as discussed in route planning. Emergency vehicle response times should be considered where vertical deflection is used. Because emergency vehicles have a wider wheel base than passenger cars, speed lumps/cushions allow them to pass unimpeded while slowing most traffic.

Strategies include the following:

- Seek approval by emergency response officials for treatments on emergency response routes.

- Allow a limited set of emergency-vehicle-friendly traffic calming techniques on emergency response routes.[146]

- Estimate travel time impacts on emergency vehicle response time, and define goals to evaluate during a trial.[147]

- Implement speed management treatments on a trial basis, and work with emergency response officials to determine whether permanent features are appropriate.

6 Speed management treatments should be used to reduce the street's target speed to 20 mph.

7 After speed management measures are implemented, posted speed limits should be reduced to match 85th percentile speed (5 mph speed increments are recommended).

8 The impacts to traffic on adjacent streets should be monitored; while speed management treatments primarily affect motor vehicle speeds, they also reduce volumes, as drivers tend to avoid slower streets.[148]

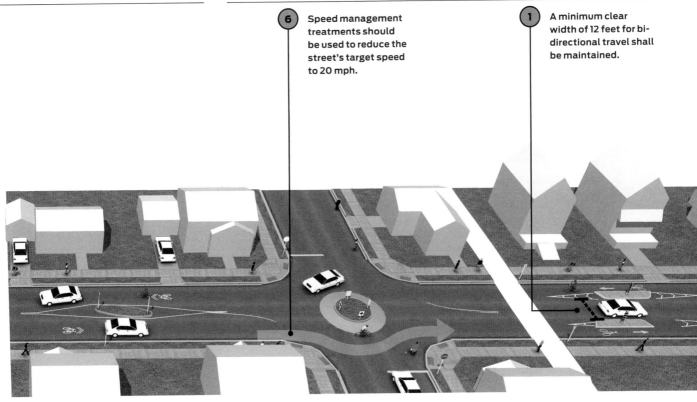

6 Speed management treatments should be used to reduce the street's target speed to 20 mph.

1 A minimum clear width of 12 feet for bi-directional travel shall be maintained.

Median Island   **Neighborhood Traffic Circle**   **Pinchpoint**

9 Vertical deflection features should be placed regularly along a corridor to reduce speeds.[149]

10 Guidance for vertical traffic calming features:

- Slopes should not exceed 1:10 or be less steep than 1:25.

- Side slopes on tapers should be no greater than 1:6 to reduce the risk of bicyclists losing their balance.

- The vertical lip should be no more than a quarter-inch high (Ewing, 2009).

11 Horizontal speed control measures should not infringe on bicycle space. Where possible, provide a bicycle route outside of the element to avoid bicyclists having to merge into traffic at a narrow pinchpoint. This technique can also improve drainage flow and reduce construction and maintenance costs.

Optional Features

12 Speed management may be implemented on a trial basis to gauge residents' support prior to finalizing the design. Temporary speed humps, tables, and lumps are available. Temporary traffic calming should be used with caution as they can diminish residents' opinions due to unappealing design and reduced functionality.

Depending on motor vehicle speeds, a bicyclist will be passed by a car going the same direction this many times during a 10 minute trip:

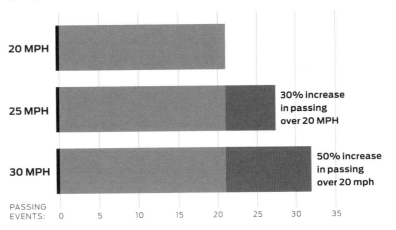

20 MPH

25 MPH — 30% increase in passing over 20 MPH

30 MPH — 50% increase in passing over 20 mph

PASSING EVENTS: 0   5   10   15   20   25   30   35

Values shown assume 3,000 VPD. Local street peak hour is 15 percent of ADT. 70 percent of peak hour traffic is in the peak direction. Cars are evenly spaced along the street: no platooning. Ten minute trip calculated during peak hour. Cars are travelling the posted speed limit (speed management techniques may be necessary). Note: Cars may pass bicyclists more or less frequently depending on how well these assumptions reflect reality.

BALTIMORE, MD

Maintenance

In cities with snowy winters, traffic calming should be designed to minimize impacts to snow removal operations through the use of reflective delineators on horizontal treatments and sinusoidal transitions to vertical treatments that allow plow blades to track over the change in elevation. Temporary traffic control devices can be used and may be removed in the winter, when speeds are generally slower.[150]

Vegetation should be regularly trimmed to maintain visibility and attractiveness.

Treatment Adoption and Professional Consensus

Many cities in the U.S. have neighborhood traffic calming programs or public works departments that have installed speed humps or traffic circles. Cities that have designated bicycle boulevards have implemented a variety of speed management treatments. Just greater than half of the jurisdictions with traffic calming programs surveyed for the U.S. Traffic Calming Manual (Ewing, 2009) use trial installations to test speed and volume management techniques. Treatment Adoption and Professional Consensus

Volume Management

PORTLAND, OR

Volume Management measures reduce or discourage thru traffic on designated bicycle boulevard corridors by physically or operationally reconfiguring select corridors and intersections along the route. On roadways with shared travel lanes such as bicycle boulevards, motor vehicle traffic volumes significantly impact bicyclist comfort. Higher vehicle volumes decrease comfort and may lead to a greater potential for conflicts, as well as a loss of perceived safety. Bicycle boulevards should be designed for motor vehicle volumes under 1,500 vehicles per day (vpd), with up to 3,000 vpd allowed in limited sections of a bicycle boulevard corridor.[151]

VANCOUVER, BC

If the street already has volumes under 1,500 vpd, then volume
management measures may be needed to maintain existing low
volumes. In the case where a bicycle boulevard passes through
a commercial or industrial area, reducing motor vehicle volumes
below 1,500 may not be possible or beneficial for the area. If
volumes are below 3,000 vpd, additional signs and markings
can be used to improve visibility of the bicycle boulevard, and
speed management can be used to maintain low speeds. Bicycle
boulevards with motor vehicle volumes over 1,500 vpd may be less
attractive to families with children and other people who do not
prefer riding in traffic, although they can make a decent commuter
connection. If volumes are over 3,000 vpd for a short segment of
the bicycle boulevard corridor, a bike lane or cycle track may be
considered through the area to maintain a low-stress bikeway.

If intervention is needed to reduce or maintain low motor vehicle volumes along the corridor, volume management treatments can prohibit motor vehicle turning or through movements while allowing passage by bicyclists and pedestrians. Such treatments should be implemented with consideration for emergency vehicles and neighborhood access.

Volume management techniques include the following:

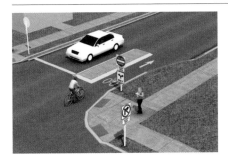

A **forced turn at an intersection** restricts through movements for motor vehicles. This diversion can exclusively use signs to allow buses and emergency vehicles to continue straight, but this may result in poor compliance by motorists (Berkeley, 2000).

A **channelized right-in/right-out island** forces motor vehicles to turn right while bicyclists can continue straight through the intersection. The island can provide a through bike lane or bicycle access to reduce conflicts with right-turning vehicles.

Partial closures or **choker entrances** across one direction of traffic at an intersection allow full bicycle passage while restricting vehicle access to one side only. Motorists on the bicycle boulevard must turn onto the cross street while bicyclists may continue straight along a short contra-flow bike lane past the closure.

Median islands/diverters restrict through vehicle movements while providing refuge for bicyclists to cross one direction of traffic at a time (also see major street crossing treatments). A snake diverter is a narrow raised median that is an extruded curb along the centerline of the cross street. This treatment minimizes impacts for travelers on the cross street while prohibiting through movements by motor vehicles on the bicycle boulevard.

Diagonal diverters placed at a four-way minor intersection require all motor vehicle traffic to turn, while allowing bicyclist and pedestrian through movements.[152]

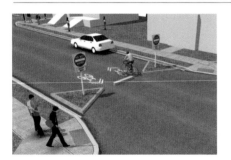

Full diverters create a "T" blocks motor vehicles from continuing on a bicycle boulevard, while bicycle travel can continue unrestricted. Full closures can be constructed to be permeable to emergency vehicles.

BALTIMORE, MD (PHOTO: NATE EVANS)

Benefits

Reduces motor vehicle volumes by completely or partially restricting through traffic on a bicycle boulevard.[153]

Establishes and reinforces bicycle priority by restricting vehicle through movements.

Improves bicyclist comfort on a corridor and benefits pedestrians and residents by reducing traffic volumes along the corridor.

Provides opportunities for landscaping, stormwater management, and other community features such as benches and message boards.

Typical Applications

Along target streets on which reductions in motor vehicle volumes are needed to meet the volume thresholds for bicycle boulevards (i.e., below 1,500 vpd preferred; 3,000 vpd maximum). Bicycle boulevards may be designated along short segments of roadways that accommodate traffic volumes above the established threshold, if necessary, to complete the corridor. Above 1,500 vpd, speeds should be low and additional signs used to increase visibility of the bicycle boulevard. Above 3,000 vpd, a bike lane, cycle track, or other treatments can be considered where speed or volume management treatments cannot reduce volumes below the threshold.

Along streets where conversion to a bicycle boulevard may otherwise encourage cut-through traffic through the removal of stop signs.

At the intersection of two bicycle boulevards.

Design Guidance

Volume Management

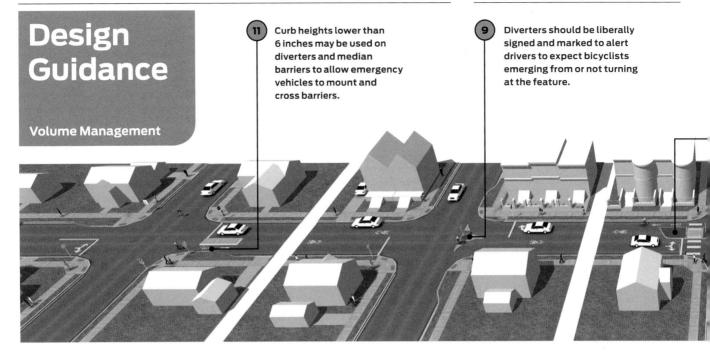

11 Curb heights lower than 6 inches may be used on diverters and median barriers to allow emergency vehicles to mount and cross barriers.

9 Diverters should be liberally signed and marked to alert drivers to expect bicyclists emerging from or not turning at the feature.

Regulatory Partial Closure

Channelized right-in/ right-out island

Partial Closure (Edge Island with Pass Through)

Required Features

1 Where emergency vehicle access is provided, an absolute minimum of 10 feet of clear space shall be maintained between bollards or features. The presence of mountable curbs, flexible or collapsible objects, or restricted lanes may reduce space requirements.

2 Volume management treatments shall provide bicycle access, either through a 4-foot minimum contra-flow bike lane or a 5- to 6-foot opening between vertical curbs.

Recommended Features

3 Appropriate signs should be used to prohibit undesired automobile movements and access while permitting desired bicycle access.[154]

4 For a partial closure, the curb extension or edge island should extend almost to the centerline of the street, leaving at least 4 feet for

the contraflow bike lane, and the adjacent travel lane may be narrowed through the closure. The length of the closure should be about 30 feet, an uncomfortable distance for drivers traveling the wrong way.

5 Diagonal diverters, median barriers, and forced-turn islands should have clear widths sufficient for single-unit trucks to make turns without encroaching on opposing lanes.

6 Volume control measures should not be used along primary emergency response routes. See route planning and speed management for a discussion of designating an emergency response network and minimizing impacts to emergency vehicles along bicycle boulevards.

7 Traffic volumes on other parallel non-arterial streets should be monitored to determine the impacts to volumes, which may require further mitigation. Neighbors and nearby businesses should be consulted to build support for volume management treatments prior to implementation.

8 Appropriate education for use of proposed treatments should be provided to neighbors and others who are likely to use the corridor.

9 Closures and diverters should be liberally signed and marked to alert drivers to expect bicyclists emerging from or not turning at the feature.

Optional Features

10 The partial closure curb extension or edge island may be tapered to deflect drivers to the right as they approach the feature.

11 Curb heights lower than 6 inches may be used on diverters and median barriers to allow emergency vehicles to mount and cross barriers.

12 Bollards may be used for diagonal diverters, but 5 feet should be provided between them to accommodate one direction of bicycle travel.

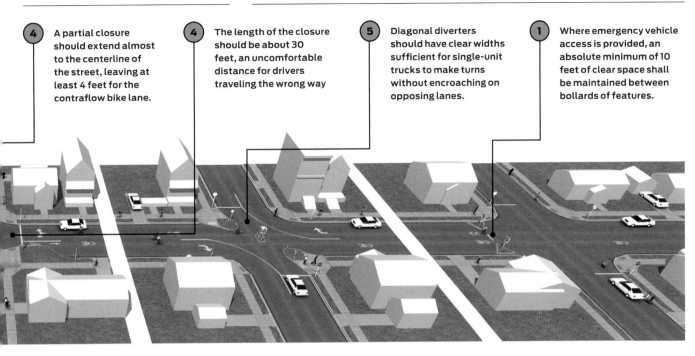

4 — A partial closure should extend almost to the centerline of the street, leaving at least 4 feet for the contraflow bike lane.

4 — The length of the closure should be about 30 feet, an uncomfortable distance for drivers traveling the wrong way

5 — Diagonal diverters should have clear widths sufficient for single-unit trucks to make turns without encroaching on opposing lanes.

1 — Where emergency vehicle access is provided, an absolute minimum of 10 feet of clear space shall be maintained between bollards of features.

Half Closure (Extension)   **Diagonal Diverter**   **Full Closure**

13 Measures may be implemented on a trial basis to gauge resident support prior to finalizing the design. Temporary closures can be created with construction barrels or planters; however, an unappealing design aesthetic may diminish residents' opinions.

14 Channelizing devices may be used along a center line to preclude turns or along lane lines to preclude lane changing, as determined by engineering judgment.[155]

15 Consider defining a threshold of acceptable motor vehicle volume impacts to traffic on adjacent streets when using speed and volume management.[156]

Depending on motor vehicle volumes, a bicyclist will be passed by a car going the same direction this many times during a 10 minute trip:

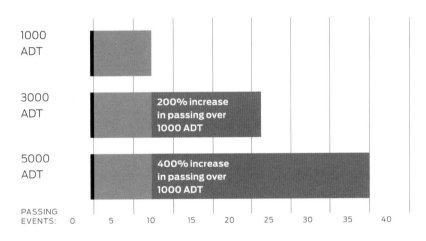

1000 ADT	
3000 ADT	**200% increase in passing over 1000 ADT**
5000 ADT	**400% increase in passing over 1000 ADT**

PASSING EVENTS: 0   5   10   15   20   25   30   35   40

Values shown assume 20 mph posted speed. Local street peak hour is 15 percent of ADT. 70 percent of peak hour traffic is in the peak direction. Cars are evenly spaced along the street: no platooning. 10 minute trip calculated during peak hour. Cars are travelling the posted speed limit (speed management techniques may be necessary). Note: Cars may pass bicyclists more or less frequently depending on how well these assumptions reflect reality.

BERKELEY, CA

Maintenance

In winter climates, these treatments can be challenging to keep clear of snow and debris. Careful consideration should be applied within the design process to minimize impacts to snow removal operation. Special maintenance may be required to keep bicycle pass-throughs clear of snow and debris.

Vegetation should be regularly trimmed to maintain visibility and attractiveness.

Treatment Adoption and Professional Consensus

Volume management techniques are used by many jurisdictions as part of neighborhood traffic calming programs.

Minor Street Crossings

BALTIMORE, MD

Minor Street Crossings for bicycle boulevards typically involve the intersection of two residential or local streets with low motor vehicle volumes and speeds. At intersections with local streets and minor collectors, bicycle boulevards should have right-of-way priority and reduce or minimize delay by limiting the number of stop signs along the route. Stretches of at least a half mile or more of continuous travel without stop sign control are desirable.

Stop signs along a bicycle boulevard increase travel time for bicyclists and may be viewed as unnecessary, resulting in low compliance and unpredictability. On many local streets, stop signs are 'woven' such that travelers along local streets must stop at every other intersection. On bicycle boulevards this pattern should be altered to remove stop signs on the bikeway and reorient them towards intersecting local streets. This provides clarity at the intersections, while creating a more continuous flow of bicycle travel. Speed and volume

MADISON, WI

control measures should be used in coordination with this approach to prevent these conditions from becoming attractive to motorists as a shortcut.

A bicycle boulevard should have traffic control and/or geometric design elements at all intersections to reduce conflicts. Neighborhood traffic circles can help direct traffic where stop controls are not appropriate. Parking can be prohibited on the intersection approaches and a pavement marking placed in the intersection so that the approaching driver on the cross street knows to expect bicyclists crossing.

PALO ALTO, CA

A cyclist who rolls through a stop at 5 mph needs 25 percent less energy to get back to 10 mph than does a cyclist who comes to a complete stop.

Fajans, J., and M. Curry. (2001). Why Bicyclists Hate Stop Signs. Access. 18:28-31.

Benefits

Enabling bicyclists to ride along the corridor with few stops significantly reduces travel time, minimizes bicyclist effort, and can improve compliance.[157]

Typical Applications

Wherever the bicycle boulevard is stop controlled at an intersection with a minor street, consider turning the stop signs to stop the cross traffic, thereby maximizing through bicycle connectivity and preserving bicyclist momentum.

At uncontrolled intersections of minor streets, neighborhood traffic circles may be used to reduce conflicts and maintain appropriate speeds. See speed management for a discussion of traffic circles and other related treatments.

Design Guidance

Minor Street Crossings

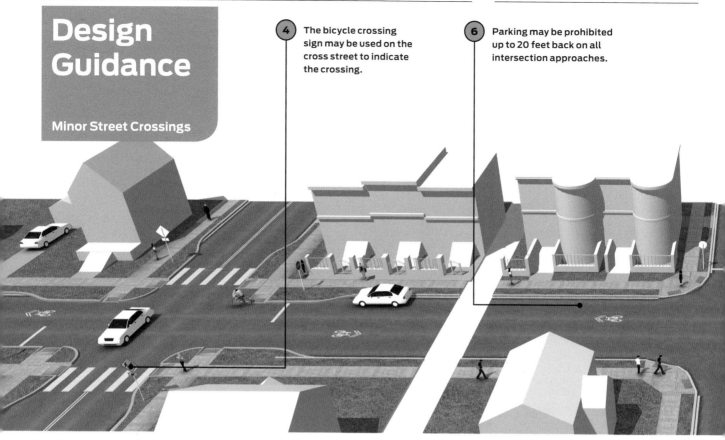

4 The bicycle crossing sign may be used on the cross street to indicate the crossing.

6 Parking may be prohibited up to 20 feet back on all intersection approaches.

Curb Extensions

Required Features

1 There is no minimum required element to a minor street crossing since they can vary significantly depending on the geometry and the speed/volume of cross traffic. Treatments shall be considered using engineering judgment and shall consider the safety and comfort of bicycle movements along the bicycle boulevard.

Recommended Features

2 Stop signs or geometric design elements should be considered at all minor street crossings to control the intersecting street and allow for the continuous flow of bicyclists.[158]

3 Stop signs should control cross traffic only along the bicycle boulevard. If vehicle traffic increases along the bicycle boulevard, implement volume control measures. If vehicle speeds increase along the bicycle boulevard, implement speed control measures.

Optional Features

4 The bicycle crossing sign (MUTCD sign W11-1; may be supplemented with AHEAD plaque) may be used on the cross street to indicate the crossing.

5 The CROSS TRAFFIC DOES NOT STOP plaque (MUTCD sign W4-4P) may be used in combination with a STOP sign on the cross street to indicate the crossing.

6 Parking may be prohibited up to 20 feet back on all intersection approaches to improve visibility.

7 A sign using the bicycle boulevard branding with an arrow may be used on the cross street to indicate the crossing.

BERKELEY, CA

BERKELEY, CA

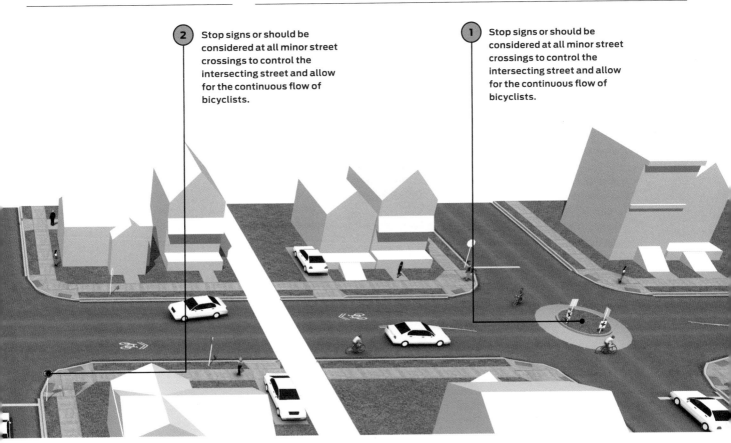

2 Stop signs or should be considered at all minor street crossings to control the intersecting street and allow for the continuous flow of bicyclists.

1 Stop signs or should be considered at all minor street crossings to control the intersecting street and allow for the continuous flow of bicyclists.

Stop Sign for Cross Traffic

Neighborhood Traffic Circle

Travel Time Impacts of Stop Signs on Bicyclists

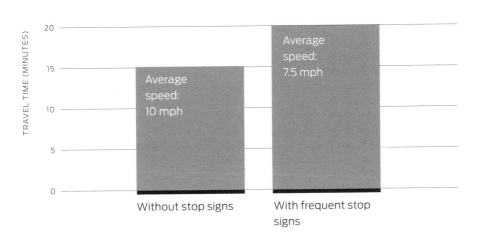

TRAVEL TIME (MINUTES)

Without stop signs — Average speed: 10 mph

With frequent stop signs — Average speed: 7.5 mph

Calculations assume a 2.5 mile trip distance. Delay calculation adapted from: City of Berkeley. (2000). Bicycle Boulevard Design Tools and Guidelines.

TUCSON, AZ

Treatment Adoption and Professional Consensus

Several jurisdictions have turned stop signs and consider bicycle connectivity a key factor in the development of bicycle boulevards.

A typical bicycle trip of 30 minutes is increased by 33% to 40 minutes if there is a STOP sign at every block.

City of Berkeley. (2000). Bicycle Boulevard Design Tools and Guidelines.

Major Street Crossings

DAVIS, CA

At locations where a bicycle boulevard crosses a major street with right-of-way priority, a variety of measures may improve visibility and reduce delay for bicyclists.

Treatments can be categorized into the following groups:

1. **Supplemental signs and markings** that enhance crosswalks, including advance stop bars and advance signing.
2. **Geometric elements,** including median refuge islands and curb extensions.
3. **Crossing devices,** including crosswalks, warning signs/markings/beacons, actuated warning beacons, and signals.

Major street crossings may pose a significant barrier the effectiveness and quality of a bicycle boulevard. Treatments of high quality should be selected to mitigate these barriers. Otherwise, it is recommended that another route or crossing that permits a higher level treatment should be selected. Selection of a given treatment depends upon several factors, including roadway width, speed, visibility, and the number and regularity of gaps.[159]

Unsignalized Intersections

At unsignalized crossings of major streets, treatments should aim to decrease crossing distance, increase the number of available crossing gaps, improve visibility for bicyclists and people using the cross street, and/or enhance the general awareness of the crossing.

Treatments appropriate for streets with three or fewer travel lanes and posted speeds below 35 mph vary with conditions and operational characteristics of the cross street. Treatments may include the following elements:

Advance warning signs notify motorists that they are about to cross a bicycle boulevard and remind them to watch for people walking and bicycling.[160]

Curb extensions shorten crossing distances and allow crossing bicyclists and pedestrians to make use of shorter gaps. They may be used in conjunction with a variety of other intersection treatments, and should only be used as a stand-alone crossing device where they will provide additional crossing gaps in a location with insufficient existing crossing opportunities.

A bicycle forward stop bar—used in conjunction with a curb extension—is placed closer to the intersection than the motor vehicle stop bar in a location that does not block the crosswalk. Encouraging bicyclists to stop at the nose of the curb extension helps bicyclists take full advantage of the design by decreasing the crossing distance. It also improves bicyclists' view of cross traffic and provides better visibility of bicyclists waiting for a crossing opportunity. Colored paint may be used to bring further attention to this space.[161]

Intersection crossing markings or **standard crosswalks** can be used to highlight to cross traffic that bicyclists are crossing the roadway in that location. They may be used with crossing warning signs for bicycles or bicycles and pedestrians (MUTCD sign W11-1 or W11-15).

A **raised intersection** is a speed management device that increases motorist awareness of the crossing while reducing motor vehicle speeds on the cross street. This treatment is also a Speed Management tool; see Route Planning for a discussion of bicycle boulevards and emergency vehicle routes.

Crossings of higher order streets with three or more travel lanes and posted speeds over 35 mph should improve safety and comfort for bicyclists. Treatments include the following elements:

A **median refuge island** allows bicyclists to cross one direction of traffic at a time when gaps in traffic allow. Islands placed in the middle of the intersection narrow the cross street, providing some speed management benefit. They can also be used to prohibit left turns by motor vehicles on the cross street and through movements on the bicycle boulevard, thus also acting as a volume management treatment. Median refuge islands should be wide enough along bicycle boulevards to accommodate more than one bicyclist or longer bicycles such as cargo bikes and trail-a-bikes.

Active warning beacons can be placed across a bicycle boulevard crossing of a major street. Rectangular Rapid Flash Beacons (RRFBs) are commonly used to alert drivers to crossing bicyclists and increase yielding behavior."

Hybrid beacons can facilitate bicycle crossing of a busy street where cross traffic does not stop but side street volumes do not warrant installation of a conventional traffic signal, or where a full traffic signal installation is not desired.

BERKELEY, CA

Signalized Intersections

Full traffic signals may be added to create gaps, overcome visibility issues, or force motorists to stop if needed (see signals). Signal installation can also alleviate a congestion problem on the main road caused by a high volume bicycle/pedestrian crossing by limiting when bicyclists or pedestrians can cross.

On streets with few crossing gaps and high motor vehicle speeds and volumes, a bicycle/pedestrian-actuated hybrid beacon should be considered. This will reduce delay at non-peak times when bicyclists do not otherwise need to wait for a gap in traffic on the cross street as well as for users on the cross street, who are not delayed with a full signal. It also reduces the likelihood of generating cut-through traffic on the bicycle boulevard route.[162]

If the intersection is fully signalized, it shall provide bicycle signal detection and actuation. Volume management may be required so that the signal does not attract unwanted vehicular cut-through traffic. However, forced turns may increase the frequency of right-turn conflicts between bicyclists and motorists. Enhancements to signals on bicycle boulevards to address these issues include the following treatments:

Bicycle signal heads can be added to a hybrid beacon to improve function and safety for bicyclists. See Bicycle Signal Heads for additional guidance.

Signs that prohibit through movements, right-in/right-out splitter islands, and partial closures are volume management strategies to reduce cut-through motor vehicle traffic. Signs are typically less effective than physical diversion.

Bike boxes allow bicyclists to get to the head of the queue at signalized intersections. This allows them to take advantage of the typically short green time provided to the minor roadway at an intersection with a major roadway. Such boxes also increase bicyclist visibility to drivers. Parking removal should be considered where a bicycle boulevard has insufficient space to provide the ingress lane to a bike box.

TUCSON, AZ

Benefits

Provides bicycle access across streets that can be major barriers along the bicycle boulevard and that compromise bicyclist safety. Because bicycle boulevard retrofits to local streets are typically along facilities without existing signalized accommodation at crossings of collector and arterial roadways, these treatments significantly improve connectivity and access.

Reduces the crossing distance and improves visibility of bicyclists, encouraging drivers to allow other users to cross safely.

Aids pedestrian crossing and improves pedestrian connectivity.

Raises awareness for both bicyclists and drivers of potential conflict areas.

Encourages or requires driver yielding behavior, allowing bicyclists to cross.

Minimizes delay for bicyclists on the bicycle boulevard.

Promotes the multi-modal nature of the corridor.

Signals separate bicycle movements from conflicting motor vehicle, streetcar, light rail, or pedestrian movements.

Provides priority to bicycle movements at an intersection (e.g., with a leading bicycle interval or bike box).

Protects bicyclists in the intersection, which may improve real and perceived safety and comfort.

Typical Applications

Anywhere bicycle boulevards intersect streets that are not stop controlled (generally higher-order streets).

Design Guidance

Major Street Crossings

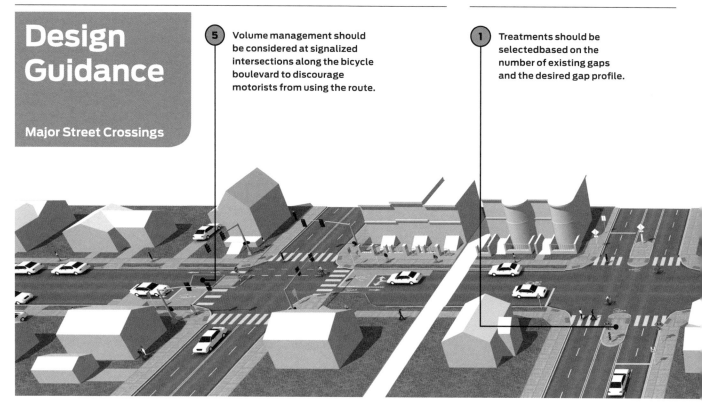

⑤ Volume management should be considered at signalized intersections along the bicycle boulevard to discourage motorists from using the route.

① Treatments should be selectedbased on the number of existing gaps and the desired gap profile.

Bike Box with Partial Closure

Median Refuge Island

Required Features

① Crossing devices shall be considered at any bicycle boulevard crossing of a roadway that is not stop controlled. Treatments should be selected based on the number of existing gaps and the desired gap profile.[163]

② All beacons and signals shall be installed with appropriate detection and actuation, unless the bicycle boulevard crossing phase is set to recall each cycle.

Recommended Features

③ Supplemental signs and markings such as warning signs and crosswalk markings should be provided at bicycle boulevard crossings of major roads to improve crossing visibility.

④ At signalized intersections, longer minimum green times should be provided for bicyclists due to slower acceleration speeds. See detection and actuation for more information.

⑤ Volume management should be considered at signalized intersections along the bicycle boulevard to discourage motorists from using the route.

Optional Features

⑥ Geometric elements such as median refuge islands, curb extensions, neckdowns, and raised crosswalks may be provided to improve sight distance for bicyclists on the bicycle boulevard as well as for drivers on the cross street.

⑦ At stop-controlled unsignalized crossings with curb extensions, forward stop bars for bicyclists may be provided.

TUCSON, AZ (CREDIT: CITY OF TUCSON)

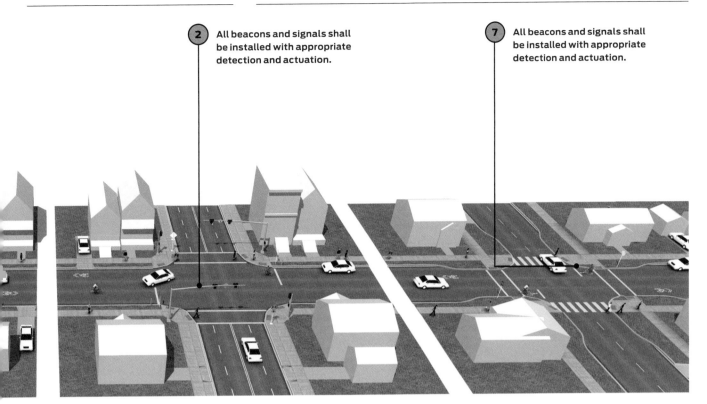

(2) All beacons and signals shall be installed with appropriate detection and actuation.

(7) All beacons and signals shall be installed with appropriate detection and actuation.

Hybrid Beacon

Bicycle Forward Stop Bar

PORTLAND, OR

Crossing major streets without signalization requires an adequate number of acceptable gaps. Treatments that reduce the duration of the minimum acceptable gap can improve the number of crossing opportunities for bicyclists.

To calculate the minimum acceptable gap for a bicyclist to cross a major roadway the following equation is

adapted from the ITE Manual of Traffic Engineering Studies (describing minimum acceptable gaps for pedestrians):

$$G = (W / S) + R$$

G = minimum acceptable gap, sec
W = crossing distance or width of roadway, ft
S = bicycling speed, ft/s
    (assumed to be 10 ft/sec for a bicyclist)
R = start-up time, s

A **bicycle forward stop bar** can reduce the minimum acceptable gap by one second per side of the street.

A **median refuge area** can cut the acceptable gap needed to cross a major street by 50 percent.

PORTLAND, OR

TUCSON, AZ (PHOTO: MICHAEL MCKISSON, TUCSONVELO.COM)

Maintenance

Maintain signs, markings, and other treatments, and replace as needed. Monitor intersections for bicyclist delay to determine if additional treatments are warranted.

Bicycle signal heads require the same maintenance as standard traffic signal heads, such as replacing bulbs and responding to power outages.

Treatment Adoption and Professional Consensus

See adoption and consensus information for specific treatment types under the relevant treatment pages.

Offset Intersections

PORTLAND, OR

Offset Intersections are junctions at which two streets in a designated bicycle boulevard corridor align asymmetrically with an intersecting roadway. Since bicycle boulevards typically utilize local streets, bicyclists are likely to encounter discontinuities in the street grid that require them to turn briefly onto another street before resuming their original direction. Offset intersection treatments are categorized into treatments for major street crossing and treatments for minor street crossings.

Selection of the appropriate treatment depends on the width and traffic characteristics of the intersecting street and on whether the bicycle boulevard jogs to the right or to the left. If an intersecting street has traffic speeds and volumes equivalent to the bicycle boulevard, no treatment is needed, although wayfinding (signing and pavement markings) should clearly direct bicyclists through the offset. This is the preferred situation.

When a bicycle boulevard crosses a major street at an offset intersection, additional corridor and crossing treatments may be required to preserve the attractiveness and comfort of the bicycle boulevard.

Treatments for a jog to the right include the following:

On a minor collector street without bike lanes or where bike lanes are present, a **two-stage turn queue box** placed in the on-street parking lane can allow bicyclists to reposition themselves and wait for a crossing opportunity. This is particularly important where the connecting street has continuous bike lanes so that bicycle boulevard traffic will not block the bike lane while waiting for a gap in traffic. It can be combined with a crosswalk and/or median island depending on the operational characteristics of the cross street.

Center left-turn lanes designed specifically for bicyclists can be marked to allow bicyclists to turn left from the cross street back onto the bicycle boulevard. Bicyclists approaching from the first bicycle boulevard section turn right onto the cross street, then merge across one direction of traffic into the turn lane, where they have a protected space to wait for a gap in the opposing direction. This treatment is appropriate for a street with one travel lane in each direction or where motor vehicle speeds and volumes are low enough on the cross street so that there are sufficient gaps.[164]

Other treatments for either left- or right-side offsets include the following:

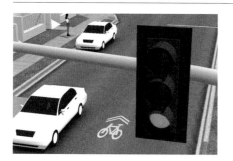

At an offset intersection where a signal exists, **signal phasing** can accommodate bicyclists riding through the intersection. This treatment will require a longer phase on the major street than a standard intersection, as it should provide sufficient time for bicyclists to travel through the jog.

A pair of **one-way cycle tracks** can be used along the section of roadway connecting the offset segments of a bicycle boulevard. This treatment requires crossing treatments on both sides of the facility, and may facilitate wrong-way riding on the cycle track.

A **two-way cycle track** has the advantage of diverting bicyclists traveling in either direction on a bicycle boulevard to a single crossing location. This minimizes the cost of the crossing treatments and enables the use of beacons and signals, which cannot be used in close proximity.

A **median island** is similar to the center turn lane treatment, except an extruded curb end cap provides more of a buffer than just paint. This type of crossing can be used to accommodate a jog in either direction, as bicyclists can cross one lane of traffic and ride in the median.

If the connecting street is one way for motor vehicle traffic, consider allowing bicyclists to travel against the flow of traffic using a contra-flow bike lane. **Contra-flow bike lanes** are installed on one side of the street facing one-way vehicle traffic.

SAN FRANCISCO, CA (PHOTO: SANFRANCISCOIZE.COM, MARK DREGER)

Benefits

Provides safer conditions for crossing and turning, and prevents the short route section along the connecting street from becoming the "weak link in the chain," which lowers the comfort and safety level of the entire route.

VANCOUVER, CANADA

Provides continuity to bicycle boulevard routes over a discontinuous local street network.

Adds comfort and wayfinding elements to jogs along the bicycle boulevard, particularly important along busier cross streets.

Typical Applications

Where a bicycle boulevard has to turn or travels for a brief distance on another street.

Design Guidance

Offset Intersections

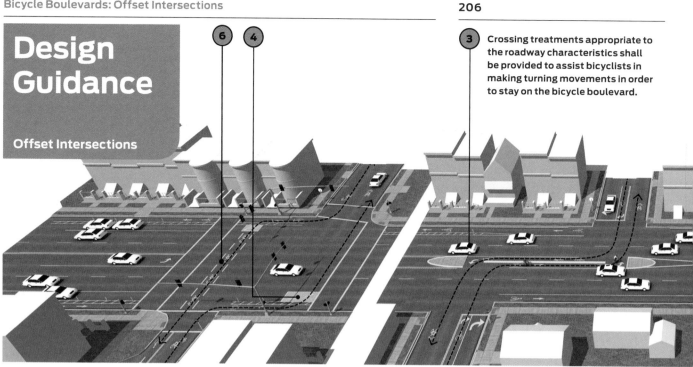

3 Crossing treatments appropriate to the roadway characteristics shall be provided to assist bicyclists in making turning movements in order to stay on the bicycle boulevard.

Two-Stage Turn Queue Boxes at Signalized Intersection

Median Refuge Turn Pocket

Required Features

1 Wayfinding signs shall be provided to indicate the change in direction when a bicycle boulevard turns.

2 Appropriate bicycle facilities (shared lane markings, bike lanes, cycle tracks, etc.) shall be used on the street onto which bicyclists turn when a bicycle boulevard jogs.

3 Crossing treatments appropriate to the roadway characteristics shall be provided to assist bicyclists in crossing the roadway or making turning movements in order to stay on the bicycle boulevard.[165]

Recommended Features

4 If the bicycle boulevard turns onto a street with another bikeway, treatments should provide sufficient space for users turning onto the bicycle boulevard to wait for a crossing opportunity without blocking users continuing on the bikeway.

Optional Features

5 Pavement markings indicating the change in direction from the bicycle boulevard may supplement wayfinding signs on the approach to a jog.

6 Intersection crossing markings may be used to assist in crossing major streets. See Intersection Crossing Markings for more guidance.

1 Turn Sign

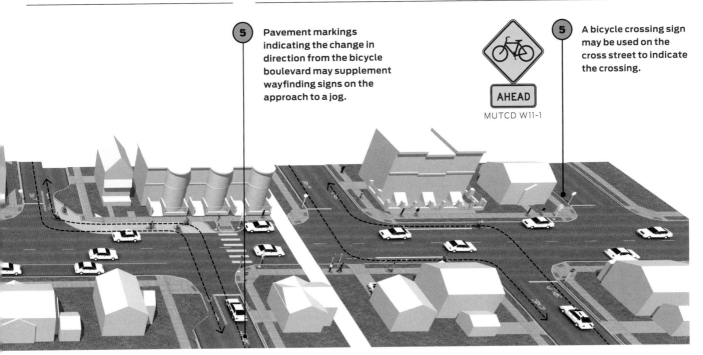

⑤ Pavement markings indicating the change in direction from the bicycle boulevard may supplement wayfinding signs on the approach to a jog.

AHEAD

MUTCD W11-1

⑤ A bicycle crossing sign may be used on the cross street to indicate the crossing.

Cycle Track Connection

Bike Lane Connection

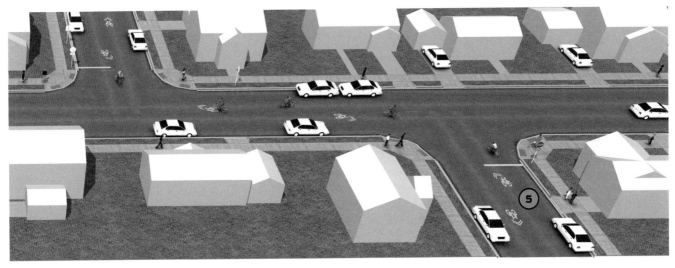

Local Street Offset

SAN FRANCISCO, CA (PHOTO: MATT HONAN)

TUCSON, AZ

Maintenance

Paint can wear more quickly in high traffic areas or in winter climates. Facilities should be cleared of snow through routine snow removal operations.

Treatment Adoption and Professional Consensus

AASHTO's Bicycle Facilities Design Guidelines document describes a long median that bicyclists can use to navigate an offset intersection along a trail.

Portland, OR, and Tucson, AZ, use a short cycle track to provide enhanced bicycle access along a busy street to make a connection to bikeways on lower-speed streets.

Additional offset intersection treatments are currently used in the following U.S. cities:
· Portland, OR
· San Francisco, CA
· Seattle, WA
· Tucson, AZ

Green Infrastructure

PORTLAND, OR

Green infrastructure is a planning and design approach to managing stormwater, the urban heat island effect, health, and air quality based on ecosystem network models. A green infrastructure approach is a shift from viewing systems as separate and disjointed components toward viewing systems as interconnected amenities that improve public health.

Bicycle boulevards present an opportunity to integrate stormwater treatment facilities, street trees, and public gathering spaces with traffic speed and volume management treatments. By incorporating green street elements such as bioswales, infiltration basins, permeable pavement, plantings and street trees into curb extensions, pedestrian refuge islands, and chicanes, roadway runoff is slowly attenuated on-site, water quality is improved, paving is reduced, and habitat connectivity is improved.

PORTLAND, OR

Bioswales are gently sloping depressions planted with dense vegetation or grass that filters stormwater runoff as it flows through the swale, allowing it to slowly infiltrate into the ground. A vegetated infiltration basin or a rain garden is a landscaped depression that holds stormwater as it slowly infiltrates into the ground. Bioswales and rain gardens can be placed in curb extensions, islands, and chicanes to absorb and filter rain water, minimizing sewer runoff.

Benefits

Provides an ecological and aesthetic enhancement of traditional traffic speed and volume control measures.

Provides a more pleasant environment for bicycling, walking or sitting. Improves drainage, reduces sewer costs, and minimizes the risk of basement flooding.[166]

Improves street crossings because of reduced vehicle volume and speed and/or reduced crossing distance.

Improves air quality, reduces the urban heat island effect, and can provide habitat connectivity by increasing urban green space.

Reduces motor vehicle speeds along the corridor when used as curb extensions, edge islands, medians, and other speed management treatments.

Reduces motor vehicle volumes along the corridor when used as diverters, closures, and other volume management treatments.

Can use non-transportation funding sources, such as stormwater management or sewer treatment money, when needed improvements are prioritized along bicycle boulevards.

Typical Applications

Place street trees and plantings in medians, chicanes, and other speed or volume management treatments.

Develop bioswales and rain gardens in curb extensions and along planting strips.

Design Guidance

Green Infrastructure

Required Features

(1) Plantings shall not impede sightlines or block signs or other traffic control devices.

Recommended Features

(2) Infiltration basins should drain a storm event within 30 hours and may not be appropriate in areas with high water tables.

(3) Some green street features, such as pervious pavers, may not be appropriate along bicycle boulevards.

Optional Features

(4) Neighborhood associations or community groups may assist with maintenance.

Chicane BERKELEY, CA

Neckdown PALO ALTO, CA

Neighborhood Traffic Circle TUCSON, AZ

Diagonal Diverter PORTLAND, OR

Curb Extension Bioswale Retrofit PORTLAND, OR

Median Refuge Island DAVIS, CA

PORTLAND, OR

Maintenance

Inspect swales periodically, especially after major storm events.

Remove sediment and trash, clean and repair inlets, curb cuts, check dams, and outlets as needed.

Maintain side slopes to prevent erosion and provide proper drainage.

Plants used in green street treatments should be selected to the local environment. Design should consider local conditions such as freezing, salt spray, flooding, and drought as well as pollutant and debris accumulation. Swales at the base of hills may incorporate a sediment collection area to reduce damage.

Resources

Notes	**217**
Design Guide Project Teams	**236**
References	**237**

Notes

Bike Lanes	CONVENTIONAL BIKE LANES	218
	BUFFERED BIKE LANES	218
	CONTRA-FLOW BIKE LANES	219
	LEFT-SIDE BIKE LANES	219
Cycle Tracks	ONE-WAY PROTECTED CYCLE TRACKS	219
	RAISED CYCLE TRACKS	220
	TWO-WAY CYCLE TRACKS	221
Intersections	BIKE BOXES	222
	INTERSECTION CROSSING MARKINGS	223
	TWO-STAGE TURN QUEUE BOXES	224
	MEDIAN REFUGE ISLAND	224
	CYCLE TRACK INTERSECTION APPROACH	224
Signals	BICYCLE SIGNAL HEADS	225
	HYBRID BEACON FOR BIKE ROUTE CROSSING	225
Signing and Marking	COLORED BIKE FACILITIES	226
	SHARED LANE MARKINGS	227
	BIKE ROUTE WAYFINDING	229
Bicycle Boulevards	ROUTE PLANNING	230
	SIGNS AND PAVEMENT MARKINGS	230
	SPEED MANAGEMENT	230
	VOLUME MANAGEMENT	233
	MINOR STREET CROSSINGS	233
	MAJOR STREET CROSSINGS	234
	OFFSET INTERSECTIONS	234
	GREEN INFRASTRUCTURE	235

Introduction

1   http://www.fhwa.dot.gov/environment/bikeped/mutcd_
     bike.htm

2   "The recommended width of a bike lane is 1.5m (5 feet)
     from the face of a curb or guardrail to the bike lane stripe."

     "If the [longitudinal] joint is not smooth, 1.2m (4 feet) of
     ridable surface should be provided."

     AASHTO. (1999). GUIDE FOR THE DEVELOPMENT OF
     BICYCLE FACILITIES.

3   "If parking is permitted, ... the bike lane should be placed
     between the parking area and the travel lane and have a
     minimum width of 1.5 m (5 feet)."

     "Where parking is permitted but a parking stripe or stalls
     are not utilized, the shared area should be a minimum 3.6
     m (12 feet) adjacent to a curb face ... If the parking volume is
     substantial or turnover is high, an additional 0.3 to 0.6 m
     (1 to 2 feet) of width is desirable."

     AASHTO. (1999). GUIDE FOR THE DEVELOPMENT OF
     BICYCLE FACILITIES.

4   "On new structures [with railings], the minimum clear width
     should be the same as the approach paved shared use path,
     plus the minimum 0.6-m (2-foot) wide clear areas."

     AASHTO. (1999). GUIDE FOR THE DEVELOPMENT OF
     BICYCLE FACILITIES.

5   Markings shall be placed:
     · At the beginning of bike lane
     · At the far side of all bike path crossings
     · At approaches and at far side of all arterial crossings
     · At major changes in direction
     · At intervals not to exceed 1/2 mile
     · At beginning and end of bike lane pockets at approach
       to intersection

     LOS ANGELES BICYCLE PLAN UPDATE (2010).
     CHAPTER 5—TECHNICAL DESIGN HANDBOOK-DRAFT.

6   "A bike lane should be delineated from the motor vehicle
     travel lanes with a 150-mm (6-inch) solid white line.
     Some jurisdictions have used a 200-mm
     (8-inch) line for added distinction."

     AASHTO. (1999). GUIDE FOR THE DEVELOPMENT OF
     BICYCLE FACILITIES.

7   "An additional 100-mm (4-inch) solid white line can be
     placed between the parking lane and the bike lane. This
     second line will encourage parking closer to the curb,
     providing added separation from motor vehicles, and where
     parking is light it can discourage motorists from using the
     bike lane as a through travel lane."

     AASHTO. (1999). GUIDE FOR THE DEVELOPMENT OF
     BICYCLE FACILITIES.

8   "Since bicyclists usually tend to ride a distance of 0.8-1.0
     m (32-40 inches) from a curb face, it is very important that
     the pavement surface in this zone be smooth and free of
     structures. Drain inlets and utility covers that extend into
     this area may cause bicyclists to swerve, and have the
     effect of reducing the usable width of the lane. Where
     these structures exist, the bike lane width may need to be
     adjusted accordingly."

     AASHTO. (1999). GUIDE FOR THE DEVELOPMENT OF
     BICYCLE FACILITIES.

9   "Bicycle lane—the preferential lane-use marking for a
     bicycle lane shall consist of a bicycle symbol or the word
     marking BIKE LANE."

     FEDERAL HIGHWAY ADMINISTRATION. (2009). MANUAL ON UNIFORM
     TRAFFIC CONTROL DEVICES. SECTION 3D.01.

10   Standard guidance for Buffer-separated right-hand side
     preferential lane buffer configurations (MUTCD 3D.02 03-D):

     1. A wide solid double white line along both edges of the
     buffer space where crossing the buffer space is prohibited.

     2. A wide solid single white line along both edges of
     the buffer space where crossing of the buffer space is
     discouraged.

     FEDERAL HIGHWAY ADMINISTRATION. (2009). MANUAL ON UNIFORM
     TRAFFIC CONTROL DEVICES. SECTION 3D.02.

11   "When crosshatch markings are used in paved areas
     that separate traffic flows in the same general direction,
     they shall be white and they shall be shaped as chevron
     markings, with the point of each chevron facing toward
     approaching traffic..."

     FEDERAL HIGHWAY ADMINISTRATION. (2009). MANUAL ON UNIFORM
     TRAFFIC CONTROL DEVICES. SECTION 3B.24.

12   "The longitudinal spacing of the chevrons or diagonal lines
     should be determined by engineering judgment considering
     factors such as speeds and desired visual impacts. The
     chevrons and diagonal lines should form an angle of
     approximately 30 to 45 degrees with the longitudinal lines
     that they intersect."

     FEDERAL HIGHWAY ADMINISTRATION. (2009). MANUAL ON UNIFORM
     TRAFFIC CONTROL DEVICES. SECTION 3B.24.

13   Center line pavement markings, when used, shall be the pavement markings used to delineate the separation of traffic lanes that have opposite directions of travel on a roadway and shall be yellow (3B.01 01).

Two-direction no-passing zone markings consisting of two normal solid yellow lines where crossing the center line markings for passing is prohibited for traffic traveling in either direction (3B.01 04.C).

FEDERAL HIGHWAY ADMINISTRATION. (2009). MANUAL ON UNIFORM TRAFFIC CONTROL DEVICES.

14   "Where there is room for bike lanes on both sides of the street, they should be included to clarify where bicyclists should travel. If there is no room for a full bike lane, other pavement markings or signs should be considered to clarify direction."

PEDESTRIAN AND BICYCLE INFORMATION CENTER. (2006). BIKESAFE: BICYCLE COUNTERMEASURE SELECTION SYSTEM. PUBLICATION NO. FHWA-SA-05-006, FEDERAL HIGHWAY ADMINISTRATION, WASHINGTON, DC.

15   Variant of MUTCD R10-15 to include helmeted bicycle rider symbol (MUTCD figure 9C-3 B). Alternate sign in common use, similar to MUTCD R1-5, 1-5a.

Cycle Tracks

16   "Cyclists feel most secure on roads with cycle tracks and most at risk on roads with mixed traffic."

JENSEN, S. U., ROSENKILDE, C., AND JENSEN, N. (2007). ROAD SAFETY AND PERCEIVED RISK OF CYCLE FACILITIES IN COPENHAGEN. COPENHAGEN: TRAFITEC RESEARCH CENTER.

17   "The construction of [raised] cycle tracks has resulted in a slight drop in the total number of accidents and injuries on the road sections between junctions of 10% and 4% respectively."

JENSEN, S. U., ROSENKILDE, C., AND JENSEN, N. (2007). ROAD SAFETY AND PERCEIVED RISK OF CYCLE FACILITIES IN COPENHAGEN. COPENHAGEN: TRAFITEC RESEARCH CENTER.

18   Overall, 2.5 times as many cyclists used the cycle tracks compared with the reference streets."

LUSK, A., FURTH, P., MORENCY, P., MIRANDA-MORENO, L., WILLETT, W., DENNERLEIN, J. (2010). RISK OF INJURY FOR BICYCLING ON CYCLE TRACKS VERSUS IN THE STREET. INJURY PREVENTION.

19   "Preferential lanes are lanes designated for special traffic uses such as high-occupancy vehicles (HOVs), light rail, buses, taxis, or bicycles."

FEDERAL HIGHWAY ADMINISTRATION. (2009). MANUAL ON UNIFORM TRAFFIC CONTROL DEVICES. SECTION 2G.01.

20   Cycle Track Width Guidelines in the Netherlands

Rush hour intensities (two directions, bikes per hour)	Cycle Track Width (feet)
0 - 150	6.5
150 - 750	10
>750	13

CROW. (2006). RECORD 25: DESIGN MANUAL FOR BICYCLE TRAFFIC. CROW, THE NETHERLANDS.

	Desirable minimum width (m) (see note 1)	Absolute minimum width (m) (see note 1)	Safety strip to carriageway kerb edge minimum width (m) (see note 2)
One Way	2.0	1.5	0.5
Two Way	3.0	2.0	0.5

Notes:
1. 0.5m should be added for each side of the track that is bounded (e.g. by a wall, railings fence or hedge)
2. Safety strip to carriageway kerb edge minimum width should be 1.0m adjacent to frequently accessed parked cars

TRANSPORT FOR LONDON. (2005). LONDON CYCLING DESIGN STANDARDS. APPENDIX C. DRAWING NO. CCE\C1

21   "Safety strip to carriageway kerb edge minimum width should be 1.0m adjacent to frequently accessed parked cars."

TRANSPORT FOR LONDON. (2005). LONDON CYCLING DESIGN STANDARDS.

"Width of critical reaction strip is .50 to .75 m."

CROW. (2007). DESIGN MANUAL FOR BICYCLE TRAFFIC.

22   *see note 17*

23 "Parking must be banned along the street with the bike path for a distance long enough to ensure adequate stopping sign distances for motorists crossing the path."

VELO QUEBEC. (2003). TECHNICAL HANDBOOK OF BIKEWAY DESIGN. 2ND ED. QUEBEC: MINISTERE DU TRANSPORT DU QUEBEC AND THE SECRETARIAT AU LOISIR ET AU SPORT.

24 Variant of MUTCD R10-15 to include helmeted bicycle rider symbol (MUTCD figure 9C-3 B).

ALTERNATE SIGN IN COMMON USE, SIMILAR TO MUTCD R1-5, 1-5A.

25 In these situations, recommended minimum widths should be increased using the following calculation: [Distance from curb to edge of gutter seam] – 18 inches (if the value is positive). For example, if the gutter seam is 24 inches from the curb, add 6 inches to the recommended dimension for a one-way cycle track that serves single-file cycling.

26 "01 Channelizing devices may also be used along a center line to preclude turns or along lane lines to preclude lane changing, as determined by engineering judgment.

03 The color of channelizing devices used outside of temporary traffic control zones shall be either orange or the same color as the pavement marking that they supplement, or for which they are substituted."

FHWA. (2009). MANUAL ON UNIFORM TRAFFIC CONTROL DEVICES. 3H.01 CHANNELIZING DEVICES.

"Tubular markers may be used effectively to divide opposing lanes of road users, divide vehicular traffic lanes when two or more lanes of moving vehicular traffic are kept open in the same direction, and to delineate the edge of a pavement drop off where space limitations do not allow the use of larger devices."

FHWA. (2009). MANUAL ON UNIFORM TRAFFIC CONTROL DEVICES. 6F.65 TUBULAR MARKERS.

27 "It is recommended that on roads within built-up areas ... cycle tracks are bent in 20-30 meters before and intersecting road (bending-in is defined as bending a separate cycle track toward the carriageway, with the distance between the cycle track and the side of the main carriageway measuring between 0 and 2 m)."

"Function of Bending Cycle Track In:
· Improving conspicuity of cyclists
· improving visibility of cyclists
· clarifying right of way situations"

CROW. (2007). DESIGN MANUAL FOR BICYCLE TRAFFIC.

28 "The ONLY word marking (see MUTCD Figure 3B-23) may be used... to supplement a preferential lane word or symbol marking."

FEDERAL HIGHWAY ADMINISTRATION. (2009). MANUAL ON UNIFORM TRAFFIC CONTROL DEVICES. SECTION 3B.20.

RAISED CYCLE TRACKS

29 "Compared with bicycling on a reference street... these cycle tracks had a 28% lower injury rate."

LUSK, A., FURTH, P., MORENCY, P., MIRANDA-MORENO, L., WILLETT, W., DENNERLEIN, J. (2010). RISK OF INJURY FOR BICYCLING ON CYCLE TRACKS VERSUS IN THE STREET. INJURY PREVENTION.

"Cyclists feel most secure on roads with cycle tracks and most at risk on roads with mixed traffic."

JENSEN, S. U., ROSENKILDE, C., AND JENSEN, N. (2007). ROAD SAFETY AND PERCEIVED RISK OF CYCLE FACILITIES IN COPENHAGEN. COPENHAGEN: TRAFITEC RESEARCH CENTER.

30 "Since the raised bicycle lane is constructed of concrete and has a left edge that is beveled up to a height of half the normal curb height, it adds a very visible edge to the travel lane that a normal, striped bike lane does not provide. The 4:1 slope of the left edge is very forgiving for both bicyclists and motorists who get too close to the edge, but is visually nearly as powerful as a vertical curb."

PEDESTRIAN AND BICYCLE INFORMATION CENTER. (2006.) BIKESAFE: BICYCLE COUNTERMEASURE SELECTION SYSTEM. PUBLICATION NO. FHWA-SA-05-006, FEDERAL HIGHWAY ADMINISTRATION, WASHINGTON, DC.

31 "Mountable Curb Design: Mountable curb should have a 4:1 or flatter slope and have no lip that could catch bicycle tires."

LOS ANGELES BICYCLE PLAN UPDATE. (2010). CHAPTER 5— TECHNICAL DESIGN HANDBOOK-DRAFT, 122.

32 *see note 17*

33 "Safety strip to carriageway kerb edge minimum width should be 1.0m adjacent to frequently accessed parked cars."

TRANSPORT FOR LONDON. (2005). LONDON CYCLING DESIGN STANDARDS.

"Width of critical reaction strip is .50 to .75 m."

CROW. (2007). DESIGN MANUAL FOR BICYCLE TRAFFIC.

34 *see note 17*

35   *see note 17*

36   "Parking must be banned along the street with the bike path
      for a distance long enough to ensure adequate stopping sign
      distances for motorists crossing the path."

      VELO QUEBEC. (2003). TECHNICAL HANDBOOK OF BIKEWAY DESIGN.
      2ND ED. QUEBEC: MINISTERE DES TRANSPORT DU QUEBEC AND THE
      SECRETARIAT AU LOISIR ET AU SPORT.

37   Variant of MUTCD R10-15 to include helmeted bicycle rider
      symbol (MUTCD figure 9C-3 B). Alternate sign in common
      use, similar to MUTCD R1-5, 1-5a.

38   "The results show that the paths with raised crossings
      attracted more than 50 percent more bicyclists and that
      the safety per bicyclist was improved by approximately
      20 percent due to the increase in bicycle flow, and with an
      additional 10 to 50 percent due to the improved layout."

      GARDER, P., LEDEN, L., PULKKINEN, U. (1998). MEASURING THE
      SAFETY EFFECT OF RAISED BICYCLE CROSSINGS USING A NEW
      RESEARCH METHODOLOGY. TRANSPORTATION RESEARCH
      RECORD, 1636.

39   "It is recommended that on roads within built-up areas
      ... cycle tracks are bent in 20-30 meters before and
      intersecting road (bending-in is defined as bending a
      separate cycle track toward the carriageway, with the
      distance between the cycle track and the side of the main
      carriageway measuring between 0 and 2 m)."

      "Function of Bending Cycle Track In:
      · Improving conspicuity of cyclists
      · improving visibility of cyclists
      · clarifying right of way situations"

      CROW. (2007). DESIGN MANUAL FOR BICYCLE TRAFFIC.

TWO-WAY CYCLE TRACKS

40   "Compared with bicycling on a reference street...these cycle
      tracks had a 28% lower injury rate."

      LUSK, A., FURTH, P., MORENCY, P., MIRANDA-MORENO, L., WILLETT,
      W., DENNERLEIN, J. (2010). RISK OF INJURY FOR BICYCLING ON CYCLE
      TRACKS VERSUS IN THE STREET. INJURY PREVENTION.

      "Cyclists feel most secure on roads with cycle tracks and
      most at risk on roads with mixed traffic."

      JENSEN, S. U., ROSENKILDE. C., AND JENSEN, N. (2007). ROAD SAFETY
      AND PERCEIVED RISK OF CYCLE FACILITIES IN COPENHAGEN.
      COPENHAGEN: TRAFITEC RESEARCH CENTER

41   "Overall, 2.5 times as many cyclists used the cycle tracks
      compared with the reference streets."

      LUSK, A., FURTH, P., MORENCY, P., MIRANDA-MORENO, L., WILLETT,
      W., DENNERLEIN, J. (2010). RISK OF INJURY FOR BICYCLING ON CYCLE
      TRACKS VERSUS IN THE STREET. INJURY PREVENTION.

42   *see note 17*

43   "Safety strip to carriageway kerb edge minimum width
      should be 1.0m adjacent to frequently accessed parked
      cars."

      TRANSPORT FOR LONDON. (2005). LONDON CYCLING DESIGN
      STANDARDS.

44   "Parking must be banned along the street with the bike path
      for a distance long enough to ensure adequate stopping sign
      distances for motorists crossing the path."

      VELO QUEBEC. (2003). TECHNICAL HANDBOOK OF BIKEWAY DESIGN.
      2ND ED. QUEBEC: MINISTERE DES TRANSPORT DU QUEBEC AND THE
      SECRETARIAT AU LOISIR ET AU SPORT.

45   Variant of MUTCD R10-15 to include helmeted bicycle rider
      symbol (MUTCD figure 9C-3 B). Alternate sign in common
      use, similar to MUTCD R1-5, 1-5a.

46   The results show that the paths with raised crossings
      attracted more than 50 percent more bicyclists and that
      the safety per bicyclist was improved by approximately
      20 percent due to the increase in bicycle flow, and with an
      additional 10 to 50 percent due to the improved layout.

      GARDER, P., LEDEN, L., PULKKINEN, U. (1998). MEASURING THE SAFETY
      EFFECT OF RAISED BICYCLE CROSSINGS USING A NEW RESEARCH
      METHODOLOGY. TRANSPORTATION RESEARCH RECORD, 1636.

47   "01 Channelizing devices may also be used along a center
      line to preclude turns or along lane lines to preclude lane
      changing, as determined by engineering judgment.

      03 The color of channelizing devices used outside of
      temporary traffic control zones shall be either orange or the
      same color as the pavement marking that they supplement,
      or for which they are substituted."

      FHWA. (2009). MANUAL ON UNIFORM TRAFFIC CONTROL DEVICES. 3H.01
      CHANNELIZING DEVICES.

      "Tubular markers may be used effectively to divide opposing
      lanes of road users, divide vehicular traffic lanes when two
      or more lanes of moving vehicular traffic are kept open in
      the same direction, and to delineate the edge of a pavement
      drop off where space limitations do not allow the use of
      larger devices."

      FHWA. (2009). MANUAL ON UNIFORM TRAFFIC CONTROL DEVICES.
      6F.65 TUBULAR MARKERS.

48   "It is recommended that on roads within built-up areas ... cycle tracks are bent in 20-30 meters before and intersecting road (bending-in is defined as bending a separate cycle track toward the carriageway, with the distance between the cycle track and the side of the main carriageway measuring between 0 and 2 m)."

"Function of Bending Cycle Track In:
· Improving conspicuity of cyclists
· improving visibility of cyclists
· clarifying right of way situations"

CROW. (2007). DESIGN MANUAL FOR BICYCLE TRAFFIC.

Intersections
BIKE BOXES

49   This is especially important in areas with high volumes of right-turning vehicles and/or trucks, whose high cabs make it difficult to see a bicyclist on the right, and who begin their turning maneuvers by going straight, which can deceive a bicyclist into thinking the truck is not turning.

"Cyclists travelling straight ahead were found to be able to position themselves in front of the traffic thus reducing the risk of conflict with ... turning vehicles."

ALLEN, D., S. BYGRAVE, AND H. HARPER. (2005). BEHAVIOUR AT CYCLE ADVANCED STOP LINES (REPORT NO. PPR240). TRANSPORT FOR LONDON, LONDON ROAD SAFETY UNIT.

50   "Feedback from the public indicates that eight feet is not large enough to comfortably maneuver into the box."

BRADY, J., MILLS, A., LOSKORN, J., DUTHIE, J., MACHEMEHL, R., CENTER FOR TRANSPORTATION RESEARCH. (2010). EFFECTS OF BICYCLE BOXES ON BICYCLIST AND MOTORIST BEHAVIOR AT INTERSECTIONS. THE CITY OF AUSTIN.

"The two stop lines must be between 4 and 5m apart; the area between them across the full width of the approach is available for cyclists who wait at the rest light."

ALLEN, D., S. BYGRAVE, AND H. HARPER. (2005). BEHAVIOUR AT CYCLE ADVANCED STOP LINES. REPORT NO. PPR240. TRANSPORT FOR LONDON, LONDON ROAD SAFETY UNIT.

51   "The video data showed that motorist encroachment into the pedestrian crosswalk fell significantly compared to the control intersection. ... This reduction of motor vehicles entering the crosswalk area has the potential to improve pedestrian safety"

MONSERE, C., & DILL, J. (2010). EVALUATION OF BIKE BOXES AT SIGNALIZED INTERSECTIONS. FINAL DRAFT. OREGON TRANSPORTATION RESEARCH AND EDUCATION CONSORTIUM.

52   "Use of bold demarcation of the box is vital. This could involve wider striping than the norm or perhaps painting the box a bright color."

HUNTER, W. W. (2000). EVALUATION OF INNOVATIVE BIKE-BOX APPLICATION IN EUGENE, OREGON. TRANSPORTATION RESEARCH RECORD, 1705, 99-106.

53   "In regards to motorist stopping behavior, the percentage of motorists that encroached on the stop line decreased significantly with the implementation of the skeleton [uncolored] bicycle box."

BRADY, J., MILLS, A., LOSKORN, J., DUTHIE, J., MACHEMEHL, R., CENTER FOR TRANSPORTATION RESEARCH. (2010). EFFECTS OF BICYCLE BOXES ON BICYCLIST AND MOTORIST BEHAVIOR AT INTERSECTIONS. THE CITY OF AUSTIN.

"The motorist survey revealed a strong preference for color. In addition, cyclists appear to use the box more as intended with the color, which should increase their visibility and improve safety."

MONSERE, C., & DILL, J. (2010). EVALUATION OF BIKE BOXES AT SIGNALIZED INTERSECTIONS. FINAL DRAFT. OREGON TRANSPORTATION RESEARCH AND EDUCATION CONSORTIUM.

"Use of bold demarcation of the box is vital. This could involve wider striping than the norm or perhaps painting the box a bright color."

HUNTER, W. W. (2000). EVALUATION OF INNOVATIVE BIKE-BOX APPLICATION IN EUGENE, OREGON. TRANSPORTATION RESEARCH RECORD, 1705, 99-106.

Support for Colored Pavement in Bike Lanes: "Significantly more motorists yielded to bicyclists after the blue pavement had been installed (92 percent in the after period versus 72 percent in the before period."

HUNTER, W.W. ET AL. (2000). EVALUATION OF BLUE BIKE-LANE TREATMENT IN PORTLAND, OREGON. TRANSPORTATION RESEARCH RECORD, 1705, 107-115.

"Best estimates for safety effects of one blue cycle crossing in a junction are a reduction of 10% in accidents and 19% in injuries."

JENSEN, S. U. (2008). SAFETY EFFECTS OF BLUE CYCLE CROSSINGS: A BEFORE-AFTER STUDY. ACCIDENT ANALYSIS & PREVENTION, 40(2), 742-750.

54   "It appears that [ingress lanes] provide cyclists with a considerable advantage in legally accessing [the bike box]." The site with no feeder lane "clearly showed that many cyclists were unable to reach the reservoir."

ATKINS SERVICES. (2005). ADVANCED STOP LINE VARIATIONS RESEARCH STUDY. REPORT NO. 503 1271. TRANSPORT FOR LONDON, LONDON ROAD SAFETY UNIT.

"Two of the sites with distinctly coloured feeder lanes had lower levels of encroachment suggesting that colour differentiation may reduce levels of encroachment."

ALLEN, D., S. BYGRAVE, AND H. HARPER. (2005). BEHAVIOUR AT CYCLE ADVANCED STOP LINES. REPORT NO. PPR240. TRANSPORT FOR LONDON, LONDON ROAD SAFETY UNIT.

55   "Where there was no cycle lane across the junction, cyclists were observed looking over their shoulders at the exit-arm pinch-point which is likely to impact on their level of comfort, and both perceived and actual safety."

ATKINS SERVICES. (2005). ADVANCED STOP LINE VARIATIONS RESEARCH STUDY. REPORT NO. 503 1271. TRANSPORT FOR LONDON, LONDON ROAD SAFETY UNIT. 8-2.

56   Variant of MUTCD R10-15 to include helmeted bicycle rider symbol (MUTCD figure 9C-3 B). Alternate sign in common use, similar to MUTCD R1-5, 1-5a.

57   "Use of bold demarcation of the box is vital. This could involve wider striping than the norm or perhaps painting the box a bright color."

HUNTER, W. W. (2000). EVALUATION OF INNOVATIVE BIKE-BOX APPLICATION IN EUGENE, OREGON. TRANSPORTATION RESEARCH RECORD, 1705, 99-106.

58   To traverse a multi-lane bike box, significant lateral movement by the bicyclist is needed. This maneuver can take time and could potentially create conflicts by providing a green light for motorists while bicyclists are moving laterally through the bike box . For this reason, careful consideration should be given before applying.

59   "Bicycle traffic signals are used to reduce turning conflicts at signalized intersections and often provide separate and sometimes exclusive phases for bicyclists."

FEDERAL HIGHWAY ADMINISTRATION. (2010). INTERNATIONAL TECHNOLOGY SCANNING PROGRAM, PEDESTRIAN AND BICYCLE MOBILITY AND SAFETY IN EUROPE. FHWA-PL-10-010.

INTERSECTION CROSSING MARKINGS

60   "In areas where cyclists/motorist conflicts are not a major concern, white dashed markings are adequate since the comprehension is adequate and not adverse in nature, and minimizes undue materials and maintenance costs. For areas where conflicts may be of greater concern, the sharrow treatment is the preferred option (of the four testes) for raising awareness."

TRANSPORTATION ASSOCIATION OF CANADA. (2008). COLOURED BICYCLE LANES SIMULATOR TESTING. FILE 785.

61   "Significantly more motorists yielded to bicyclists after the blue pavement had been installed (92 percent in the after period versus 72 percent in the before period."

HUNTER, W.W. ET AL. (2000). EVALUATION OF BLUE BIKE-LANE TREATMENT IN PORTLAND, OREGON. TRANSPORTATION RESEARCH RECORD, 1705, 107-115.

62   "Significantly fewer bicyclists slowed or stopped when approaching the conflict areas in the after period."

HUNTER, W.W. ET AL. (2000). EVALUATION OF BLUE BIKE-LANE TREATMENT IN PORTLAND, OREGON. TRANSPORTATION RESEARCH RECORD, 1705, 107-115.

63   "Best estimates for safety effects of one blue cycle crossing in a junction are a reduction of 10% in accidents and 19% in injuries."

JENSEN, S. U. (2008). SAFETY EFFECTS OF BLUE CYCLE CROSSINGS: A BEFORE-AFTER STUDY. ACCIDENT ANALYSIS & PREVENTION, 40(2), 742-750.

64   "Pavement markings extended into or continued through an intersection or interchange area shall be the same color and at least the same width as the line markings they extend."

FEDERAL HIGHWAY ADMINISTRATION. (2009). MANUAL ON UNIFORM TRAFFIC CONTROL DEVICES. SECTION 3B.08.

65   A bike lane should be delineated from the motor vehicle travel lanes with a 150-mm (6-inch) solid white line. Some jurisdictions have used a 200-mm (8-inch) line for added distinction.

AASHTO. (1999). GUIDE FOR THE DEVELOPMENT OF BICYCLE FACILITIES.

66   "In areas where the practitioner deems that a bicycle lane carried through a conflict zone warrants increased visibility and/or demarcation, the following is recommended: ... If there is a requirement for lane markings then a succession of bicycle stencils may optionally be placed between the dashed bicycle lane markings."

TRANSPORTATION ASSOCIATION OF CANADA. (2008). COLOURED BICYCLE LANES SIMULATOR TESTING. FILE 785.

67   "Rotated bicycle symbols in bike lanes at intersections and driveways oriented towards turning or entering motorists: Can be implemented at present time."

FEDERAL HIGHWAY ADMINISTRATION. (2011). BICYCLE FACILITIES AND THE MANUAL ON UNIFORM TRAFFIC CONTROL DEVICES.

68   "Significantly more motorists yielded to bicyclists after the blue pavement had been installed (92 percent in the after period versus 72 percent in the before period)."

HUNTER, W.W. ET AL. (2000). EVALUATION OF BLUE BIKE-LANE TREATMENT IN PORTLAND, OREGON. TRANSPORTATION RESEARCH RECORD, 1705, 107-115.

69   Elephant's Feet Bicycle Crossing Markings are defined as 200-400 mm wide squares with equal distance spacing.

TRANSPORTATION ASSOCIATION OF CANADA. (2008). COLOURED BICYCLE LANES SIMULATOR TESTING. FILE 785.

70   "Yield lines (see Figure 3B-16) shall consist of a row of solid white isosceles triangles pointing toward approaching vehicles extending across approach lanes to indicate the point at which the yield is intended or required to be made."

FEDERAL HIGHWAY ADMINISTRATION. (2009). MANUAL ON UNIFORM TRAFFIC CONTROL DEVICES. SECTION 3B.16.

TWO-STAGE TURN QUEUE BOXES

71   "Bicycle Hook Turn Storage Areas should be up to 3.0 metres long and at least 1.0 metre wide."

RTA. (2009). BICYCLE STORAGE AREAS AND ADVANCED BICYCLE STOP LINES. TECHNICAL DIRECTION.

Stacking facility for bicyclists turning left at traffic control system: "depending on intensity, width of stacking area > 1.2 m."

CROW. (2006). RECORD 25: DESIGN MANUAL FOR BICYCLE TRAFFIC. CROW, THE NETHERLANDS.

72   "Bicycle traffic signals are used to reduce turning conflicts at signalized intersections and often provide separate and sometimes exclusive phases for bicyclists."

FEDERAL HIGHWAY ADMINISTRATION. (2010). INTERNATIONAL TECHNOLOGY SCANNING PROGRAM, PEDESTRIAN AND BICYCLE MOBILITY AND SAFETY IN EUROPE. FHWA-PL-10-010.

MEDIAN REFUGE ISLAND

73   Width of refuge:
2.0 m (6 ft) = poor
2.5 m (8 ft) = satisfactory
3.0 m (10 ft) = good

AASHTO. (1999). GUIDE FOR THE DEVELOPMENT OF BICYCLE FACILITIES. P.51-52.

74   "The ends of the islands first approached by traffic should be preceded by diverging longitudinal pavement markings on the roadway surface, to guide vehicles into desired paths of travel along the islands edge."

FEDERAL HIGHWAY ADMINISTRATION. (2009). MANUAL ON UNIFORM TRAFFIC CONTROL DEVICES.

75   "Retroreflective solid yellow markings should be placed on the approach ends of raised medians and curbs of islands that are located in the line of traffic flow where the curb serves to channel traffic to the right of the obstruction."

"Retroreflective solid white markings should be used when traffic is permitted to pass on either side of the island."

FEDERAL HIGHWAY ADMINISTRATION. (2009). MANUAL ON UNIFORM TRAFFIC CONTROL DEVICES. SECTION 3B.23.

76   "Length of island should be 2 m (6 ft) or greater."

AASHTO. (1999). GUIDE FOR THE DEVELOPMENT OF BICYCLE FACILITIES. P.51-52.

77   AASHTO. (2004). GEOMETRIC DESIGN GUIDE OF HIGHWAYS AND STREETS.

78   AASHTO. (2004). GEOMETRIC DESIGN GUIDE OF HIGHWAYS AND STREETS.

79   FEDERAL HIGHWAY ADMINISTRATION. (2009). MANUAL ON UNIFORM TRAFFIC CONTROL DEVICES. SECTIONS 3B.16, 2B.11, AND 2B.12.

80   "Landscaping should not exceed 3 ft."

CITY OF MINNEAPOLIS. (2010). BICYCLE FACILITY MANUAL. P.227.

CYCLE TRACK INTERSECTION APPROACH

81   "Another way [sic] improving interactions between vehicles turning right and cyclists is to truncate the cycle track. One way of doing it is by locating the cycle crossing at an intersection immediately next to the adjacent street and remove [sic] the curb stone at a distance of 20-30 m."

LEDEN, L., GÅRDER P., JOHANSSON, C. (2005). TRAFFIC ENVIRONMENT FOR CHILDREN AND ELDERLY AS PEDESTRIANS AND CYCLISTS. 18TH ICTCT WORKSHOP.

82   Where it is necessary to route bicyclists from a cycle track to a standard bike lane the transition should be "clear, smooth, safe and comfortable." Included in the design of the facility should be measures to slow bicyclists down to a safe speed prior to entering/exiting the cycle track. This may be accomplished through the use of 'Tramline & Ladder' tactile pavers at the ramps. On the bicyclist path these should run in the direction of travel ('tramline').

TRANSPORT FOR LONDON. (2005). LONDON CYCLING DESIGN STANDARDS.

Signals
BICYCLE SIGNAL HEADS

83 Concluding a case study of a bicycle signal head installation in Davis, CA: "Both motorists and bicyclists found the new signal heads to be effective in reducing conflicts between the various modes passing through the intersection. Evaluation of crash data seemed to reflect this as well. For the two-year period before the installation of bicycle signal heads at the intersection of Sycamore and Russell, there were about 16 bicycle and motor vehicle collisions. For the two-year period following the installation, there were only two collisions, neither of which involved bicycles."

PEDESTRIAN AND BICYCLE INFORMATION CENTER. (2006.) BIKESAFE: BICYCLE COUNTERMEASURE SELECTION SYSTEM. PUBLICATION NO. FHWA-SA-05-006, FEDERAL HIGHWAY ADMINISTRATION, WASHINGTON, DC.

84 "In Davis, the current signal phasing provides for a minimum bicycle green time of 12 seconds and a maximum green time of 25 seconds. Additionally, a two-second all red interval is provided at the end of this phase as opposed to only one second at the end of other phases."

METROPOLITAN TRANSPORTATION COMMISSION. SAFETY TOOLBOX: ENGINEERING. BICYCLE SIGNALS.

85 A research study collecting cyclist speeds on 15 trails throughout the United States found that the 15th percentile cycling speed is approximately 9.4 miles per hour.

HYBRID BEACON FOR BIKE ROUTE CROSSING OF MAJOR STREET

86 Some controllers have built-in features to specify and program a bicycle minimum green based on bicycle detection. However, if this is not available, and bicycle minimum green time is greater than what would ordinarily be used, the green time should be increased.

FEDERAL HIGHWAY ADMINISTRATION. (2006). SHARED USE PATH LEVEL OF SERVICE CALCULATOR. PUBLICATION: FHWA-HRT-05-138.

87 The need for a signalized crossing of a collector at a minor street if often limited to peak traffic times. A full signal would have the unintended consequence of unnecessarily delaying bicyclists wishing to cross the collector during off-peak conditions as well as motorists on the main street, who would have to wait through an otherwise unnecessary full signal cycle.

88 "The three devices designated as red signal or beacon had statistically similar mean compliance rates. These devices include the midblock signal, half signal, and HAWK signal beacon. All three devices had average compliance rates greater than 97 percent."

"A compliance rate above 94 percent exists, regardless of the number of lanes on the facility."

FITZPATRICK, K., TURNER, S., BREWER, M., CARLSON, P., LALANI, N., ULLMAN, B., TROUT, N., PARK, E.S., LORD, D., AND WHITACRE, J. (2006). IMPROVING PEDESTRIAN SAFETY AT UNSIGNALIZED CROSSINGS. TCRP/NCHRP REPORT 112/ 562, TRANSPORTATION RESEARCH BOARD, WASHINGTON, DC.

89 For roads with speeds less than 35 miles per hour (MUTCD Figure 4F-1):

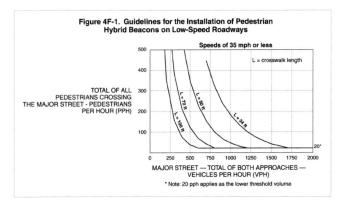

For roads with speeds greater than 35 miles per hour (MUTCD Figure 4F-2):

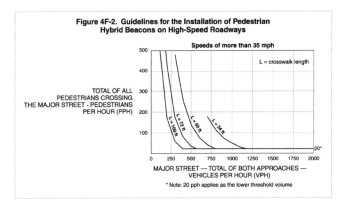

FEDERAL HIGHWAY ADMINISTRATION. (2009). MANUAL ON UNIFORM TRAFFIC CONTROL DEVICES.

90 FEDERAL HIGHWAY ADMINISTRATION. (2009). MANUAL ON UNIFORM TRAFFIC CONTROL DEVICES.

91   FEDERAL HIGHWAY ADMINISTRATION. (2009). MANUAL ON
      UNIFORM TRAFFIC CONTROL DEVICES.

92   The City of Madison published and distributed a brochure
      describing the function and operation of the Pedestrian
      Hybrid Beacon.

      CITY OF MADISON, WISCONSIN. PEDESTRIAN & BICYCLIST
      HYBRID BEACON.

Signing and Marking
COLORED BIKE FACILITIES

93   "Significantly fewer bicyclists slowed or stopped when
      approaching the conflict areas in the after period."

      HUNTER, W.W. ET AL. (2000). EVALUATION OF BLUE BIKE-LANE
      TREATMENT IN PORTLAND, OREGON. TRANSPORTATION RESEARCH
      RECORD, 1705, 107-115.

94   "Significantly more motorists yielded to bicyclists after the
      blue pavement had been installed (92 percent in the after
      period versus 72 percent in the before period."

      HUNTER, W.W. ET AL. (2000). EVALUATION OF BLUE BIKE-LANE
      TREATMENT IN PORTLAND, OREGON. TRANSPORTATION RESEARCH
      RECORD, 1705, 107-115.

      "A higher percentage of motorists yielded to bicycles in
      the after period (86.7% before versus 98.5% after). A
      chi-square test revealed the differences to be statistically
      significant at the 5% significance level (p < 0.001)."

      WILLIAM W. HUNTER, W., SRINIVASAN, R., MARTELL, C. (2008).
      EVALUATION OF A GREEN BIKE LANE WEAVING AREA IN ST.
      PETERSBURG, FLORIDA. UNIVERSITY OF NORTH CAROLINA
      HIGHWAY SAFETY RESEARCH CENTER.

      "The proportion of yielding events that were resolved by
      the motorist yielding to the bicyclist increased from 63%
      to 78% after the colored lane treatment was installed.
      Additionally, the proportion of motorists who used a turn
      signal before crossing the conflict zone when a bicyclist was
      present increased significantly from 38% to 74% after the
      colored lane treatment."

      BRADY, J., MILLS, A., LOSKORN, J., DUTHIE, J., MACHEMEHL, R.,
      CENTER FOR TRANSPORTATION RESEARCH. (2010). EFFECTS
      OF COLORED LANE MARKINGS ON BICYCLIST AND MOTORIST
      BEHAVIOR AT CONFLICT AREAS. CITY OF AUSTIN, TEXAS.

95   "Overall, more cyclists followed the recommended path
      after the blue marking: 87 percent before versus 94
      percent after."

      BIRK, M., BURCHFIELD, R., FLECKER, J., HUNTER, W.W., HARKEY,
      D.L., AND STEWART, J.R. (1999). PORTLAND'S BLUE BIKE LANES:
      IMPROVED SAFETY THROUGH ENHANCED VISIBILITY. CITY OF
      PORTLAND OFFICE OF TRANSPORTATION.

96   "NYCDOT data indicates that the green paint treatment
      resulted in fewer instances of drivers encroaching on the
      bike lane by driving on the bike lane boundary line. Overall,
      7% of drivers on the green paint treated streets drove on
      the bike lane boundary line as opposed to 16% of drivers
      on streets with the typical non-painted bike lane treatment.
      The data also showed fewer instances in driving in the
      bike lane; on average, 4% of drivers drove in the bike
      lane on green paint treated streets as opposed to 7%
      of typical streets."

      NEW YORK CITY DEPARTMENT OF TRANSPORTATION. (2011).
      EVALUATION OF SOLID GREEN BICYCLE LANES, TO INCREASE
      COMPLIANCE AND BICYCLE SAFETY.

97   Yellow, white, red, blue, and purple all have defined standard
      uses in the MUTCD. Blue is specifically discouraged for
      use on bicycle lanes to prevent confusion with parking for
      persons with disabilities.

      "When used, blue markings shall supplement white
      markings for parking spaces for persons with disabilities."

      FEDERAL HIGHWAY ADMINISTRATION. (2009). MANUAL ON
      UNIFORM TRAFFIC CONTROL DEVICES. SECTION 3A.05.

98   "Significantly more motorists yielded to bicyclists after the
      blue pavement had been installed (92 percent in the after
      period versus 72 percent in the before period)."

      HUNTER, W.W. ET AL. (2000). EVALUATION OF BLUE BIKE-LANE
      TREATMENT IN PORTLAND, OREGON. TRANSPORTATION RESEARCH
      RECORD, 1705, 107-115.

      "Bicyclists familiar with more traditional sharrows have
      noted that the additional emphasis resulting from the green
      pavement paint appears to be creating an heightened
      awareness by the motorists in the lane."

      CITY OF LONG BEACH. (2010). FINAL REPORT: SECOND STREET
      SHARROWS AND GREEN LANE IN THE CITY OF LONG BEACH,
      CALIFORNIA (RTE 9-113E).

99   Variant of MUTCD R10-15 to include helmeted bicycle rider
      symbol (MUTCD figure 9C-3 B). Alternate sign in common
      use, similar to MUTCD R1-5, 1-5a.

100   The City of San Francisco is currently experimenting with
      dashed green bicycle lanes.

      THE CITY AND COUNTY OF SAN FRANCISCO. (2010). EVALUATION OF
      SOLID AND DASHED GREEN PAVEMENT FOR BICYCLE LANES.

101   "NYCDOT data indicates that the green paint treatment
      resulted in fewer instances of drivers encroaching on the
      bike lane by driving on the bike lane boundary line. Overall,
      7% of drivers on the green paint treated streets drove on
      the bike lane boundary line as opposed to 16% of drivers on
      streets with the typical non-painted bike lane treatment.
      The data also showed fewer instances in driving in the bike
      lane; on average, 4% of drivers drove in the bike lane on
      green paint treated streets as opposed to 7% of typical
      streets."

NEW YORK CITY DEPARTMENT OF TRANSPORTATION. (2011). EVALUATION OF SOLID GREEN BICYCLE LANES, TO INCREASE COMPLIANCE AND BICYCLE SAFETY.

102   Salt Lake City, UT, and Long Beach, CA, have used a carpet of green coloring to create a lane-within-a-lane to indicate the priority area and preferred riding placement for bicyclists.

"THE GREEN LANE FACILITY HAS APPEARED TO RESULT IN AN APPROXIMATE DOUBLING OF USAGE OVER THE FIRST 12 MONTHS OF EXISTENCE."

"Bicyclists familiar with more traditional sharrows have noted that the additional emphasis resulting from the green pavement paint appears to be creating an heightened awareness by the motorists in the lane."

CITY OF LONG BEACH. (2010). FINAL REPORT: SECOND STREET SHARROWS AND GREEN LANE IN THE CITY OF LONG BEACH, CALIFORNIA (RTE 9-113E).

In an evaluation of a lane-within-a-lane treatment in Salt Lake City, researchers found that "eleven months after implementation, the fraction of in-street cyclists riding in the preferred zone, at least 4 ft from the curb, had risen from 17% to 92%."

FURTH, P., DULASKI, D. M., BERGENTHAL, D., BROWN, S. (2011). MORE THAN SHARROWS: LANE-WITHIN-A-LANE BICYCLE PRIORITY TREATMENTS IN THREE U.S. CITIES. PRESENTED AT THE 2011 ANNUAL MEETING OF THE TRANSPORTATION RESEARCH BOARD.

SHARED LANE MARKINGS

103   "The average distance bicyclists rode from the edge of the lane (called lateral position) increased only marginally, usually between four and eight inches, but a large shift in the mode occurred along multiple sites—at least three feet in many cases."

THE CENTER FOR TRANSPORTATION RESEARCH, THE UNIVERSITY OF TEXAS AT AUSTIN. (2010). EFFECTS OF SHARED LANE MARKINGS ON BICYCLIST AND MOTORIST BEHAVIOR ALONG MULTI-LANE FACILITIES.

104   "Along Dean Keeton Street, where bicyclists rode along side on-street parked vehicles, the marginal increase in lateral position resulted in a significant decrease in the percentage of bicyclists who rode within the range of an opening car door."

THE CENTER FOR TRANSPORTATION RESEARCH, THE UNIVERSITY OF TEXAS AT AUSTIN. (2010). EFFECTS OF SHARED LANE MARKINGS ON BICYCLIST AND MOTORIST BEHAVIOR ALONG MULTI-LANE FACILITIES.

"Overall, the presence of a marking increased the distance of cyclists to parked cars by 8 inches."

"When passing vehicles were present, the markings caused an increase of 3 to 4 inches in the distance between cyclists and parked cars. In addition, the markings caused an increase of over 2 feet in the distance between cyclists and passing vehicles.

The bike-and-chevron had a greater effect (by 3 inches) on the distance between cyclists and passing vehicles."

SAN FRANCISCO DEPARTMENT OF PARKING AND TRAFFIC. (2004). SAN FRANCISCO'S SHARED LANE PAVEMENT MARKINGS: IMPROVING BICYCLE SAFETY.

In the Cambridge, MA, study, the percentage of bicyclists who rode within 40 inches (i.e., near the door zone) of parked motor vehicles decreased.

FEDERAL HIGHWAY ADMINISTRATION. (2010). EVALUATION OF SHARED LANE MARKINGS. FHWA-HRT-10-041.

105   "Regarding motorist behavior, motorists were more likely to change lanes when passing, less likely to pass, and less likely to encroach on the adjacent lane when passing, all of which indicate safer motorist behavior."

THE CENTER FOR TRANSPORTATION RESEARCH, THE UNIVERSITY OF TEXAS AT AUSTIN. (2010). EFFECTS OF SHARED LANE MARKINGS ON BICYCLIST AND MOTORIST BEHAVIOR ALONG MULTI-LANE FACILITIES.

In the Chapel Hill, NC, experiment, motorists moved away from the markings, providing more operating space for bicyclists.

FEDERAL HIGHWAY ADMINISTRATION. (2010). EVALUATION OF SHARED LANE MARKINGS. FHWA-HRT-10-041.

106   "Both the markings significantly reduced the number of sidewalk riders: the bike-and-chevron by 35% and the bike-in house by 25%."

SAN FRANCISCO DEPARTMENT OF PARKING AND TRAFFIC. (2004). SAN FRANCISCO'S SHARED LANE PAVEMENT MARKINGS: IMPROVING BICYCLE SAFETY.

"Before the arrow was placed, 39.3% of bicyclists rode in street, with traffic [versus on sidewalk.] After the arrow was placed, the proportion of bicyclists riding in street with traffic increased to 45.3%."

PEIN, W.E., HUNTER, W.W., AND STEWART, J.R. (1999). EVALUATION OF THE SHARED-USE ARROW. FLORIDA DEPARTMENT OF TRANSPORTATION,TALLAHASSEE, FL.

107   "The bike-and-chevron marking significantly reduced the number of wrong-way riders by 80%. The bike-in-house marking did not have any significant impact on the percentage of wrong-way riders."

SAN FRANCISCO DEPARTMENT OF PARKING AND TRAFFIC. (2004). SAN FRANCISCO'S SHARED LANE PAVEMENT MARKINGS: IMPROVING BICYCLE SAFETY.

108   "The complexity of vehicle interactions within a roundabout leaves a cyclist vulnerable, and for this reason, bike lanes within the circulatory roadway should never be used."

US DEPARTMENT OF TRANSPORTATION. (2000). ROUNDABOUTS: AN INFORMATIONAL GUIDE. FHWA-RD-00-067.

109 "The Shared Lane Marking should not be placed on roadways that have a speed limit above 35 mph."

FEDERAL HIGHWAY ADMINISTRATION. (2009). MANUAL ON UNIFORM TRAFFIC CONTROL DEVICES. SECTION 9C.07 02.

The Toronto Cycling Study (2010) found that while 72.5% of all existing bicyclists are comfortable riding on major roads with bike lanes, only 54% reported feeling comfortable on major roads with sharrow markings.

CITY OF TORONTO/IPSOS REID. (2010). CITY OF TORONTO CYCLING STUDY: TRACKING REPORT (1999 AND 2009).

110 'Shared Lane Marking' Placement – Revised 5/17/2010. Added 24 ft and 26 ft street details with parking on both sides, and 20 ft street detail with parking on one side.

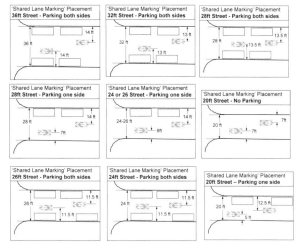

PORTLAND BUREAU OF TRANSPORTATION. (2011). WAYFINDING SHARROW GUIDELINES.

111 Placement Guidelines for San Francisco
Laterally:
11' minimum with parking
11.5' general standard with parking
May increase if higher cycling speeds are expected

SFMTA. (2008). SHARED LANE MARKINGS: WHEN AND WHERE TO USE THEM. PRESENTED AT PRO WALK/PRO BIKE 2008.

If used in a shared lane with on-street parallel parking, Shared Lane Markings should be placed so that the centers of the markings are at least 11 feet from the face of the curb or from the edge of the pavement where there is no curb.

FEDERAL HIGHWAY ADMINISTRATION. (2009). MANUAL ON UNIFORM TRAFFIC CONTROL DEVICES.

112 See SFMTA. (2008). Shared Lane Markings: When and Where to Use Them. Presented at Pro Walk/Pro Bike 2008.

PORTLAND BUREAU OF TRANSPORTATION. (2011). WAYFINDING SHARROW GUIDELINES.

If used on a street without on-street parking that has an outside travel lane that is less than 14 feet wide, the centers of the Shared Lane Markings should be at least 4 feet from the face of the curb or from the edge of the pavement where there is no curb.

FEDERAL HIGHWAY ADMINISTRATION. (2009). MANUAL ON UNIFORM TRAFFIC CONTROL DEVICES.

113 Salt Lake City, UT, and Long Beach, CA, have used a carpet of green coloring to create a lane-within-a-lane to indicate the priority area and preferred riding placement for bicyclists.

"The green lane facility has appeared to result in an approximate doubling of usage over the first 12 months of existence."

"Bicyclists familiar with more traditional sharrows have noted that the additional emphasis resulting from the green pavement paint appears to be creating an heightened awareness by the motorists in the lane."

CITY OF LONG BEACH. (2010). FINAL REPORT: SECOND STREET SHARROWS AND GREEN LANE IN THE CITY OF LONG BEACH, CALIFORNIA. RTE 9-113E.

114 Configurations in Brookline, MA, have used dotted lines to create a lane-within-a-lane to indicate the priority area and preferred riding placement for bicyclists.

"The lane-within-a-lane treatment appears to be effective in bringing about a shift in bicyclist position away from right-side hazards."

FURTH, P., DULASKI, D. M., BERGENTHAL, D., BROWN, S. (2011). MORE THAN SHARROWS: LANE-WITHIN-A-LANE BICYCLE PRIORITY TREATMENTS IN THREE U.S. CITIES. PRESENTED AT THE 2011 ANNUAL MEETING OF THE TRANSPORTATION RESEARCH BOARD.

BIKE ROUTE WAYFINDING

115 **Figure 1: Supported Destinations**

Primary Destinations: distances up to five miles
7 destinations total (adjoining or en route jurisdictions, downtown)

Destination	Sign Content	Distance Measured From
Alameda	Alameda	city line
Berkeley	Berkeley	city line
Downtown	Downtown	Grand Ave, I-980, I-880, Oak/Lakeside/Harrison
Emeryville	Emeryville	city line
Moraga	Moraga	city line
Piedmont	Piedmont	city line
San Leandro	San Leandro	city line

Secondary Destinations: distances up to two miles
37 destinations total (10 BART stations, 4 other transit stations, 23 districts)

Destination	Sign Content	Distance Measured From
BART stations		
12th St BART	12th Street	12th St and Broadway
19th St BART	19th Street	19th St and Broadway
Ashby BART	Ashby	Adeline St and Woolsey St
Coliseum BART	Coliseum	San Leandro St and 73rd Ave
Fruitvale BART	Fruitvale	E 12th St and 34th Ave
Lake Merritt BART	Lake Merritt	Oak St and 9th St
MacArthur BART	MacArthur	40th St and Frontage Rd
Rockridge BART	Rockridge	College Ave and Shafter Ave
San Leandro BART	San Leandro	San Leandro St and Davis St
West Oakland BART	West Oakland	7th St and Center St
Other transit stations		
Alameda/Oakland Ferry	Oakland Ferry	Clay St and Water St
Coliseum Amtrak	Coliseum	73rd Ave and San Leandro St
Emeryville Amtrak	Emeryville	Horton St and 59th St
Jack London Amtrak	Jack London	2nd St and Alice St
Districts		
Allendale	Allendale	38th Ave and Penniman Ave
Chinatown	Chinatown	8th St and Webster St
Dimond	Dimond	MacArthur Blvd and Fruitvale Ave
Eastlake	Eastlake	E 12th St and 7th Ave
Eastmont	Eastmont	closest edge
Embarcadero Cove	Embarcadero Cove	Embarcadero and Livingston St
Elmhurst	Elmhurst	94th Ave and Plymouth St
Fairfax	Fairfax	Bancroft Ave and Fairfax Ave
Glenview	Glenview	Park Blvd and Wellington St
Grand Lake	Grand Lake	Lake Park Ave and Walker Ave
Jack London Sq	Jack London Sq	Broadway and 2nd St
Laurel	Laurel	MacArthur Blvd and 38th Ave
Millsmont	Millsmont	MacArthur Blvd and Seminary Ave
Montclair	Montclair	Mountain Blvd and La Salle Ave
Oakmore	Oakmore	Leimert St and Oakmore Ave
Old Oakland	Old Oakland	9th St and Washington St
Park Street Business District (Alameda)	Park Street	Park St and Lincoln Ave
Parkway / Lake Merritt District	Parkway	E 18th St and Park Blvd
Piedmont Ave	Piedmont Ave	Piedmont Ave and 41st St
Rockridge	Rockridge	College Ave and Shafter Ave
Sobrante Park	Sobrante Park	105th Ave and Edes Ave

CITY OF OAKLAND. (2009). DESIGN GUIDELINES FOR BICYCLE
WAYFINDING SIGNAGE.

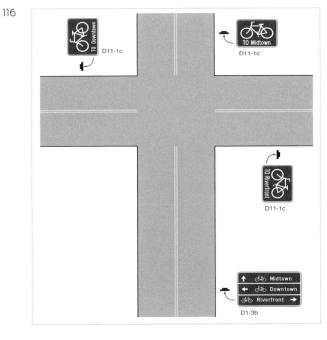

FEDERAL HIGHWAY ADMINISTRATION. (2009). MANUAL ON
UNIFORM TRAFFIC CONTROL DEVICES. FIGURE 9B-6.

117 "Bike Route Guide (D11-1) signs (see Figure 9B-4) may
be provided along designated bicycle routes to inform
bicyclists of bicycle route direction changes and to confirm
route direction, distance, and destination."

FEDERAL HIGHWAY ADMINISTRATION. (2009). MANUAL ON
UNIFORM TRAFFIC CONTROL DEVICES. P. 798.

118 *see note 109*

119 The Clearview Hwy typeface was granted interim approval
by the FHWA for use on positive contrast road signs (light
text on dark background) in September 2004 based on
studies showing improved legibility.

FEDERAL HIGHWAY ADMINISTRATION. (2004). INTERIM APPROVAL
FOR USE OF CLEARVIEW FONT FOR POSITIVE CONTRAST LEGENDS
ON GUIDE SIGNS.

120 The MUTCD defines the general meaning of 11 colors. Green
is identified for use on direction guidance.

FEDERAL HIGHWAY ADMINISTRATION. (2009). MANUAL ON
UNIFORM TRAFFIC CONTROL DEVICES.

Bicycle Boulevards
ROUTE PLANNING

121 Low-stress bikeways, which include cycle tracks, buffered bike lanes, and off-street paths, appeal to a wider spectrum of the population than conventional bike lanes or shared lanes along busy streets. A low-stress network should be fine-grained and many jurisdictions aim to provide a density of low-stress facilities at quarter- or half-mile intervals.

122 Intersection treatments that reduce delay can make bicycle boulevards more attractive for cut-through motor vehicle traffic, necessitating periodic monitoring of motor vehicle speeds and volumes.

123 See the U.S. Traffic Calming Manual for specific emergency-vehicle-friendly recommendations.

124 "Women and people who bicycle less frequently appear to be more concerned about bicycling on facilities with a lot of motor vehicle traffic, including bicycle lanes on major streets. Many of these bicyclists stated and revealed a preference for low-traffic streets, bicycle boulevards, and separate paths. This indicates that these types of facilities may be more effective at getting more women and infrequent or non-cyclists to ride."

DILL, J., AND GLIEBE, J. (2008). UNDERSTANDING AND MEASURING BICYCLING BEHAVIOR: A FOCUS ON TRAVEL TIME AND ROUTE CHOICE. OREGON TRANSPORTATION RESEARCH AND EDUCATION CONSORTIUM (OTREC).

"For the typical cyclist, 1-min cycling in mixed traffic is as onerous as 4.1 min on bike lanes or 2.8 min on bike paths."

HUNT, J.D., AND ABRAHAM, J.E. (2007). INFLUENCES ON BICYCLE USE. TRANSPORTATION 34.4: 453.

Speed management and other bicycle boulevard treatments on a street in Berkeley, California, reduced the number of automobiles by almost 20 percent, while the number of bicyclists and pedestrians increased by 83 percent and 87 percent, respectively.

BOUAOUINA AND ROBINSON (1990) IN EWING. (1999). TRAFFIC CALMING: STATE OF THE PRACTICE.

"Using police-reported collision data and the city's cyclist count data, this study finds that Berkeley's bicycle boulevards do indeed have lower collision rates for cyclists than their parallel arterial routes."

MINIKEL, E. (2011). CYCLIST SAFETY ON BICYCLE BOULEVARDS AND PARALLEL ARTERIAL ROUTES IN BERKELEY, CALIFORNIA. ACCIDENT ANALYSIS AND PREVENTION. 45: 241-247.

125 "Most homebuyers prefer homes on streets with lower traffic volumes and speeds. For this reason homes on cul de sac streets command a price premium and new developments are being built with streets designed to control traffic."

LITMAN, T. (1999). TRAFFIC CALMING BENEFITS, COSTS, AND EQUITY IMPACTS.

126 Portland, OR, and Albuquerque, NM, have designated lower speed limits for residential streets—20 and 18 mph, respectively—for residential streets classified as bicycle boulevards/neighborhood greenways.

SIGNS AND PAVEMENT MARKINGS

127 Portland, OR, Madison, WI, Nampa, ID, and Wilmington, NC, use standard shared lane markings on their neighborhood greenways/bicycle boulevards. Tacoma, WA, is adjusting the standard marking to include a colored flag and modified bicyclist.

128 "Center line markings should be placed on paved urban arterials and collectors that have a traveled way of 20 feet or more in width and an ADT of 4,000 vehicles per day or greater."

"On roadways without continuous center line pavement markings, short sections may be marked with center line pavement markings to control the position of traffic at specific locations."

FEDERAL HIGHWAY ADMINISTRATION. (2009). MANUAL ON UNIFORM TRAFFIC CONTROL DEVICES. 3B.01.

129 "A pictograph (see definition in Section 1A.13) may be used on a D3-1 sign. If a pictograph is used on a D3-1 sign, the height and width of the pictograph shall not exceed the upper-case letter height of the principal legend of the sign. The pictograph should be positioned to the left of the street name."

FEDERAL HIGHWAY ADMINISTRATION. (2009). MANUAL ON UNIFORM TRAFFIC CONTROL DEVICES. 2D.42.

130 "Parking space markings tend to prevent encroachment into fire hydrant zones, bus stops, loading zones, approaches to intersections, curb ramps, and clearance spaces for islands and other zones where parking is restricted."

FEDERAL HIGHWAY ADMINISTRATION. (2009). MANUAL ON UNIFORM TRAFFIC CONTROL DEVICES. 3B.19.

SPEED MANAGEMENT

131 Refer to the American Planning Association (APA) U.S. Traffic Calming Manual (Ewing and Brown, 2009) and Chapter 15 of the Institute of Transportation Engineers (ITE) Traffic Engineering Handbook (2009) for detailed guidelines about speed and volume management treatments.

132   As of 2012, Oregon cities have authority to lower the speed limit on residential streets to 20 mph if the road has an average volume less than 2,000 vpd, an 85th percentile speed of less than 30 mph, and if there is a device (e.g., shared lane markings, warning signs) that indicates the presence of bicyclists or pedestrians. City of Portland staff intend to sign all residential neighborhood greenways that meet these criteria at 20 mph and have begun implementing speed management measures to create streets with target speeds of 20 mph in anticipation of the lowered speed limit.

Albuquerque, NM, signs bicycle boulevards at 18 mph but has not used speed management to reduce the streets' speeds. Targeted enforcement is used when a bicycle boulevard first opens, and electronic speed feedback signs reinforce the speed limit to drivers.

In California, the prima facie speed limit in residential areas is 25 mph, which is the lowest speed limit allowed allowed, with specific exceptions. In order to enforce speed using a radar, a city must conduct a speed survey to justify the speed limit. Cities can post advisory speeds, such as a triangular, yellow 15 mph sign with a speed bump warning sign.

133   Speed humps should be no more than 500 feet (152 m) apart or between slow points where the desired 85th percentile operating speed is between 25 and 30 mph.

INSTITUTE OF TRANSPORTATION ENGINEERS. (2011). UPDATED GUIDELINES FOR THE DESIGN AND APPLICATION OF SPEED HUMPS AND SPEED TABLES.

"Improperly designed, speed humps and all speed bumps are dangerous for bicyclists... both 3-inch and 4-inch humps are likely to be safe for bicyclists, although the 4-inch hump should probably be used with caution where bicycle traffic is frequent or rapid. ... Speed humps should be located far enough from intersections that turning cyclists are no longer leaning when they encounter the hump."

Speed humps should be used with caution on hills where bicyclist speeds may exceed 20 mph. The City of Oakland, CA, only installs speed humps on streets with a vertical grade less than 5 percent.

DEROBERTIS, M., AND WACHTEL, A. (1996). TRAFFIC CALMING: DO'S AND DON'TS TO ENCOURAGE BICYCLING.

134   "Speed lumps reduce the 85th percentile speed by 25 percent, or 9 mph... The speed reduction with lumps is comparable to that with speed humps."

Speed lumps or cushions have been found to have minimal, if any, impact to emergency vehicles in Austin, TX, and San Diego, Sacramento, and Danville, CA.

GULDEN, J., AND EWING, R. (2009). NEW TRAFFIC CALMING DEVICE OF CHOICE.

On a 36-foot wide roadway, three lumps are optimal, with a 6-foot wide center lump to minimize emergency vehicle delay and discomfort, and the outside lump widths can vary. The wheel gaps should be 1 to 2 feet wide. This configuration also allows bicyclists to pass through the speed lumps without having to leave the center of the lane; the City of Seattle marks shared lane marking arrows at the gap to guide bicyclists.

EWING, R. AND BROWN, S. (2009). U.S. TRAFFIC CALMING MANUAL.

"Speed cushions do not present any notable disadvantages for emergency vehicles."

BERTHOD, C. (2011). TRAFFIC CALMING: SPEED HUMPS AND SPEED CUSHIONS.

Parking alongside speed lumps may be restricted to enable bicyclists to pass through the outside of the feature.

135   "After several runs, it was decided that the distance between the two lane bump halves needed to be at least 28 feet for the vehicle to maneuver through at or near 20 mph."

MULDER, K. (1998). SPLIT SPEED BUMP.

136   "Granite and cobblestone finishes are not recommended [for raised crosswalks] because, although aesthetically pleasing, the surface may become slippery when wet, and may be difficult to cross for pedestrians who are visually impaired or using wheelchairs."

PARKHILL, M., SOOKLALL, R., AND BAHAR, G. (2011). UPDATED GUIDELINES FOR THE DESIGN AND APPLICATION OF SPEED HUMPS.

Raised crosswalks are 3 inches below the level of standards sidewalks, and an accessible curb ramp should be provided, as well as a surface textural indication for pedestrians with vision impairments.

EWING, R. AND BROWN, S. (2009). U.S. TRAFFIC CALMING MANUAL.

137   The number of automobile accidents at intersections [with traffic circles] fell 94 percent... Accident reduction was also found in subsequent years.

MUNDELL, J. (NO DATE). NEIGHBORHOOD TRAFFIC CIRCLES.

Neighborhood traffic circles can include a paved apron or mountable curb to accommodate the turning radii of larger vehicles like fire trucks or school buses. Larger circles should include splitter islands at the approaches. Vehicles over 22 feet may be allowed to turn left in front of traffic circles in some states; others expressly prohibit this movement.

Traffic circles at T-intersections should include curb extensions before and after the intersection or use curb indentation at the top of the T to provide the same deflection benefits as at 4-way intersections.

EWING, R. AND BROWN, S. (2009). U.S. TRAFFIC CALMING MANUAL.

The circle should be landscaped to attract attention and for aesthetic reasons; trees should have clear stem heights of at least 8 feet and be no more than 4 inches in diameter, while other plantings should be no more than 2 feet high.

Stop signs may be used in conjunction with traffic circles, but are not mandatory.

Some jurisdictions use yield signs, while others discourage use of both stop and yield.

138   Curb extensions and edge islands should be tapered at 45 degrees to reinforce the edge lines and should use plantings to increase their visibility.

Edge lines should be marked to designate the travel lane.

A landscaped center island may be used to separate opposing traffic and discourage drivers from crossing the centerline.

On narrow streets with low parking turnover, parking bays may be used to create the lateral shift.

139   Pinchpoints should provide a clear two-way travel path of less than 18 feet (12 feet recommended).

CURB EXTENSIONS AND EDGE ISLANDS SHOULD BE TAPERED AT 45 DEGREES TO REINFORCE THE EDGE LINES AND USE PLANTINGS TO INCREASE THEIR VISIBILITY.

140   The curb radius of neckdowns on local streets should be approximately 20 feet.

Stop lines on side streets may be set back from intersections such that turning trucks can briefly cross into the opposing lane.

141   Center island narrowings should be large enough to command attention—at least 6 feet wide and 20 feet long.

EWING, R. AND BROWN, S. (2009). U.S. TRAFFIC CALMING MANUAL.

In addition to the above retrofit treatments that narrow a street, some jurisdictions are building skinny streets or queuing streets, which are between 20 and 28 feet wide (with parking).

On-street parking should be prohibited within 20 to 50 feet of the right-hand side of intersections to accommodate turning movements and increase visibility.

142   On-street parking should be prohibited within 20 to 50 feet of the right-hand side of intersections to accommodate turning movements and increase visibility.

Seattle's standard, low-volume, non-arterial streets are 25 feet wide when parking is allowed on both sides.

143

Speed Impacts of Traffic Calming Measures				
Treatment	Sample Size	Average Speed After Traffic Calming (mph)	Average Change in Speed with Traffic Calming (mph)	Average % Change in Speed with Traffic Calming (mph)
12' Humps	184	27.3 (4.0)	-7.8 (3.7)	-22 (9)
14' Humps	15	25.6 (2.1)	-7.7 (2.1)	-23 (9)
Lumps	49	27.0 (3.4)	-8.9 (5.3)	-25 (12)
22' Tables (Raised Crosswalks)	78	29.2 (3.1)	-7.3 (3.4)	-20 (8)
Longer Tables	11	31.3 (2.9)	-3.6 (2.6)	-10 (7)
Raised Intersections	3	34.3 (6.0)	-0.3 (3.8)	-1 (10)
Mini-Circles	45	30.3 (4.4)	-3.9 (3.2)	-11 (10)
Narrowings (chicanes, pinchpoints, neckdowns)	7	32.3 (2.8)	-2.6 (5.5)	-4 (22)
One-Lane Slow Points	5	28.6 (3.1)	-4.8 (1.3)	-14 (4)
Half Closures	16	26.3 (5.2)	-6.0 (3.6)	-19 (11)
Diagonal Diverters	7	27.9 (5.2)	-1.4 (4.7)	-4 (17)

* Values in parentheses are standard deviations from the average.

U.S. TRAFFIC CALMING MANUAL. EWING, 2009: 63.

144   "The average risk of severe injury for a pedestrian struck by a vehicle reaches 10% at an impact speed of 16 mph, 25% at 23 mph, 50% at 31 mph, 75% at 39 mph, and 90% at 46 mph."

AAA FOUNDATION FOR TRAFFIC SAFETY. (2011). IMPACT SPEED AND A PEDESTRIAN'S RISK OF SEVERE INJURY OR DEATH.

145   In general, a speed differential between motor vehicles and cyclists of no more than approximately 15 mph is desirable. [Note: this refers to the difference between a person on a bicycle traveling at 10 mph and a motorist at 25 mph. Smaller differential is desirable.]

ALTA PLANNING + DESIGN AND PORTLAND STATE UNIVERSITY INITIATIVE FOR BICYCLE AND PEDESTRIAN INNOVATION. (2009). BICYCLE BOULEVARD PLANNING & DESIGN GUIDEBOOK.

146   Emergency-vehicle-friendly treatments can include 22-foot speed humps, split humps (laterally offset speed tables), speed lumps/cushions (which have a gap that accommodates emergency vehicles' wheels), or speed humps with a configuration of three lumps with a six-foot-wide center lump with one or two foot wheel gaps.

EWING, R. AND BROWN, S. (2009). U.S. TRAFFIC CALMING MANUAL.

147   For a maneuverability test, cones are placed in the street to model the proposed dimensions of the treatments or street reconfiguration. Typical emergency response vehicles are then driven through the area, using every possible turning movement. Travel time tests should be discouraged. Research has shown a large variance between speeds with simulated devices (represented by cones) and actual devices as constructed.

EWING, R. AND BROWN, S. (2009). U.S. TRAFFIC CALMING MANUAL.

148

Table 5-2
MOTOR VEHICLE TRAFFIC VOLUME:
IMPACTS OF TRAFFIC CALMING MEASURES

Measure	Sample Size	Average Change in Volume (Vehicles/Day)	Average Change in Volume (%)
Traffic circles	49	-293	-5
Narrowings	11	-263	-10

BERKELEY BICYCLE BOULEVARD DESIGN TOOLS AND GUIDELINES (APRIL 2000).

149   Speeds increase about 0.5 to 1.0 mph for every 100 feet of separation for hump spacing up to 1,000 feet.

EWING, R. (1999.) TRAFFIC CALMING: STATE OF THE PRACTICE. INSTITUTE OF TRANSPORTATION ENGINEERS.

150   "In 92% of cases where the measure is permanent, it remains as effective at slowing speeds in the winter as in the summer. In 79% of cases, there was no deterioration resulting from winter conditions or snow removal. In 71% of cases, snow removal did not pose any problems. ... A sinusoidal shape is preferred over a circular or parabolic shape because it provides a more gentle transition and is easier for winter maintenance operators and cyclists to negotiate."

BERTHOD, C. (2011). TRAFFIC CALMING: SPEED HUMPS AND SPEED CUSHIONS.

VOLUME MANAGEMENT

151   On a 20 mph street with 1,000 vpd, a cyclist traveling at 12 mph during peak hour would be passed by a car traveling in the same direction approximately every 86 seconds (assuming peak hour is 15 percent of vpd, the street is two-way with 70% of traffic volumes traveling in the peak direction, and cars are evenly spaced along the street). By comparison, at 3,000 vpd, a bicyclist would be passed by a car every 29 seconds, and at 5,000 vpd, a bicyclist would be passed by a car every 17 seconds.

152   Diagonal diverters should provide a 6- to 10-foot refuge area for crossing bicyclists to wait for a gap in traffic, which is forced to turn across the feature.

153

Volume Impacts of Traffic Calming Measures

Treatment	Sample Size	Average Change in Volume with Traffic Calming (vpd)	Average % Change in Volume with Traffic Calming
12' Humps	143	-355 (591)	-18 (24)
14' Humps	15	-529 (741)	-22 (26)
Lumps	18	-165 (211)	-7 (17)
22' Tables (Raised Crosswalks)	46	-415 (649)	-12 (20)
Traffic Circles	49	-293 (584)	-5 (46)
Narrowings (chicanes, pinchpoints, neckdowns,)	11	-263 (2,178)	-10 (51)
One-Lane Slow Points	5	-392 (384)	-20 (19)
Full Closures	19	-671 (786)	-44 (36)
Half Closures	53	-1,611 (2,444)	-42 (41)
Diagonal Diverters	27	-501 (622)	-35 (46)
Other Volume Controls	10	-1,167 (1,781)	-31 (36)

* Values in parentheses are standard deviations from the average.

U.S. TRAFFIC CALMING MANUAL. EWING, 2009: 63.

154   FEDERAL HIGHWAY ADMINISTRATION. (2009). MANUAL ON UNIFORM TRAFFIC CONTROL DEVICES. SECTION 2B.18.

155   "Channelizing devices, as described in Sections 6F.63 through 6F.73, and 6F.75, and as shown in Figure 6F-7, such as cones, tubular markers, vertical panels, drums, lane separators, and raised islands, may be used for general traffic control purposes such as adding emphasis to reversible lane delineation, channelizing lines, or islands. Channelizing devices may also be used along a center line to preclude turns or along lane lines to preclude lane changing, as determined by engineering judgment"

FEDERAL HIGHWAY ADMINISTRATION. (2009). MANUAL ON UNIFORM TRAFFIC CONTROL DEVICES. 3H.01.

156   The threshold can consider total traffic volume; an increase of over 400 vpd on a local street may be unacceptable, and the resulting traffic volume on any local street should not exceed 3,000 vpd.

CITY OF PORTLAND. (2011). IMPACT THRESHOLD CURVE.

MINOR STREET CROSSINGS

157   "A typical bicycle trip of 30 minutes is increased by 33% to 40 minutes if there is a STOP sign at every block."

CITY OF BERKELEY. (2000). BICYCLE BOULEVARD DESIGN TOOLS AND GUIDELINES.

"A cyclist who rolls through a stop at 5 mph needs 25 percent less energy to get back to 10 mph than does a cyclist who comes to a complete stop."

FAJANS, J., AND M. CURRY. (2001). WHY BICYCLISTS HATE STOP SIGNS. ACCESS. 18:28-31.

158 "The use of YIELD or STOP signs should be considered at the intersection of two minor streets or local roads where the intersection has more than three approaches and where one or more of the following conditions exist:

A. The combined vehicular, bicycle, and pedestrian volume entering the intersection from all approaches averages more than 2,000 units per day;

B. The ability to see conflicting traffic on an approach is not sufficient to allow a road user to stop or yield in compliance with the normal right-of-way rule if such stopping or yielding is necessary; and/or

C. Crash records indicate that five or more crashes that involve the failure to yield the right-of-way at the intersection under the normal right-of-way rule have been reported within a 3-year period, or that three or more such crashes have been reported within a 2-year period."

"A YIELD or STOP sign should not be installed on the higher volume roadway unless justified by an engineering study. … The following are considerations that might influence the decision regarding the appropriate roadway upon which to install a YIELD or STOP sign where two roadways with relatively equal volumes and/or characteristics intersect:

A. Controlling the direction that conflicts the most with established pedestrian crossing activity or school walking routes*;

B. Controlling the direction that has obscured vision, dips, or bumps that already require drivers to use lower operating speeds; and

C. Controlling the direction that has the best sight distance from a controlled position to observe conflicting traffic."

*Note: this should extend to bicycle crossings as well.

FEDERAL HIGHWAY ADMINISTRATION. (2009). MANUAL ON UNIFORM TRAFFIC CONTROL DEVICES. 2B.04.

MAJOR STREET CROSSINGS

159 See National Cooperative Highway Research Program Report # 562 Improving Pedestrian Safety at Unsignalized Crossings (2006) for guidance on when to use crosswalks, active or enhanced treatments, or beacons and signals. The future expected volume of bicyclists and pedestrians should be used in the analysis to determine the appropriate crossing treatment that will encourage use of the corridor.

160 Vehicular traffic warning signs may be used to alert road users to locations where unexpected entries into the roadway [or shared use of the roadway by pedestrians, animals, and other crossing activities] might occur. When used in advance of a crossing, non-vehicular warning signs may be supplemented with supplemental plaques with the legend AHEAD, XX FEET, or NEXT XX MILES to provide advance notice to road users of crossing activity.

FEDERAL HIGHWAY ADMINISTRATION. (2009). MANUAL ON UNIFORM TRAFFIC CONTROL DEVICES. 2C.48.

161 This is a variation of a staggered stop line.

Option: Stop and yield lines may be staggered "longitudinally on a lane-by-lane basis (see Drawing D of Figure 3B-13).

Support: Staggered stop lines and staggered yield lines can improve the driver's view of pedestrians, provide better sight distance for turning vehicles, and increase the turning radius for left-turning vehicles."

FEDERAL HIGHWAY ADMINISTRATION. (2009). MANUAL ON UNIFORM TRAFFIC CONTROL DEVICES. SECTION 3B.16

162 This application [of a hybrid beacon] provides a pedestrian crossing without signal control for the side street because signal control on the side street can encourage unwanted additional traffic through the neighborhood.

FEDERAL HIGHWAY ADMINISTRATION. (2010). SAFETY EFFECTIVENESS OF THE HAWK PEDESTRIAN CROSSING TREATMENT. FHWA-HRT-10-042.

163 Bicyclist gaps can be estimated by modifying guidance from National Cooperative Highway Research Program Report # 562 Improving Pedestrian Safety at Unsignalized Crossings (2006) using crossing distance and bicyclist start-up and clearance speed (assume a start-up time of 6 seconds, a speed of 10 mph or below, and a clearance interval of 6 feet). Bicycle boulevards should assume a high number of bicyclists and pedestrians, rather than relying on counts which indicate existing use rather than potential use after the facility has been improved.

Recommended treatments for pedestrian crossings are designed to improve visibility and encourage motorists to stop for pedestrians; with engineering judgment many of the same treatments are appropriate for use along bicycle boulevards.

NATIONAL COOPERATIVE HIGHWAY RESEARCH PROGRAM (NCHRP). (2006). REPORT # 562 IMPROVING PEDESTRIAN SAFETY AT UNSIGNALIZED CROSSINGS.

OFFSET INTERSECTIONS

164 Each bicycle left-turn lane should be at least 4 feet wide (total width of 8 feet), with 6 feet preferred (total width of 12 feet).

This treatment is appropriate for relatively short jogs.

HENDRIX, MICHAEL. (2007). RESPONDING TO THE CHALLENGES OF BICYCLE CROSSINGS AT OFFSET INTERSECTIONS. THIRD URBAN STREET SYMPOSIUM.

This treatment is not appropriate if the cross street has more than one lane per direction or has a posted speed above 30 mph.

A raised median with a small opening for bikes may be used to prohibit motor vehicles from continuing on the bicycle boulevard or turning left from the cross street.

Green coloration may be used in the bike lane area to improve its visibility, as well as median islands at either end for protection from motor vehicle traffic.

165   A refuge island may be provided to make a two-step crossing for path users at a complex crossing.

AMERICAN ASSOCIATION OF STATE HIGHWAY AND TRANSPORTATION OFFICIALS (AASHTO). (1999). GUIDE FOR THE DEVELOPMENT OF BICYCLE FACILITIES.

GREEN INFRASTRUCTURE

166   Facilities that filter stormwater through vegetation and soil have been shown to reduce total suspended solids (TSS) by 90%, organic pollutants/oils by 90%, and heavy metals by more than 90%.

UNITED STATES ENVIRONMENTAL PROTECTION AGENCY. (1999). STORM WATER TECHNOLOGY FACT SHEET: BIORETENTION.

Design Guide Project Teams

To create the Guide, the authors have conducted an extensive worldwide literature search from design guidelines and real-life experience. They have worked closely with a panel of urban bikeway planning professionals from NACTO member cities, as well as traffic engineers, planners, and academics with deep experience in urban bikeway applications. A complete list of participating professionals is below.

Project Review Team

Dennis Leach, A.I.C.P.	Arlington County
Joshuah Mello, A.I.C.P.	Atlanta Department of Planning & Community Development
Annick Beaudet, A.I.C.P.	Austin Public Works Department
Nathan Wilkes	Austin Public Works Department
Nate Evans	Baltimore City Department of Transportation
Zach Vanderkooy	Bikes Belong
Nicole Freedman	Boston Transportation Department
David Gleason	Chicago Department of Transportation
Cara Seiderman	City of Cambridge
Andy Lutz, P.E.	City of Indianapolis Department of Public Works
Kyle Wagenschutz	City of Memphis
Mike Goodno	District of Columbia Department of Transportation
Jim Sebastian, A.I.C.P.	District of Columbia Department of Transportation
Ian Sacs, P.E.	Hoboken Department of Transportation and Parking
Dan Raine, A.I.C.P., L.C.I.	Houston Traffic and Transportation Division
Michelle Mowery	Los Angeles Department of Transportation
Don Pflaum, P.E., P.T.O.E.	Minneapolis Department of Public Works
Eric Gilliland	National Association of City Transportation Officials
David Vega-Barachowitz	National Association of City Transportation Officials
Linda Bailey	New York City Department of Transportation
Josh Benson, A.I.C.P.	New York City Department of Transportation
Hayes Lord, A.I.C.P.	New York City Department of Transportation
Jon Orcutt	New York City Department of Transportation
Charles Carmalt, A.I.C.P. /P.P.	Philadelphia Mayor's Office of Transportation and Utilities
Joseph Perez	Phoenix Street Transportation Department
Rob Burchfield, P.E.	Portland Bureau of Transportation
Roger Geller	Portland Bureau of Transportation
Heath Maddox	San Francisco Municipal Transportation Agency
Seleta Reynolds, A.I.C.P.	San Francisco Municipal Transportation Agency
Michael Sallaberry, P.E.	San Francisco Municipal Transportation Agency
Bridget Smith, P.E.	San Francisco Municipal Transportation Agency
Sam Woods	Seattle Department of Transportation
Randy Neufeld	SRAM Cycling Fund

Consulting Team

Joe Gilpin	Alta Planning and Design
Jeff Olson, R.A.	Alta Planning and Design
Mia Birk	Alta Planning and Design
Drew Meisel	Alta Planning and Design
Nick Falbo	Alta Planning and Design
Hannah Kapell	Alta Planning and Design
Jamie Parks, A.I.C.P.	Kittelson & Associates, Inc.
Mike Coleman, P.E.	Kittelson & Associates, Inc.
Conor Semler	Kittelson & Associates, Inc.
Peter Furth, Ph.D	Northeastern University
David Parisi, P.E.	Parisi Associates
Nick Grossman	OpenPlans
Andy Cochran	OpenPlans
Chris Abraham	OpenPlans
Arjen Jaarsma	Netherlands
Niels Jenson	City of Copenhagen
Lynn Weigand, Ph.D	IPBI
Donald Meeker	Meeker Designs

References

Bike Lanes

Research and Studies

ACADEMIC

Bicycle Facility Selection A Comparison of Approaches. (2002).

Evaluation of Innovative Bicycle Facilities. (2011).

Infrastructure, Programs, and Policies to Increase Bicycling: An International Review. (2010).

Design Guides

CITY

Baltimore Bicycle Facility Design Toolkit. (2007).

Bicentennial Bikeways Plan. (2008).

Bicycle Facilities Design Manual for the City of Redmond. (2009).

City of Austin Street Smarts Task Force Bicycle Facilities. (2007).

City of Memphis Bicycle Design Manual. (2008).

Denver Bicycle Master Plan. (2001).

Los Angeles Technical Design Handbook. (2011).

Louisville Complete Streets Manual: Facility Design. (2008).

Maricopa County AZ Bicycle Transportation System Plan. (1999).

New York City Bicycle Master Plan. (1997).

NYCDOT Street Design Manual. (2009).

Portland Bicycle Plan for 2030: Survey of Best Practices. (2009).

Sacramento Best Practices for Bicycle Master Planning and Design. (2005).

San Diego Bicycle Design Guidelines. (2009).

Seattle Bicycle Master Plan. (2007).

Wisconsin Bicycle Facility Design Handbook. (2004).

STATE

Arizona Bicycle and Pedestrian Plan Design Guidelines. (2003).

Ohio Design Guidance for Roadway Based Bicycle Facilities. (2005).

Oregon Bicycle and Pedestrian Facility Design Standards. (1995).

Vermont Pedestrian and Bicycle Facility Planning and Design Manual: On Road Bicycle Facilities. (2002).

NATIONAL

Bikesafe Bicycle Countermeasure Selection System. (2006).

FHWA Manual on Uniform Traffic Control Devices. (2009).

Transportation Planning Handbook - Bicycle and Pedestrian Facilities. (2009).

International Materials

Department for Transport Cycle Infrastructure Design. (2008).

Design Manual for Bicycle Traffic. (2005).

Langley Bicycle and Pedestrian Facility Design Guidelines. (2004).

London Cycling Design Standards. (2005).

Nottinghamshire Cycling Design Guide. (2006).

Road Directorate Collection Cycle Concepts. (2000).

Sustrans Cycling Guidelines. (1997).

Victoria vicroads Cycle Notes No 9. (2001).

Cycle Tracks

Research and Studies

ACADEMIC

Bicycle Facility Selection A Comparison of Approaches. (2002).

Cyclist safety on bicycle boulevards and parallel arterial routes in Berkeley, California. (2011).

Effects of Colored Lane Markings on Bicyclist and Motorist Behavior at Conflict Areas. (2010).

Effects of Shared Lane Markings on Bicyclist and Motorist Behavior along Multi-Lane Facilities. (2010).

Efficacy of Rectangular-Shaped Rapid Flash LED Beacons.

Evaluation of a Green Bike Lane Weaving Area in St. Petersburg, FL. (2008).

Evaluation of Bike Boxes at Signalized Intersections. (2010).

Evaluation of Blue Bike-Lane Treatment in Portland, OR. (2000).

Evaluation of combined bike Lane and right turn lane, Eugene, OR. (2000).

Evaluation of Green Bike Lane Weaving Area in St Petersburgh, Florida. (2008).

Evaluation of Innovative Bicycle Facilities. (2011).

Evaluation of Innovative Bike-Box Application in Eugene, Oregon. (2000).

Evaluation of the Rectangular Rapid Flash Beacon at a Pinellas Trail Crossing in St. Petersburg, Florida. (2009).

Impact Speed and a Pedestrian's Risk of Severe Injury or Death. (2011).

Influences on bicycle use. (2007).

Infrastructure, Programs, and Policies to Increase Bicycling: An International Review. (2010).

Measuring the Safety Effect of Raised Bicycle Crossings Using a New Research Methodology. (1998).

More Than Sharrows-Lane-Within-A-Lane Bicycle Priority Treatments in Three US Cities. (2011).

Resident Perceptions of Bicycle Boulevards. (2009).

Responding to the Challenges of Bicycle Crossings at Offset Intersections. (2007).

Risk of Injury for Bicycling on Cycle Tracks Versus in the Street. (2011).

Safety Effects of Blue Cycle Crossings. (2008).

Traffic Calming Benefits, Costs, and Equity Impacts. (1999).

Traffic Calming: Do's and Don'ts to Encourage Bicycling. (1996).

Traffic Calming: Speed Humps and Speed Cushions. (2011).

Understanding and Measuring Bicycling Behavior: A Focus on Travel Time and Route Choice.(2008).

Updated Guidelines for the Design and Application of Speed Humps. (2007).

MUNICIPALITY

15th Street NW Separated Bike Lane Pilot Project. (2010).

PROFESSIONAL

Cycle Track Lessons Learned. (2009).

Design Guides

CITY

Bicentennial Bikeways Plan. (2008).

Los Angeles Technical Design Handbook. (2011).

New York City Bicycle Master Plan. (1997).

NYCDOT Street Design Manual. (2009).

San Diego Bicycle Design Guidelines. (2009).

NATIONAL

Bikesafe Bicycle Countermeasure Selection System. (2006).

International Materials

Design Manual for Bicycle Traffic. (2005).

London Cycling Design Standards. (2005).

Nottinghamshire Cycling Design Guide. (2006).

Road Directorate Collection Cycle Concepts. (2000).

Road safety and perceived risk of cycle facilities in Copenhagen. (2007).

Sustrans Cycling Guidelines. (1997).

Technical Handbook of Bikeway Design. (2003).

Traffic Environment for Children and Elderly as Pedestrians and Cyclists. (2005).

Victoria vicroads Cycle Notes No 9. (2001).

Intersections

Research and Studies

ACADEMIC

Evaluation of Bike Boxes at Signalized Intersections. (2010).

Evaluation of Blue Bike-Lane Treatment in Portland, OR. (2000).

Evaluation of combined bike Lane and right turn lane, Eugene, OR. (2000).

Evaluation of Innovative Bike-Box Application in Eugene, Oregon. (2000).

Infrastructure, Programs, and Policies to Increase Bicycling: An International Review. (2010).

Measuring the Safety Effect of Raised Bicycle Crossings Using a New Research Methodology. (1998).

Risk of Injury for Bicycling on Cycle Tracks Versus in the Street. (2011).

MUNICIPALITY

Portland's Blue Bike Lanes: Improved Safety Through Enhanced Visibility. (1999).

PROFESSIONAL

Cycle Track Lessons Learned. (2009).

Effects of Bicycle Boxes on Bicyclist and Motorist Behavior at Intersections. (2010).

General Design and Engineering Principles of Streetcar Transit. (2011).

Protected Bikeway Design. (2011).

Design Guides

CITY

Baltimore Bicycle Facility Design Toolkit. (2007).

Bicentennial Bikeways Plan. (2008).

Bicycle Facilities Design Manual for the City of Redmond. (2009).

Chicago Bike Lane Design Guide. (2002).

City of Austin Street Smarts Task Force Bicycle Facilities. (2007).

City of Davis Comprehensive Bike Plan. (2006).

City of Memphis Bicycle Design Manual. (2008).

DC Bicycle Facility Design Guide. (2005).

District of Columbia Bicycle Master Plan. (2005).

Los Angeles Technical Design Handbook. (2011).

Nashville-Davidson County Strategic Plan for Sidewalks and Bikeways. (2008).

New York City Bicycle Master Plan. (1997).

Portland Bicycle Plan for 2030: Survey of Best Practices. (2009).

Sacramento Best Practices for Bicycle Master Planning and Design. (2005).

Seattle Bicycle Master Plan. (2007).

Shared Lane Markings: When and Where to Use Them. (2008).

Wisconsin Bicycle Facility Design Handbook. (2004).

STATE

Arizona Bicycle and Pedestrian Plan Design Guidelines. (2003).

Oregon Bicycle and Pedestrian Facility Design Standards. (1995).

Vermont Pedestrian and Bicycle Facility Planning and Design Manual: On Road Bicycle Facilities. (2002).

NATIONAL

AASHTO Guide for the Development of Bicycle Facilities. (1999).

Bikesafe Bicycle Countermeasure Selection System. (2006).

FHWA Manual on Uniform Traffic Control Devices. (2009).

International Materials

Advanced Stop Line Variations Research Study. (2005).

Behaviour at Cycle Advanced Stop Lines. (2005).

Bicycle Storage Area and Advanced Bicycle Stop Lines. (2009).

Coloured Bicycle Lanes Simulator Testing. (2008).

Department for Transport Cycle Infrastructure Design. (2008).

Design Manual for Bicycle Traffic. (2005).

Ireland National Cycling Promotion Policy. (2008).

Langley Bicycle and Pedestrian Facility Design Guidelines. (2004).

London Cycling Design Standards. (2005).

Nottinghamshire Cycling Design Guide. (2006).

Road Directorate Collection Cycle Concepts. (2000).

Sustrans Cycling Guidelines. (1997).

Technical Handbook of Bikeway Design. (2003).

Traffic Environment for Children and Elderly as Pedestrians and Cyclists. (2005).

Signals

Research and Studies

ACADEMIC

Efficacy of Rectangular-Shaped Rapid Flash LED Beacons.

Evaluation of the Rectangular Rapid Flash Beacon at a Pinellas Trail Crossing in St. Petersburg, Florida. (2009).

MUNICIPALITY

Modified HAWK Signal and Bike Signal. (2010).

PROFESSIONAL

Cycle Track Lessons Learned. (2009).

Design Guides

CITY

Baltimore Bicycle Facility Design Toolkit. (2007).

Bicentennial Bikeways Plan. (2008).

Bicycle Facilities Design Manual for the City of Redmond. (2009).

City of Austin Street Smarts Task Force Bicycle Facilities. (2007).

City of Davis Comprehensive Bike Plan. (2006).

City of Memphis Bicycle Design Manual. (2008).

DC Bicycle Facility Design Guide. (2005).

Denver Bicycle Master Plan. (2001).

Los Angeles Technical Design Handbook. (2011).

Nashville-Davidson County Strategic Plan for Sidewalks and Bikeways. (2008).

New York City Bicycle Master Plan. (1997).

Sacramento Best Practices for Bicycle Master Planning and Design. (2005).

San Diego Bicycle Design Guidelines. (2009).

Wisconsin Bicycle Facility Design Handbook. (2004).

STATE

Ohio Design Guidance for Roadway Based Bicycle Facilities. (2005).

NATIONAL

FHWA Manual on Uniform Traffic Control Devices. (2009).

International Materials

Design Manual for Bicycle Traffic. (2005).

Langley Bicycle and Pedestrian Facility Design Guidelines. (2004).

London Cycling Design Standards. (2005).

Nottinghamshire Cycling Design Guide. (2006).

Road Directorate Collection Cycle Concepts. (2000).

Signing and Marking

Research and Studies

ACADEMIC

Effects of Colored Lane Markings on Bicyclist and Motorist Behavior at Conflict Areas. (2010).

Effects of Shared Lane Markings on Bicyclist and Motorist Behavior along Multi-Lane Facilities. (2010).

Evaluation of a Green Bike Lane Weaving Area in St. Petersburg, FL. (2008).

More Than Sharrows-Lane-Within-A-Lane Bicycle Priority Treatments in Three US Cities. (2011).

MUNICIPALITY

Evaluation of Solid Green Bicycle Lanes to Increase Compliance and Bicycle Safety. (2011).

Evaluation of the Shared-Use Arrow. (1999).

San Francisco's Shared Lane Pavement Markings: Improving Bicycle Safety. (2004).

Second Street Sharrows and Green Lane in the City of Long Beach, California. (2010).

PROFESSIONAL

Cycle Track Lessons Learned. (2009).

Evaluation of Solid and Dashed Green Pavement for Bicycle Lanes. (2008).

Design Guides

CITY

Baltimore Bicycle Facility Design Toolkit. (2007).

Bicentennial Bikeways Plan. (2008).

Bicycle Facilities Design Manual for the City of Redmond. (2009).

City of Austin Street Smarts Task Force Bicycle Facilities. (2007).

City of Memphis Bicycle Design Manual. (2008).

DC Bicycle Facility Design Guide. (2005).

Detroit Non-Motorized Transportation Plan. (2006).

Los Angeles Technical Design Handbook. (2011).

Louisville Complete Streets Manual: Facility Design. (2008).

Milwaukie Bicycle Wayfinding Signage Plan. (2009).

Nashville-Davidson County Strategic Plan for Sidewalks and Bikeways. (2008).

New York City Bicycle Master Plan. (1997).

NYCDOT Street Design Manual. (2009).

Sacramento Best Practices for Bicycle Master Planning and Design. (2005).

San Diego Bicycle Design Guidelines. (2009).

Seattle Bicycle Master Plan. (2007).

Shared Lane Markings: When and Where to Use Them. (2008).

Wisconsin Bicycle Facility Design Handbook. (2004).

NATIONAL

AASHTO Guide for the Development of Bicycle Facilities. (1999).

Bikesafe Bicycle Countermeasure Selection System. (2006).

FHWA Manual on Uniform Traffic Control Devices. (2009).

International Materials

City of Toronto Cycling Study. (2010).

Department for Transport Cycle Infrastructure Design. (2008).

Design Manual for Bicycle Traffic. (2005).

Langley Bicycle and Pedestrian Facility Design Guidelines. (2004).

London Cycling Design Standards. (2005).

Nottinghamshire Cycling Design Guide. (2006).

Road Directorate Collection Cycle Concepts. (2000).

Sustrans Cycling Guidelines. (1997).

Bicycle Boulevards

Research and Studies

ACADEMIC

Cyclist safety on bicycle boulevards and parallel arterial routes in Berkeley, California. (2011).

Efficacy of Rectangular-Shaped Rapid Flash LED Beacons.

Evaluation of Bike Boxes at Signalized Intersections. (2010).

Impact Speed and a Pedestrian's Risk of Severe Injury or Death. (2011).

Influences on bicycle use. (2007).

Resident Perceptions of Bicycle Boulevards. (2009).

Responding to the Challenges of Bicycle Crossings at Offset Intersections. (2007).

Traffic Calming Benefits, Costs, and Equity Impacts. (1999).

Traffic Calming: Do's and Don'ts to Encourage Bicycling. (1996).

Traffic Calming: Speed Humps and Speed Cushions. (2011).

Understanding and Measuring Bicycling Behavior: A Focus on Travel Time and Route Choice.(2008).

Updated Guidelines for the Design and Application of Speed Humps. (2007).

MUNICIPALITY

Impact of Traffic Calming Devices on Emergency Vehicles. (1996).

Modified HAWK Signal and Bike Signal. (2010).

Neighborhood Traffic Circles.

Residential Street Standards and Neighborhood Traffic Control.

Split Speed Bump. (1998).

PROFESSIONAL

Literature Review and Impact of the Bicycle Boulevard. (2010).

New Traffic Calming Device of Choice. (2009).

U.S. Traffic Calming Manual. (1999).

Why Bicyclists Hate Stop Signs. (2001).

Design Guides

CITY

Bicentennial Bikeways Plan. (2008).

Bicycle Boulevard Design Tools and Guidelines. (2000).

Bicycle Facilities Design Manual for the City of Redmond. (2009).

City of Oakland (2009)

City of Portland Traffic Calming Devices and Photos.

Emeryville Bicycle Boulevard Treatments. (2011).

Impact Threshold Curve. (2011).

Los Angeles Technical Design Handbook. (2011).

Milwaukie Bicycle Wayfinding Signage Plan. (2009).

Minneapolis Design Guidelines for Bicycle Boulevards. (2011).

Neighborhood Traffic Calming: Seattle's Traffic Circle Program. Road Management & Engineering Journal. (2008).

Portland Bike Plan for 2030. (2010).

Portland Neighborhood Greenways-Goals. (2010).

Portland Stormwater Solutions Handbook. (2004).

Sacramento Best Practices for Bicycle Master Planning and Design. (2005).

STATE

Oregon Neighborhood Street Design Guidelines. (2000).

Right-In Right-Out Channelization. (1998).

NATIONAL

AASHTO Guide for the Development of Bicycle Facilities. (1999).

Bikesafe Bicycle Countermeasure Selection System. (2006).

FHWA Manual on Uniform Traffic Control Devices. (2009).

Traffic Calming State of the Practice. (1999).

Traffic Engineering Handbook. (2009).

TrafficCalming.org

Updated Guidelines for the Design and Application of Speed Humps and Speed Tables. (2011).

International Materials

Behaviour at Cycle Advanced Stop Lines. (2005).